W9-BFP-171

VOICES
FROM THE
FRONT

OTHER BOOKS BY FRANK SCHAEFFER

*Keeping Faith—A Father-Son Story About Love
and the United States Marine Corps*
(coauthored with Cpl. John Schaeffer USMC)

Faith of Our Sons—A Father's Wartime Diary

and . . .

The Calvin Becker Trilogy of novels:

Portofino

Zermatt

Saving Grandma

VOICES
FROM THE
FRONT

Letters Home from America's Military Family

Letters Collected, Edited,
and with a Foreword by

FRANK SCHAEFFER

CARROLL & GRAF PUBLISHERS
NEW YORK

Voices from the Front
Letters Home from America's Military Family

Carroll & Graf Publishers
An Imprint of Avalon Publishing Group, Inc.
245 West 17th Street
New York, NY 10011

AVALON
publishing group incorporated

Copyright © 2004 by Frank Schaeffer

First Carroll & Graf edition 2004

All rights reserved. No part of this book may be reproduced in whole or in part
without written permission from the publisher, except by reviewers who may
quote brief excerpts in connection with a review in a newspaper, magazine, or
electronic publication; nor may any part of this book be reproduced, stored in a
retrieval system, or transmitted in any form or by any means electronic,
mechanical, photocopying, recording, or other, without written permission from
the publisher.

Library of Congress Cataloging-in-Publication Data are available.

ISBN: 0-7867-1462-X

Interior design by Simon M. Sullivan
Printed in the United States of America
Distributed by Publishers Group West

To Brianna White, for all the days you will miss your father. Thank you.

Contents

Foreword

During the forty days of Lent—in the spring of 2004—I began editing this book. At first the heavy workload seemed incompatible with the spirit of a season of spiritual reflection. (My wife and I belong to the Greek Orthodox Church and in our tradition observing Lent and Easter is important.) But as I read the letters it struck me; nothing could be more appropriate to a season when we meditate on the meaning of sacrifice than reading the words of men and women willing to lay down their lives for strangers.

My stake in this book is personal. Our men and women in uniform brought my youngest son home alive from two back-to-back deployments to the wars in the Middle East. They are his brothers and sisters and therefore my family. My son, Corporal John Schaeffer, USMC, has been serving our country since he volunteered in 1999. In two previous books I chronicled how our family's life has been changed by his service: "Keeping Faith—A Father-Son Story about Love and the United States Marine Corps," coauthored with John, and "Faith of Our Sons—A Father's Wartime Diary." This book of letters evolved from those two books and the e-mails I received from our readers. When I asked them for help in collecting the letters herein they put the word out.

These letters were written under the most difficult circumstances; the disorientation of training, deployment, and combat, not to mention occupation duties in Afghanistan and Iraq that must seem to stretch into a lonely infinity for those who are currently wearing the uniforms of the United States. I selected and ordered the letters, and in some instances trimmed them for length, but I made no other changes. I did not try to whitewash the jagged and sometimes strange wartime experiences related here either. And I did not pick the letters with any agenda in mind, other than trying to bring my readers face-to-face with our defenders. All the letters were written by military personnel or their families since the events of September 11, 2001. Collectively I hope they give voice to a generation that went to war against terror in Afghanistan and to war in Iraq, for reasons that are still being debated, and who are fighting and dying in those wars as I write.

Often as I read these letters I cried. My tears were shed for the men who didn't make it home and for their families. I was also deeply moved by the unselfconscious spirit of noble purpose permeating the words and actions of so many of our soldiers, sailors, airmen and Marines. It was a privilege to better get to know our warriors through their humor, descriptions of dangerous experiences, and their love for family.

One theme seems to unite their diverse voices: the belief that the person standing next to you is more important than you are. This brings me back to my Lenten meditation. Why is it that life seems to have no purpose unless it is lived for others? Why is it that the words of the Gospel of John (15:13) resonate so deeply? "Greater love hath no man than this, that a man lay down his life for his friends."

It seems fitting to begin this book with a letter reflecting on the events of September, 11, 2001, that plunged our country into a series of wars that are now the context of all of our lives and all the other letters in the book. The writer, Charles Evered, is in residence at Emerson College, Boston. In the fall of 2001, he was in the US Navy (Reserves). After spending time at "Ground Zero" documenting the site, he wrote this letter to his wife, Wendy.

Frank Schaeffer
Memorial Day, May 31, 2004

September 16, 2001

Wend,

Down at the site today with "Rad," my photographers mate. Documenting it all . . .

Words are not enough.

Started with our approaching it all from Liberty Street. And it's sad but true—all you could think of is a movie set. As though sadly, that's become our emblematic touchstone of so many things we experience now, real or imagined. But in this case, it just happens to be true.

At first I just stood there. Looking up at the flames, still poking through the twisted steel. They still had dogs going down, trying to sniff some living people out. But to no avail.

I can't express the feeling around the perimeter except to say there was palpable anger. People had spray painted some messages to Osama, messages to "whomever" did this, and they weren't in the Queen's English, let me tell you. . . .

At one point I walked out on a beam. How ridiculous. As though somehow I was going to find someone. Be able to do something. Be able to help someone.

While I was out there in the middle of all of it, I had the strangest sensation. I don't know how else to explain it except to say that if it is possible to feel the evil intent of something, viscerally, almost physically, well, that is what I felt. It was as though to me, the steel and the fires and the awful other things on the site were not the only things left behind by the cowards who did this. It's as though they left their intent behind as well.

In my mind, I started imagining how something so huge like this, so colossal, had likely started with a meeting in a coffee shop somewhere, or in someone's apartment. Someone actually had the IDEA to do this. Just a hypothetical conjecture on someone's part, and then followed through to this actuality with months and most likely years in between and money and planning and in the end, intent. Well, that's what I felt I was feeling out there—that intent. That is what lingers, what is most disturbing. Because while planes being used as bombs are scary, to be sure, it's the intent to use them that way that is scarier still.

Around the perimeter, there was a little blown out restaurant—or at least what I think used to be a restaurant—and the front had been blown out, but someone had set up the tables again so rescue workers and other support staff could have a place to eat. The place was lit by candles, and in one of the more surreal situations I imagine I will ever experience in my life, I walked in and saw crisply, well dressed catering staffs serving salmon and prime rib and other high end meals to the exhausted workers.

Some restaurants from uptown had been sending food down— as well as people to serve it. Of course it was a beautiful gesture, but the contrast was at one point almost too much for me to take. And so everyone just sat there, eating silently, as these caterers cleared the plates, served some more, asked whether everyone had had enough. And just outside, not twenty yards away, was the pile of death and flames and the smell of it all commingling.

And the huge lights, still, like a movie set, illuminating it all. Every once in awhile, we would hear a whistle, and then another one, which I believe meant that someone thought they had heard something down in the hole. And so everyone, and I mean *everyone* was to be perfectly quiet while the dogs continued sniffing and listening devices were lowered down into the crevices. So there we all sat in the restaurant, forks and knives suspended above our plates— perfectly still, just waiting, not a word, until another whistle blew, signaling that people could go back to what they were doing. And so then you'd hear the sound of forks scrapping against the plates, the tinkling of ice in glasses, and never a word spoken. This was now normal. No questions asked. This is what life is like now. . . .

Everything is a blur to tell you the truth, I have stuff on my shoes I need to get off. Or, I need to just throw them out. I don't want to bring this back home to you and the kids. But that's the point, isn't it? All of this is home now. On all of our front stoops. This has happened three thousand miles from where we now live, but to me, it's as though they tried to kill you—and *our* babies. Because they didn't care.

I can't help but think of what one of the hijackers must've been thinking when they were sitting there, waiting to take off. Knowing what they were going to do. And no doubt there must have been a baby or a toddler on board. And I wonder whether they dared to make eye contact with that baby? Did they think, even for a second, about what that baby did to deserve the fate they decided it should meet? I doubt they did.

This is a different kind of war. It's going to last a long, long time, but it's worth it. Because whatever the relativists might want to say, Wend, there *is* evil. And it won't go away by wishing it away, or justifying it or rationalizing it. If only it were that simple.

I'll let you know if I get a flight tomorrow. Kiss Margaret and John for me, and while you're at it, think of the babies on board those planes and imagine kissing them too. I love you all—

Charles Evered

BOOT CAMP

1

Boot camp is the start of each military experience. Young men and women go into the military for many reasons but they all pass through boot camp first. Some make it; some fail or are sent home for health reasons. The ones who graduate are rewarded by being sent to war.—FS

February 25, 2004

Hi Frank,

This letter was written while my son was at boot camp on Parris Island days after 9/11. They were not given very many details of what was happening.

Of course we sent him the Sunday paper and many articles we got off the internet along with pictures and he indeed saw that it was just as bad if not worse than Pearl Harbor. I hate that he was there for such a monumental point in the history of our nation and was not allowed to watch it unfold as we did. My son is now a LCpl. in the U. S. Marines.

Kathy Neno
Proud Mom of LCp. Neno
Semper Fi

September 14, 2001

Dear Mom,

All this stuff with the terrorists has made some changes here. They said we are at Defcon level "D". That's the highest he said. Nobody gets on the base without an ID and they are searching cars. No one can park close to the buildings. They keep giving us little updates. I hope ya'll send the Sunday paper for the Sunday after all this stuff. The chaplain today talked about how this could eclipse Pearl Harbor. I'm only getting a limited view of it all but that's bullshit right? I think Pearl Harbor was a little worse right? It changed history. Maybe if that other plane would have made it to the White House or where ever it was headed, maybe. But write and tell me what all is going on. Give me another view. Well I got to go. I miss ya'll and love ya'll more.

Recruit Mark Neno

LCpl. Mark Neno, USMC, is now at Marine Corps Air Station, Yuma, Arizona working as a brig guard.—FS

———

Recruit Jonathon Fox is from upstate New York. He was on Parris Island in the summer of 2003. He struggled with pneumonia. Jonathan was nineteen when he wrote these letters. This first letter is to his sister.—FS

*I think its the 26th? Friday, the something?**

———

*It is not unusual for a recruit in one of the two bases where Marines are made—Marine Corps Recruit Depot Parris Island South Carolina, or San Diego California—to be so disorientated that he or she literally looses track of time. It is also not unusual for recruits to become ill or so injured they can no longer train. Some are "recycled" into other platoons after a stay in MRP (medical recovery platoon); many are sent home too ill or injured to continue.—FS

Dear Linze and Evan,

. . . . I miss you so much. . . . Life has become extremely hard and tedious. I had some stress released yesterday by doing a bayonet charge on some rubber dummies. I have THE meanest drill instructor on the Island. We nicknamed him Sergeant Slaughter. Ha, ha. What a goof! I hate him. But I have forgiven him. Once he yelled at me and his spit ran down my face and dripped off my chin. . . . But I've gotten used to wearing sweat and pee soaked cammies for a week. It actually doesn't smell to me any more. Tonight I've had the longest shower in 2 weeks. 2 minutes long! Thank God! Got to use soap! . . .

Pray for me to come home in 12 weeks. 11 now!

Please comfort Mom for me. Give her a big hug for me tonight. Let her know how much I love her and miss her. And tell Dad that I am becoming a stronger person, inside and out. . . .

Love Your Brother,
Jon
Jonathon Fox

June 30, 2003

Dear Mom and Dad,

Today is Sunday. . . . It's morning, the Catholics are about to go to Church. We [the Protestants] will follow soon after.

I am extremely tired. Yesterday we ran two miles at a brisk pace and did millions of push ups, chin ups and crunches. We did two hours straight of drill. (Very tiring.)

["Drill" is marching with your rifle and doing parade-style exercises such as "port arms."—FS]

Last night we cleaned our rifles and, as we got up and lifted our footlockers, I fell over another recruit's who hadn't picked his up and went face down onto mine. I ripped my chin wide open and was taken by Sgt. Slaughter or "Sgt. Slobber" to a hospital off base, but it was a military hospital. He made me sit with my head in my lap so I couldn't see my surroundings.

[When a recruit goes off base the Marine DIs (drill instructors) do not want the spell they are casting over the recruit broken by outside distractions, so they do not let them catch sight of anything in the outside world; thus "he made me sit with my head in my lap."—FS]

When we got to the hospital, a nurse took me into the ER and it was my first time alone with a civilian. I stayed at position of attention and sat there like a machine. I was sweating horribly and the nurse took a towel and wiped off my brow. It was the first sign of kindness in two weeks. She told me to relax and not to worry about my DI. He yelled at me in front of some patients for not saying good evening to them.

Anyway I was taken to a hospital bed. The doctor and nurses allowed me to relax on the bed (it was soft) and took care of the other patients first so that I could have some time to myself. It felt so good. I could look around, touch my face to let myself know that I am still human, go to the bathroom, adjust myself, and best of all it gave me time with God, I prayed for a long time, prayed for you guys and everyone back home, prayed for Molly not to forget about me. . . .

Anyway, I got 3 stitches and am good to go. . . . Let everyone know I am still clumsy! I got a good chewing in the head for it too by my senior drill instructor. He . . . told me how stupid I was. It wasn't bad though. I just pictured home and sitting on the deck, eating cheeseburger and being offered another drink by you, Mom. . . . [So] the yelling just got blocked out.

I miss home so much. The smell of clean clothing, a long shower, sleeping in, Mom speaking so calmly to me and Dad wanting to hang out with me. Everything was taken for granted, but now even the smallest things count. . . .

Call Molly when you receive this and tell her everything and how much I love her. I still don't have her address. Please send it and have her write me. I miss her soooooo much. . . .

Mom, I need you to know that I am sorry for all the harsh exchanges of words that we've ever had. I wish they could all go away. You were always right. It took great hardship and pain to see this. I miss you more that anything right now. . . . Please remember and pray for me to overcome the fitness test and come home in eleven weeks. . . .

Love Your Son,
Jon
Jonathon Fox

Jon got pneumonia and was given a medical discharge and sent home.—FS

2

These are letters from LCpl. Christopher Cardall, age nineteen, USMC, written in boot camp.—FS

Nov 26, 2002

Hey Family,

Just doing the boot camp thing. I got your cards and pictures yesterday. They were very much appreciated. So, for sure you, Dad, Grandma and Granddad are coming [to graduation]? (If so that is excellent. . . .)

Tomorrow we get issued our first dress uniform. I am looking forward to that. We get our "Charlie's" and our dress blue pants. That is another reason why I need to know if you are buying me a plane ticket home or whatever so that I know if I will have enough money to buy my dress blues. . . .

There is another subject I need to touch on which you have probably heard about by now. Yes, there was a boy who died here a few days ago on the obstacle course. I saw most of it happen. He didn't die from the training though. He died from a brain aneurysm he had while running the "O" course. He was behind me in [the] training [cycle] and my platoon had already run both the "O" course and the obstacle course twice. So I know for a fact that nothing here at recruit training will kill me. I will be fine. Just gotta keep my head in the game. I only have 2 1/2 weeks left down here before I go up to Pendleton [for rifle range training]. Keep addressing your letters here though until I tell you otherwise.

Well, I love you Mom. Goodnight and sleep tight—don't let the bed bugs bite. I love you Mom and miss you very much. When you come down to see me I want you to bring that money down so that I can buy my dress blues.* They are about $300. . . . if I still have enough [money left I'll] take you all out to dinner or just get a damn pizza. That is what I really miss—Pizza.

Well gotta get back to sleep. . . .

Happy Thanksgiving.
Love,
Chris
LCpl. Christopher Cardall, USMC

Dec 11, 2002

Dear Family,

. . . . I found out why most countries are scared of the United States Marines. It is because we are trained to be marksmen at, at least 500 yards distance. That is a long way without a scope. . . .

We all puff out our chests, straighten our backs and walk with pride. We all have outgoing attitudes. All we want to do is conquer. Our drill instructors have even commented on how all the sudden we have come together as a team. . . . only 5 1/2 more weeks. I am so glad. I am starting to get home-sickness at night really bad. I really miss you guys. I think about you all everyday and pray for you every night. . . .

Wow, I just counted and there are only 41 more days left. Time

* Marines have to pay for their uniforms.—FS

is flyin by. Soon enough, we'll be seein each other. I remembered some things on top of that black suit I want you to bring, [on family day the day before graduation] that "Very Sexy for Men" cologne that I have, a nice pair of jeans. I don't care which ones and my CDs. . . .

I figured out how to accomplish everything and found out the secret to the Marine Corps boot camp, and I even asked a senior drill instructor about this and he told me I was right. Boot camp is 20% physical, 30% teamwork and 50% confidence. I am sure that if everyone went through Marine Corps boot camp, there would be a lot more confidence in society, not to mention [fewer] nasty, undisciplined and unthankful people. Yeah, that is how we think and talk here.

We have some funny phrases or names we call each other, like if we are trying to get another recruit's attention we either say "ears" or "hello ass." Every recruit here goes by "ass" no matter if you are in a group or by yourself. Soon as the DI says "Hello ass" you know he is talking to you. Sometimes it is good, sometimes it's bad. I haven't gotten that many of the bad, which means you are going to get IT'd. IT means Incentive Training. I call it Intensive Training. Basically a DI sits there and puts you through torture by doing push-ups, jumping jacks, "building a house," running in place etc, etc, etc . . .

LCpl. Christopher Cardall USMC

LCpl. Christopher Cardall, USMC, is currently in Camp Pendleton. He will be deployed to the war in Iraq in the fall of 2004.—FS

3

Kelley L. Chambers, age twenty-one, was writing to her father from Navy boot camp.—FS

February 10, 2002

Dear Daddy,

Only 12 more days until graduation. Tomorrow we go to the gas chamber [to test our gas masks]. I'm so nervous. You would not believe the schedule we keep. You know how I used to like to sleep in all the time, well not any more! We're up and at PT, practicing marching, and on and on. I can't wait to see you and Mom and Melissa and Paul. I didn't realize how much I would miss you until I was away. I hope after boot camp it will be easier because I'll be able to talk to you on the phone. When you come to Chicago for graduation [where the Navy conducts boot camp] there are a few things I'd like you to bring. Ask Grandma to bake some candy cane cookies. . . . I can't wait to pig out! My friends and I talk about food from home all the time! I can't wait to graduate but I wish I was coming home. I miss the house, my bed, my car, my friends, and most of all you guys. I'll see you in less than 2 weeks!!!

Love, your little sailor, Kelley

P.S. I forgot to tell Mom to bring my eyeliner, lipstick, and mascara!

February 3, 2002

Hi Daddy!

We got to work in the drill hall this week. We get up at 3:00am and clean and stand watches all day. It sounds like it would be awful, but we got to listen to music while we were cleaning. It was the first time I'd heard music since December 17! Last Tuesday, I went to the dentist and it was so nice because I got to lie down in that chair and listen to music again. When I come home, I'll show you how I shine my boots! You'll be amazed! I graduate in only 19 days! Remember when it was 50-something?

   . . . . I love you so much and I miss you.

   Write back soon,

Love your "princess" Kelley
P.S. take care of Mom

Petty Officer Kelley L. Chambers USN is now at Naval Station Mayport, Florida, as an air traffic controller.—FS

4

Joseph Giardino wrote these boot camp letters when he was twenty-one.—FS

December 21, 2002

Mom & Dad,

How's it going? It's been raining for about 10 days and it's cold. I really enjoy it now that we can train but I miss you all very much. How's R.C. doing in school? Does Anne Marie have her license yet? I'm a squad leader here so I get punished a lot. Whenever people screw up, I pay along with them. I got IT'd 8 times in 2 days, none from my mistakes!

I've come to appreciate my family a lot now that I can't see or talk to you as I please. I appreciate a lot of things more, thank you Mom and Dad. I'm able to breeze through a lot of this because of the discipline you've taught me. The DIs have a saying: "I'm doing in 3 months what your parents couldn't do in 18 years" and it's true! Some of these guys here don't get the fact that there's only one way out of here. . . .

I really miss you all, especially you Dad. Thanks Dad, you really made me feel better that night I called home. It's helped me a lot. I can't wait until March 6th, it will be the first time I get to see you all again. I hope Nikki and Richard will be able to come with you. Rumor has it we get to watch a movie on Christmas but no one really knows for sure. I hope all is well out there and I miss and love you all.

Joe
Joseph Giardino

January 13, 2003

Mom & Dad,

. . . . I've lost 10 lbs. Today we did a combat conditioning course, it was really tough. You match up with a partner and keep your partner that whole time. I was matched up with a guy that's 6'2" and I had to carry him for 3 carries, he was so much taller than me his feet were almost on the ground even though I had him lifted up! Did I tell you I got my dress uniforms? Boy do I look sharp! Mom, you were asking if we have any mottos or slogans—our platoon has one: "Ready to fight, ready to kill, ready to die, but NEVER will." Well, I've got to get some sleep, you guys take it easy and I know I'll hear from you soon.

I Love You,
Joe
Joseph Giardino

January 18, 2003

Dad & Mom,

How's it going?
. . . . We finished swim week here and it was pretty easy. They throw you in the pool and you just float! I was amazed; I'm fully dressed with 65 lbs. of gear plus my weapon and I float!

This has been a challenging week mentally. The mind games have gone to a new level. To a lesser person it would be tough, but not a Giardino—thanks Dad!

. . . Did I tell you how much I enjoyed your "Ode to Joe"? I really am grateful for how supportive you are being. I couldn't be doing this without your help. I'd also like to say "I told you you'd be proud of me!" And again, thank you.

I love you,
Joe
Joseph Giardino

February 21, 2003

Mom & Dad,

. . . . Our week in the field was amazing. I only have 14 days left and it's suddenly so sad to me. The Crucible [a final three-day period of intense physical and mental testing—FS] made me so close to so many of the guys. It was only 54 hours but with no food or sleep it makes you look at things differently. What little food we would get, we all found ourselves giving it to the Marine next to us. That's just the way it is. . . . I've learned so much about heart and determination. . . .

I've got to go now and I'll see you in 13 days!

Love,
Joe
Joseph Giardino

LCpl. Joseph Giardino, USMC, is serving his second deployment to Iraq and will be there until October/November 2004. We meet him again later in this book.—FS

5

March 2, 2004

Dear Mr. Schaeffer,

Below is a letter our son, PFC Nate Nemitz, USMC, wrote to us
from Marine boot camp, Parris Island in August of 2003.

Sharlene A. Nemitz

PFC Nate Nemitz was eighteen when he wrote this letter. He was so disorientated he did not know the date.—FS

August (?) , 2003

Mom and Dad,

Well I have a little bit of bad news but it's no big deal, yet at least.
I did not qualify on the rifle range. I got a 184. You need a 190 to
qualify as Marksman [the lowest ranking to pass]. I go back on
Monday to try and qualify again. I'll make it this time. I made some
stupid mistakes last time. . . . I've paid for it. . . . That's OK. It's just
making me stronger.

. . . I've been thinking about what I want to do in 8 years. I think that if I don't re-enlist that I might go to school to become a preacher.

How about that Dad?
Nate Nemitz

August 17 (?), 2003

This is the last day, hopefully, of being an outcast in the platoon for not qualifying. Some people are really good about it. I can't wait for Monday (tomorrow) so I can qualify and rejoin the platoon.

I've been QD [punished on the quarter deck] so much these past few days and I'm getting stronger. I'm up to 12 pull-ups now. My run time is 18:45 and I have 124 crunches. Church last week was awesome. They brought in a heavy metal band to play some songs for us. Their name was Judah First. They were pretty good. There was a song . . . that made me cry and realize how much I miss being home.

I love the pics of everyone especially the one with Ryan eating cake and ice cream. I don't have dog tags yet. I can't wait for Wednesday. We are going to get our uniforms fitted. I was on the 4x400 team. We won that race. It felt good to do that again. We led the whole thing. I was the 3rd leg. Instead of a baton we used a moonbeam [flashlight] plus we ran on a dirt track (that sucked). I can't wait to be home. Keep sending pics as they are giving me a look at what's going on in the real world.

Nate Nemitz

August 18, 2003

Well, I didn't pull it off. My 500 yard fire was all jacked up. Today was just a bad day all around. . . . There is a good possibility that I might get dropped if I don't qualify tomorrow, Tuesday, the 19th. One month from graduation. I've come too far with this platoon to get dropped back to 2nd BN. . . . [He would then have to begin his rifle training all over again. If he did not qualify then he would be sent home—FS]

I'll write as soon as I know if I qualified or not. . . . Anyway I'm hoping that tomorrow is a better day. It's getting late and I have to be up early tomorrow. A bunch of people have been trying to help me out. Let's hope I make it. I love all your support. I couldn't ask for any more. As long as I can relax at the 300 [yards] rapid [fire] and the 500 [yards] I'll be fine. I love and miss you all.

Love, Nate
Nate Nemitz

March 2, 2004

Frank:

Nate did qualify as Marksman on the last day possible [before he would have been dropped]. He graduated with 3rd BN, L Company. He is now a PFC graduating from his MOS [military occupational specialty school] on March 5. He will be heading [overseas] April 5, 2004.

Sharlene Nemitz

VPMM [very proud Marine Mom] of PFC Nate
VPM [very proud mom] of Laura—college student
VPM of Amy—wife of USMC Sgt Rhett and
mommy to Mikayla and Ryan

PFC Nate Nemitz USMC is in now stationed in Okinawa.—FS

6

March 11, 2004

LCpl. David Sandifer went through boot camp from May 5–August 1, 2003. He graduated a PFC and is now in the 1st Marine Division and serving in Iraq. I do not have any letters from Iraq yet (he is still traveling over there), so boot camp letters is all I have.

Katie E. Sandifer

David was twenty-one when he wrote these letters.—FS

June 25, 2003

. . . The cool thing about the pits [the sand pit ouside each squad bay where recruits are punished—FS] is that the Drill Instructors mess around with the recruits and do some pretty funny stuff. They like to make kids "fly" to the port-a-potty at the end of the pit. Every so often a Recruit will run by flapping his arms and squawking like a bird. Other Recruits have to make a loud siren noise if their trip to the head [toilet] is an emergency. Usually [the DI's] pick on one or two Recruits all the time, but today they spread it around.

Our junior DI stuck two spotting disks in my portholes (glasses), so it looked like my eyes were 3 inches wide with a quarter-inch pupil. The DI thought it was so funny he could hardly talk. He made me run over to the other DI so he could get a good laugh, too . . . . It felt funny, and it was hilarious to see the DI lose control and bust out laughing. . . .

David
David E. Sandifer

July 11, 2003

. . . .They made us give blood today. . . .The blood screening lady came to get the next recruit in line and said "Hi" when it was my turn. I almost froze because I didn't know how to respond. It's been 2 1/2 months since somebody said hi to me. I've been "this Recruit" for so long that I have to think about my words when I talk. Even when I pray I find myself ending words with "sir."

David
David E. Sandifer

LCpl.David E. Sandifer, USMC, is now in Iraq with the 1st Marine Division. We will meet him again in this book.—FS

7

The scope of the military family goes beyond the headlines. While some are at war, others are in boot camp and yet others serve all over the world, as is the case with those stationed in Korea. Many of those same troops have now been sent to war in the Middle East.—FS

March 9, 2004

Dear Frank,

I have attached . . . letters written by my husband, Brandon Scott Bailey, Airman 1st Class, USAF, who is in the Air Force at this time. . . .

Brandon and I have known each other for quite a while but started dating just four months before he left for boot camp on Nov 11, 2002. We dated throughout all of his training and on May 2, 2003 we were married 2 1/2 weeks before he left for South Korea where he was stationed until May 2004.

I was able to see him for four weeks this summer in Korea and then he came home for a mid tour leave. I'm heading back there for a six days the middle of this month to split up the time before he comes home. . . .

Sincerely,
Sarah Bailey

These were written during Air Force basic training when Brandon was nineteen.—FS

November 22, 2002

I just sat outside the church here in San Antonio as a young mother walked by with about a three month old baby. Man, the things that make me think about you in the most unthinkable places. The days are getting so much easier to get through, the trainees I am in charge of are starting to move quicker and work together as a team. If we can keep it up I am not too worried about getting recycled, that possibility is always present.

I have only been getting about three hours of sleep every night since every time we are supposed to be doing things I am either showing someone else how to do something or doing push-ups [as squad leader being punished] for the people that mess up. . . .

Well, I got to finish this now, we are having an inspection tomorrow and we aren't supposed to have been writing letters yet. You could get me recycled if I have to keep writing you! Just kidding!

I love you tons and I can't wait to be with you. I hope you still feel the same cause it's hard here without you. Actually, it sucks.

XOXO,
Brandon
Brandon Scott Bailey
Airman 1st Class Red Horse Squadron 554 USAF

December 28, 2002

Hey honey,

. . . You know this is all your fault right? If it weren't for you I would really have no reason to look forward to the end of tech school. . . . I hope you realize that if I knew right now where I would be stationed that we would already be engaged? It is so stressful for me to know that I have found THE ONE . . . but then have to wait for the President of our country to tell me where I am most needed. I anticipate that day, not only because my job and residency will be established but also it will open the doors for our future. I love you so much Sarah.

I'll let you in on a little secret, right now all the guys in my flight think I am a dumb-ass because during warrior week I had about 20 females hit on me in very obvious manners, even I could tell they weren't just being friendly. The guys in my flight see me as a dumb-ass because I could play every one of those girls and you would never know about it, but do you know what I did instead? I told all those girls I was engaged to a wonderful woman, that they didn't even have a chance, and that they should leave me alone because I had a job to do. . . .

[Unlike the Marines, the other services train men and women together.—FS]

Guess where I am at again, on the toilet in the latrine!?! What a surprise huh? This is the only place I don't get bothered by other people [where I can write]. . . .

It is really weird to think of the way my life may change again in the next few months, five months from now I could be working on an Air Force base overseas during the day and then going home at night to find a meal made for me and a beautiful wife waiting for me. . . . At least I will be able to call you a lot more. . . .

I have kicked myself for joining the Air Force so many times because I desire to be with you. . . .

XOXOXO
Your Chief,
Brandon
Brandon Scott Bailey
Airman 1st Class Red Horse Squadron 554 USAF

This was written by Brandon during his time in technical school in Missouri.—FS

February 25, 2003

Good Morning Love,

. . . . I hate the fact that I don't have control over my future; I am way too independent and responsible to feel comfortable having every decision made for me. I like the freedom of being able to determine how, why, and when I would like to do things . . .

I can see how if you had no idea of how to live or what you wanted to do with your life the military would be great, but that's not me; I know what I want to do with my life. I want to spend it with you. The Air Force is just making it hard for me to obtain that part of my dream right now. . . .

I'll love you forever,
Brandon
Brandon Scott Bailey
Airman 1st Class Red Horse Squadron 554 USAF

Brandon Scott Bailey is now in Peterson Air Force Base in Colorado Springs.—FS

8

Frank:

When [my son] Andy was in Marine boot camp in San Diego and wrote us a lot, I saved all his letters and put them in a notebook for him. . . . When he was home after boot camp, I asked him to wear his uniform to a party because people in Colorado see few servicemen. Like you, I wanted Mr. Ordinary Guy to be more aware of what these young people are willing to do for their country.

[Andy] "graduated" from the School of Infantry two weeks ago as a mortar man. Thirty guys from his platoon were sent to Hawaii, the rest are waiting to go to Iraq. Andy is one of the thirty. I, of course, am so relieved, at least for now. He was mad and felt guilty, but I'm hoping he'll adjust. . . .

He's now in Hawaii, chomping at the bit because "there's not enough action." I hope he stays there forever, although he's recently signed up for something that will help him become an officer, go to college, serve another six and then become a civilian, I guess.

[Andy] and I have always been close; learning to let go and give him wings has been painfully exhilarating.

I've also enclosed a letter I wrote at Christmas after Andy graduated. It ties up a few loose ends. I talked to him over the weekend and he said to send you any of the letters, but to take out the "mushy stuff" about his girlfriend. I've crossed out her name at his request. Also I feel like I need to apologize for his language—we sure didn't raise him like that, but I guess he's in his Marine phase.

I am so grateful that you are putting the letters together—giving these kids a chance to let others know what the military is all about. I certainly never understood. . . .

Gaye Lowe-Kaplan

August 19 or 20 (?) 2003

Dear Mom and Dad,

I have 7 minutes to write, Mom, about the asthma, I was depressed and hadn't slept in 3 days. As much as I hate boot camp, I won't quit. I'm 90% sure I can handle it. The worst part is not being able to see you guys and _____.

I am going to include with this letter a small journal I kept for a few days. Mom, don't write a letter to my senior DI about easing up on me. Anyway, things are going all right. I'm pretty anxious and depressed, but I'll survive. . . .

Mom I would give anything to talk to you. Dad, I miss your cooking. Tell Danny I love him. Boot camp is really different and I mess up a lot. I have been yelled at a lot. I just want these first 4 weeks to be over. I think about you guys all the time. Tell ____ I miss her more than I can say.

Love,
Andy Kaplan

Names of the DIs in Andy's journal have been changed.—FS

Andy's Journal
August 22, 2003

["T" stands for training day.—FS]

T-Day 2: Today has been a bad day. I miss home and hate my DIs. I am now on my second week, only eleven and a half to go. I want to go home. Fastest way home is graduation. Boot camp is hell, no free time to self—can't think always worrying. Not supposed to keep journal. . . .

DI Smith is a hard ass, but just doing his job. He does not like me much. He's white and always angry.

DI Jackson is African-American. Always calling us filthy pigs, he's the mean one. I can't stand him. Another thing, when he talks it all runs together and you can't understand him.

Senior DI Polk is a fair guy, but scary as hell when he is mad. He comes from the infantry, so I look up to him. Out of all the DIs, I like him the most.

I am now sitting in class. It is hard to stay awake. Boot camp is becoming bearable, I hate PT [physical training] though. Every time I think about spending eleven more weeks here I get depressed.

I am now standing post. DI Jackson just gave us some instruction but I couldn't understand him.

The worst part about boot camp is the sleep and the PT. I never get enough sleep because I have night visions of the DIs giving me orders.

PT sucks because I hate running and we get screamed at all the time. I'm getting sick of being screamed at. I got three letters yesterday, but I have not had a chance to read them. I want to go home, this sucks.

Sometimes it is bearable though and I have a feeling that if I give it a week of two more, I'll be okay. I love you, Mom! I love you, Dad, I love you, Danny.

I am now standing in line for chow, hungry—one more day down.

I am now on the two hour fire-watch. I am pissing. The one thing I have here is sleep and they took it away from me. I am sick of Jackson yelling at me. . . .

I want to go home. I'm hungry and tired.

T-Day 5: Broke down this morning.

T-Day 6: I am sitting in terrorism class trying to stay awake. Most of these classes are interesting, but I have a hard time staying awake. Boot camp is a lot more bearable, but still pretty bad. We watched a video about 9/11 and Marines in Afghanistan and it reminds me why I'm doing this: so I can get trained and kill terrorists. I wish I could write more letters.

Now, I am in Marine Corps history class right after chow, am very sleepy, can't sleep. DIs will slay me. See movie; The Last Battalion, learning about Marines during the Banana wars. I am very tired.

T-Day 7: I have been here for 7 days. It has been a hard roller coaster ride. The first three days were, without a doubt, the worst of my life, up till now. There will probably be worse.

On day two or three I was miserable and I told a doctor that I had asthma. [Note: from Mom, he has asthma; lied to get in the Corps]. He called my mother and then called me a coward and told me that he was going to make me continue. . . . I expect boot camp will get much harder, but I think I can do it.

Now, on to my DIs: There is the senior Staff Sgt. Polk, then Sgt. Smith and Sgt. Jackson. They are all mean mother-fuckers. More later.

Cont'd: I should be studying my knowledge *right now, but I'm not.

Today has not been a good day. We did have church in the morning, which was a nice break from the DIs. After that, my spirits

---

* "Knowledge" is Marine recruit speak for book and classroom learning.—FS

were raised a bit because I got a chance to talk to some recruits who graduate next week.

Basically all I need to do is survive the next two weeks. That won't be easy seeing as now I'm a fuck-up.

Well, I need to study now, more later.

T-Day 8: I just moved during the raising of the flag. Four DIs ganged up on me and slammed my face into the table. I will never move during taps again.

Let's see, what else I have left out. Well, we are on day 8 and we still have no free time to write letters or just think by ourselves. I still don't follow directions or get things as fast as the other recruits. I am now convinced that I will be dropped.

Tonight will be my first time in the Q-deck [quarter deck area of the barracks used as a punishment area] and I am quite worried about it. We got our rifles today, not very exciting, just one more thing to worry about.

All I can think is that 12 more weeks is a long time. I miss my Mom, Dad and girlfriend and would do/give anything to see them. More later.

We just ran PT for the first time. PT demonstrates the best and worst part of boot. PT is a fast and efficient way to get recruits into shape. The bad part is that you do it as a series, which means there are 270 recruits doing PT with you so you can't hear or see anything. Then your platoon gets in trouble and there is more PT, which is very bad. More later. . . .

August 30, 2003

Dear Mom and Dad,

I'm sorry that have only been able to get off a few letters. It's been 3 weeks and tonight is the first time we've actually got free time.

First off: the whole "head bashing" thing was not as bad as I made it sound. It didn't hurt and I kinda deserved it. After that it got worse, because I was really depressed and homesick. I wasn't focusing very well and I moved when I wasn't supposed to. For a while S/Sgt. Polk and the other DIs were on my ass a lot and I hated it. But the other day S/Sgt—gotta go more tomorrow—

August 31, 2003

Again, Mom, Anyway, about the other day: We were in MCMAPS, which is Marine Corps martial arts program and we were doing some grippers, basically you hold your arms out and squeeze for a long time. Usually they suck and I get all depressed, but I just thought about ____ and all the hardship she's been through and something snapped and I just went off, and ever since that I've been doing better.

S/Sgt. Polk even mentioned that I had improved. That helped a lot.

One of the biggest adjustments for me has been all the negativity. Everything that comes out of the DIs mouth is negative; we get almost no positive encouragement. It's always "that was ——— horrible, you guys are ass!" constantly, 24/7. I couldn't deal with it for those first two and a half weeks, but then you get used to it and the platoon starts getting better and sometimes the DI will say, "Not fucking bad" or "I'm almost impressed," and that really pumps you up and you start doing really well and you feel proud to be doing what you're doing.

I know that this is what I want to do, I may hate boot camp, but it's worth it and I have almost completely adjusted. I still can't adjust to not being able to see you but even that is getting easier. I miss you guys so much! I love you.

Anyway, I want to let you know what a typical day is like in boot camp, so here it goes:

We wake up at 5:00 or 0500 and get dressed in about a minute, and then we make our racks and square way the house [barracks]. Then we make head calls [toilet] and head to breakfast—morning chow. The food here isn't great, but chow is one of the best things here. After chow, we either PT or go the classes, then drill (march) and go to noon chow. After that, it's usually classes, then drill, then evening chow. After that it's back to the house for more drill, then maybe some more PT, then a little square away time, then we hygiene.

We used to have to hygiene (brush teeth, shave and shower) in two minutes, now we get 10 to 20 minutes. Then hygiene inspection and lights out. Sleep is the best thing here, it's the one time where you aren't getting yelled at.

That's a day. . . .

Love, love, love,
Andrew Kaplan

P.P.S. I hope you guys forgive me, but I don't go to the church, I write letters in the barracks on Sundays and I pray at night.

T15: Having a bad day. Homesickness hit really bad. Miss Mom and ___. Got yelled at in the chow hall. Second time in two days for same thing: Chewing while walking. Fucking retarded. It's my own fault though. Still think it's a stupid rule. Other than that, normal day.

Ran 2 miles, proud of myself. Legs hurt a lot after run.

We have initial drill on Saturday. This is the first time that we are graded on drill and it's a big deal for our DIs. If we win, then we might get to watch a movie or something. Overall, things have been OK lately.

I have adjusted better, but I am still homesick. We got our nametag for out blouses [shirts] and trousers. That was kind of cool, seeing "KAPLAN" on a cammie patch. They are going to get sewed on today.

I guess the thing that worries me most is the possibility of getting hurt and sent to MRP [medical recovery platoon]. That would mean I have to stay at boot camp longer. I am pretty confident that I can make it. I am looking forward to Camp Pendleton and being able to fire the M-16. Any kind of change will better than here.

I love and miss you guys. I will try and keep sending journal entries. Share them with whoever cares. I'm holding up OK. I miss you.

T15 cont'd: In this entry I've decided to talk about some of my fellow recruits, the ones that help me through the day of the ones that I'm just buds with.

Eckhardt: I have to mention Eckhardt first. I probably would've already been dropped if it weren't for him. He's a medium built/height 21 year old from Cody, Wyoming. He takes care of me. If I'm movin' a bit slow, he's there to help. We talk whenever we can, which isn't much. Hopefully we're going to go drinking together after graduation. He is sick right now, as is everyone in the platoon. Mostly it's just a rough throat and I am feeling better. Anyway, on to other stuff.

These last two days have been hard. We haven't got any mail and that's been depressing. One month and it still doesn't seem like there is any end in sight. I guess I'm as adjusted as I'm going to get. I'm pretty lonely, cuz I can't talk to anyone really. It's just the same thing over and over everyday. Every once in a while the Senior DI will pump us up, but most of the time they just try and break us down.

We are going up north soon and I'm nervous. Pendleton is good and bad. It's something different, and it pulls us closer to grad day, but it is supposed to be really hard physically and from what I've heard, they try to brad down the team. But I also heard that the food is better and you get to finally fire the M-16 AZ.

The M-16 is a hell of a weapon. Sometimes we do weapons maintenance and we break the rifle down and clean it. I really like doing that most of the time, it's (for some reason) really relaxing. I just brush my barrel and the other part of the rifle and think about home. . . .

Mom, I love you and miss you everyday. Please don't worry about me, I am seriously doing OK, I'm just lonely and homesick. I think that when I see you and _____ again on visitor's Thursday, that will be the happiest day of my life. Also, I will be a Marine. My asthma hasn't bothered me at all. I love you.

I hope everything is going well and that you are getting my mail. Tell Anna and chip I say Hi. I will write more soon.

Love, Andy

September 7, 2003

Dear Mom,

Well, it's Sunday again and we're getting some "square away time" so I'm writing again. I never realized how slow mail actually is. It is the 7th and I just received a letter you wrote on the 29th of August. I haven't heard from _____ in 4–5 days. I've written her 3-5 times and she hasn't shown any indication in the letters she's written that she got them.

They haven't come back to me so I guess they're getting to her. . . . Well, anyway, to answer some of your questions. I want to fly back home as soon as possible on Nov. 7 right after graduation. I have a bank account and don't need any money right now. I need to know if you are going to buy my ticket home or if you want me to take care of it.

I have learned to make a tight rack [bed]. Whenever we are in the squad bay (barracks) all we do is tighten racks and clean. We clean so much its ridiculous. They even make us clean when there's nothing left to clean.

On to something else. I have now been here for 4 weeks. Initial drill is over and the DIs are getting harder on us. But, for the most part we are used to it. . . . Altogether, I guess I am doing fine in training. I'm rarely getting yelled at anymore and I do what I'm supposed to.

I'm starting to have a lot of respect for S/Sgt. Polk. He's scary when he's mad, but he's a pretty cool guy. He has been checking on me every once in a while to make sure I'm doing ok. Today he said that I was doing better.

Mom, I'm sorry, but I would prefer if you didn't call him, unless you absolutely can't stand it. I'm sorry.

[Note from Mom: Sgt. Polk called me once regarding the head-slamming incident. He gave me his cell phone number and told me to call if I wanted to, but—somehow I refrained.]

. . . . One of the biggest problems that I've started having in the last few days is the lack of intellectual stimulation. I can't fucking read or listen to music. Please send me some paper so I can write. I'm basically just bored, everything here is physical. The mental part still has to do with the physical part, just telling your body to keep going even though it hurts. We can't talk, so my brain is just bursting with boredom.

Give or take a few things, the days are exactly the same, no variations. I do like getting letters that is the best part. Please keep sending letters and tell people to send me letters. Check if ____ is getting my mail. Send letters soon, I've only had 1 in 4-5 days.

I love you more than the Marine Corps, more than I will ever love the USMC.

Love,
Andy Kaplan

T18: Early in the morning. I hate mornings, mornings are always shitty because it makes everything seem so far away. You have a whole day of shit you think is pointless ahead to you.

Now, up to this point my journal entries have been pretty negative, but in all fairness, there are some very good things about boot camp. In the short run, there is a sense of pride in everything you accomplish. Every time you make it through another day, you're proud of yourself. Whenever Senior DI Polk pumps us up with his Senior DI time, it really makes you want to complete the training.

The two things that drive me are 1) Being a Marine will be the best thing I've ever done, and 2) When I graduate, I can see my family and girlfriend again. That's what pushes me.

Even when I hate boot camp, I still know that I want to be a Marine. I get excited when I think about being deployed. . . . Once boot camp is over, military life will be much better.

I do worry about girls and _____ now there's a chance that I will be far away for a long time. I don't know if that will work for us. I definitely might meet someone and she might too and that sucks. I miss her a lot and the thought of seeing her when I graduate gets me through all the other bullshit. . . .

I'm really starting to respect and like S/Sgt. Polk. Whenever he takes over, I get motivated and really want to be a Marine. But when DI Smith or Jackson take over, it's just them being assholes. That's the way it's supposed to be.

T-18 and the DIs are getting harder on us. "Move it, little shit" for not being dressed in time. I still need to move faster, but I think I'm doing much better.

The one thing that I haven't really grasped is the whole no individuality. The Corps says, especially in boot, that there is no "I" in team. But, I think that even in the group/team oriented environment, you have to retain individuality. I, on the other hand, still think of myself too much. I need to be more team oriented. The way to retain my individuality is by keeping this journal.

Today I found out that my two best buds in the platoon are being dropped.[*]

T19: My mood changes so much here at boot. One minute I'm on top of the world and I know that this is the shit for me—I want to be a Marine. At other times, I'm so depressed I want to cry and just go home. The one thing that keeps bugging me is the fact that half the time I'm really not motivated.

A lot of kids are starting to like boot camp, I'm not. I like the feeling of pride I get when I accomplish something. . . . But in no way, shape or form, do I like or enjoy 85% of boot camp and it brings me down. I think I might go see the chaplain.

We screwed up today and Staff Sergeant Polk is hella pissed off at us. We're going to have to work hard to win his respect back.

T20: Early morning. I have been called to special testing [Note from Mom: He was later asked to "try out" for the Seals program, but wasn't a strong enough swimmer. He was very relieved he didn't make it.] No idea why, may have something to do with infantry.

I am convinced that infantry is the only MOS for me. Why join the Marines for any other reason?

Today is training Day 20, that's good, only like 50 something to go. . . .

I am still worried about getting hurt up north [in Pendleton]. I don't want to go MRP. I want to graduate on Nov. 7.

One thing I have really not touched on is the other kids in my platoon. There are 87 of us, I probably can't name more that 30 or 40. You don't really know each other. We never really get a chance to

*Sent home for failure to "adjust" or for some other health or disciplinary reason or being sent back in training for failure to complete some test.—FS

talk. In some instances, there is a chance to get to know one another and you do make a sort of friend.

Everyone in the platoon watches out for each other, but not because they are nice, it's because if one person messes up, the whole platoon is screwed. Mostly everyone is just kinda looking out for themselves while making sure that no one else messes up in order to save their own skin. Then there are the guide and squad leaders, they are the recruit leaders of the platoon and they are all asses. The only words that ever really come out of their mouths are, "Stop fucking moving or get your fucking ass on line," all negative. They are asses and I have no respect for them. The guide is like [is] the head recruit. Our guide is C, he's a hard-ass, but he's a good guide. Sometimes he's a prick, but that's okay.

Evening chow. Today we did a CCX (combat conditioning exercise) and for the first time I actually kind of liked the physical stuff. The depressing part about boot camp is that even when you get pumped up, it only lasts for an hour or two and then you realize that you still have eight weeks in this hellhole and if you get hurt, you'll be here longer, so you just revert back to that hopeless, "Oh shit, I hate boot camp, but I have to keep doing this crap because if I don't I get dropped." It sucks. . . .

The DIs are being really hard on us lately, so I'm going to try and write at night. I want to send more letters to _____ and get some off to Lauren and Eric. End of this.

————————

September 14, 2003

Dear Mom and Dad,

Hey, we have arrived safely up north. [The recruits at MCRD, Marine Corps Recruit Depot, San Diego are sent north to Camp Pendleton to complete the rifle training.—FS] We got up here sometime in the afternoon yesterday and for the first two hours it was like they wanted to put us through the first day of boot camp again. They made us pick up our 60-70 pound sea bags and put them over our heads and do squats. Then we had to pick them up and run back and forth. One of the times I was a tiny bit behind everyone else and Sgt Smith ripped my head off, he really doesn't like me. I hope he doesn't make my time here miserable.

Yesterday got me really stressed out and I have been at a high level of anxiety for 24 hours for some reason and I mean 90% anxiety. Right now I want to cry. Kim and I have started talking more and he helps me out.

I've just started worrying about everything. I'm constantly worried about being dropped for some reason or having to stay in boot camp longer. I'm still homesick and I worry about you. . . . It's like being at boot camp takes my anxiety and multiplies it by a hundred times. Right now I think it was just moving up north and being singled out yesterday. I will get better as I get used to being up north. . . .

I've never felt so empty and not whole in my entire life. No one really cares what happens to me except maybe Kim. It's a horrible feeling to know that. If I had known what this was going to be like, I don't know if I could've joined up. But I think that's the point, like they say, "No one is prepared for boot camp."

Now that I'm here I do want to be a Marine, more that anything. But emotionally I don't know how long I can take it. My mood is always up and down, up and down. By the time you guys get this letter, everything could be hunky dory again, I don't know. All I know is that without my family and friends, (girlfriends especially), I am not a whole person.

How are you holding up? Go to Taco Bell for me. I miss fast food and soda and my hair and TV and movies and just about everything good in life. Boot camp is hell, but I can do it and I will. If I do get kicked out, so be it; I'll get to see you guys. . . .

Love,
Andy Kaplan

[Family Christmas newsletter December 03 from Andy's mom, Gaye Lowe-Kaplan.—FS]

Christmas 2003

Merry Christmas, Feliz Navidad, Shalom,

When I look back at 2003 and wonder what to tell you, the first thing that comes to mind, and won't go away is that Andy became a U.S. Marine. He headed off for boot camp on August 4 and we didn't see him again until November 4. That day we watched as six platoons of Marine clones marched around the parade deck, showing their parents how all 498 of them could execute a ninety-degree turn simultaneously. It was quite impressive, actually, but the only thing the mothers cared about was getting the first glimpse of their sons.

Frank saw Andy before I did . . . I never knew how terribly I would miss him; he never realized how homesick he would be.

None of us, including Andy, thought he would make it through "boot." I thought for sure his asthma would take a turn for the worse and he'd be sent home, but no luck. He continued to breathe. He was constantly screamed at by his DIs (drill instructors), and his head was bashed into a table once when he moved during the raising of the flag. He hiked (humped) ten miles, straight up, with a 60 pound pack on his back to the top of The Reaper (mountain) and was told the platoon was a disgrace to the Corps.

Because of the Coke bottle glasses ("portholes") [Andy] had to wear, he was a constant source of amusement to the DIs,

"Hey, Kaplan! Can you predict the future through those things?"

"SIR, NO SIR!"

"You got beat up a lot in high school, didn't you, Kaplan?"

"SIR, NO SIR!"

"We hate you, Kaplan. Get outta here!"

"SIR, YES SIR!"

Another time one of the recruits didn't eat his food fast enough, so each recruit in the platoon was ordered to gulp down three canteens of water as quickly as possible. They all threw up, and were then ordered outside to fill their pockets with dirt. Then they covered the vomit with dirt and had to sit in it for an hour cleaning their rifles. Fun stuff, huh?

Later on in the training, he had to swim with all his gear on, take off his gas mask in the gas chamber, and jump off of a five-story building. It was a miserable time for him, but during the eighth week, he had breakfast with the base commander for being one of the six "most improved recruits."

We flew out to San Diego for his graduation and were awestruck when we first saw his metamorphosis. Today, December 2, is his first day at the School of Infantry at Camp Pendleton, Calif., and for all we know, he could be jumping out of a helicopter into the Pacific or throwing grenades. He'll finish his training in February and then wants to get some college courses under his belt while he practices blowing things up. He also wants to go to Iraq and will probably get that opportunity by next September, if not before. He said there are "men in the Marines, and there are Marines." He's not sure where he fits just yet and he's a bit disheartened with the public attitude toward the military. . . .

Gaye Lowe-Kaplan

LCpl. Andy Kaplan, USMC, is stationed in Hawaii working hard to find a way to be sent into action in the Middle East. His mother has written to me several times since sending me the letters above. Gaye has been telling me about the change in Andy, his level of maturity and dedication to the Marine Corps.—FS

9

Letter from Cpl. Cody M. Harkins, USMC, age eighteen to his family, written upon completing Marine boot camp in San Diego, where the last event is a fast "hump" (march) up a steep mountain.—FS

January 1, 2001

Dear family,

Well here we are born to be kings!

. . . . Here we are moments away from being reunited. I am different from before. I am better. My head has a weird tan and I eat a lot faster. . . . My heart has been changed and my eyes have been opened. I know now the importance of family and freedom. Even better because it is my job to protect them and keep them alive.

On Friday at about 9:00 on top of the highest mountain in the world, I became a United States Marine. For 3 months of my life I worked so hard giving 100% everyday all for a little matte black EGA [eagle, globe, and anchor, the symbol of the Marine Corps]. And let me tell you it was worth every second. The lessons I have learned and skills that were taught to me are forever etched in my mind. What got me up the Reaper? [the mountain near the San Diego training depot]. What pulled me from a hypothermic state to someone running up the mountain so fast that I popped a blood vessel in my eye? These words you sent me:

1. "All I want for my Birthday is my brother"—Sommer [his sister]
2. "I can do all things through Christ who strengthens me"—Dad
3. "I love you/I miss you/come home"—Mom
4. "I wish I would have done that (joined the military)" —Uncle Scotty

I did it for a way to get home. For a chance to finish something so many have tried and failed. For my friends. For my family. To create a tradition and make the name Harkins strong and proud. I did it for myself. I did it for the uniforms and the way people look at you. I did it for this moment. I am done here. Mission accomplished. It is the primary objective of the Corps—Mission accomplished! I am coming home.

Love,
PFC Cody M. Harkins, USMC
Semper Fi/Do or Die

Cpl. Cody M. Harkins is now in Afghanistan.—FS

DEPLOYMENT

10

Mr. Schaeffer,

We met briefly at a book signing in Quantico a few weeks ago. My name is Captain Jason D. Grose [USMC] and we talked about my son and daughter and the plight I might one day face if they decide to enter the military. I read your book Faith of Our Sons. . . . As a Marine, I saw what my own parents must have felt when I was deployed to the first go around in Iraq. As a father, I could imagine going through the same horror and discovered it would be much worse from that perspective. You might or might not remember but I relayed a conversation I had with my wife when we discussed the possibility of our son and/or daughter joining one day. I told her she'd be a wreck for the boot camp three months and she never skipped a beat and said no, I'd be the wreck. Thinking about it, I realized she was right. . . . Recently, I had occasion to talk to my mentor; the Sergeant who took me to the first Gulf War and kept his promise to bring me back. He is simply the best Marine I've ever known and even now, as a Captain of Marines with almost 17 years of enlisted and commissioned service, I cannot hold a candle to him and only hope to be a fraction of the Marine he was. I often call him for his professional and personal advice.

In 1990, we had arrived in Saudi Arabia and were living in tents.

It had been a couple of months and had not called home until we got a chance to pile in a half-ton truck and travel for an hour to a liberty area where they had set up some phone banks. I called my wife and it was the most joyous time I experienced up to that point. . . . We had finished up and everyone climbed back into the truck for the ride back to camp. I noticed Sgt. Shane Maxey (my mentor) had a more severe than normal expression on his face so I asked him what was wrong. He told me that when it came time to talk to his 8-year-old son, his wife handed the boy the phone. The only thing that came through the line was inconsolable crying. Shane tried to talk to him but all he heard was the boy weeping. Finally, his wife took he phone and time was up.

It was at that point I knew I was blessed not to have any children. I missed my wife terribly and even my cats. But to be in a foreign land fighting a war and hearing your son crying is a pain I don't know if I could have handled. Shane is hard as woodpecker lips and was a harder "hard corps" drill Instructor even by [our] standards, but even such a man has his limits. My heart broke when I saw the look in his eyes.

I tell you this story because there is an interesting twist. That little boy is graduating high school this year and has joined the National Guard. Unlike the Marines, when you join the National Guard, you know what unit you will be joining and Chris's unit is slated to go to Iraq as soon as his boot camp is completed. That small boy who could only cry when talking to his Marine father at war is now himself on a path that takes him to fight.

Shane retired a year ago (he got out of the Marine Corps at 13 years, joined the National Guard and then active duty Army to finish out his career) and I recently had to talk him out of trying to get back in when he learned his son was going over. That's just Shane being Shane.

The other story that illustrates who he is . . . was when we found out we were deploying. He invited the dozen men slated to go and their wives over to his house for dinner. We got to know each other and Shane took aside the wives to talk to them. He promised each one of them he'd bring their husbands back which was a bold promise considering all the unknowns at the time. But that he took personal responsibility for our return speaks volumes. I took him aside and told him I had a problem. I had not contacted my mom and since everything was classified, I didn't know what to tell her. We were leaving any day and I didn't want to leave without letting her know. Shane never hesitated and told me what to tell her. He made me call from his phone (note that's a long distance phone call on a Sergeant's pay) and this is what I said: "Mom, I have to go away on business and you know my business." As you can imagine, my Mom lost it and all I heard were cries of "My baby! My baby!" Never before nor since have experienced the pain I felt at that moment. I had to practically hang up on her and then I called my brother (again, at Shane's insistence). He had spent time in the Army so when I made the same statement to him, he said he understood, to be careful, and get my butt home in one piece. I then told him to call Mom and calm her down and say the things I was not allowed to say. . . .

At the end of the night, we all held up a glass of champagne and toasted for our success and safety. It was at this moment that we learned something that Shane had withheld up to this point. That night just happened to be Shane's wedding anniversary.

Iraq invaded [Kuwait] on August 2nd. We found out we were leaving on August 8th. We were gone on August 12th. Shane had every right to have a quiet anniversary dinner with his bride and young family, especially considering he was leaving to war any day. But instead, he chose to invite a dozen Marines he hardly knew (he had just checked into the unit from being a Drill Instructor weeks before) to make promises to the wives and share the evening in brotherhood. . . .

My time in the Corps is coming to an end in 2007 but just as one chapter closes, another begins. My son is 12 and it will not be long before he will have to make a decision. I feel strongly about letting him make his own decision and supporting him in any path he chooses. . . .

I hope my son will choose to serve for a variety of reasons. I think it is his American duty and he will benefit from it personally. But as a father, I shudder at the thought. . . . I know too much of the dangers and possibilities. I love my son as much as our political leadership loves theirs and [know that their] policies would be radically different if their children were one of the pawns they moved around on maps. . . . Semper Fi.

Captain Jason D. Grose, USMC

March 10, 2004

Hello Mr. Schaeffer,

On behalf of my husband who is currently deployed to Iraq, I was wondering if you would be interested in receiving some of his correspondence. My husband is a Chaplain for the National Guard and a Pastor of First Presbyterian Church in Monroe, NC. [These] "Dispatches" . . . amount to a collection of his thoughts, prayers, struggles, and experiences since October 2003. They were sent to family and members of his church when his unit was activated [first to his base in the United States, then sent to Iraq].

God bless,
Heather Wainwright

CH (CPT) Kevin Wainwright
Chaplain 1-113th FA BN
October 16, 2003

Hello to everyone,

. . . . I was present at all the mobilization ceremonies to give the invocation and the benediction. I was moved by the number of little children who were present at the ceremonies. Many tears of both pride and sadness were shed by all in attendance. . . .

I have been very busy counseling with and visiting soldiers. There are many who are having an especially difficult time with the separation, particularly the younger soldiers with families. I try to be a good listener. . . . It gets hard at times because I do not have someone to talk to [myself] down here.

We have received several secret briefings concerning the area where we will be deploying. I am now convinced that not only are we going but we should be going. The enemy we are facing is especially cunning and cruel. We will fight them over there or over here, but we will fight them.

I am constantly trying to present the soldiers with a balanced perspective. They are definitely motivated to be going, but I remind them that both our enemies and our allies are human beings created by God. The first step towards committing an atrocity is to dehumanize the foe. . . .

Grace, Mercy, and Peace,
CH Kevin Wainwright Ft. Bragg, NC
CH (CPT) Kevin Wainwright
Chaplain 1-113th FA BN

October 17, 2003

Hello Everyone,

. . . . We are having two services on Sunday. One outside next to our headquarters and one by the CS (tear gas) tent. Every soldier (including me) had to go through to make sure the seal on the mask is tight. The gas stings a little bit, but they did not make us take off our mask like they usually do. I was a little disappointed. I have been through the "tent" at least five times, and they say that you continue to build up resistance to it every time.

The smallpox vaccination is beginning to itch. I would recommend that anyone who can get it should. The homicide bombers may soon start injecting themselves with smallpox before they commit their atrocities. This means that infected flesh and shrapnel would be spread throughout the area. People traveling back who were hit could be disease carriers. What a wonderful world we live in.

They are going to prosecute the West Point grad and Islamic Chaplain who was in my company. They are giving me a hard time about that here, all in good nature of course. It makes me sick to my stomach. Apparently he was trying to email to Al Qaeda links back in Syria the names of all internees, the map of the camp, and the names and addresses of all the families of the interrogators. Bad, bad situation. . . .

We soldiers have to relearn the values of accountability and responsibility. Many, but not too many, soldiers come to me complaining about how [as reservists] they did not sign up for this and about how the [National] Guard does not care about families. We live in a culture that is so self-obsessed and rights concerned that holding someone to a promise or an oath is considered blasphemy. I am glad, even though it is causing me to be away from my family, that institutions like the church and the military still expect us to fulfill our promises.

A brief observation: Soldiers who regularly attend church, profess their faith. . . . are handling this deployment better than the average G.I. They have more hope and a more positive outlook. We are only journeying through this world. The stripping away of my old life has reawakened me to the value of people over things and how much God truly loves us. . . .

Wish you could have been there last Sunday when all the soldiers were singing. . . . Do not believe any stories about bad morale in our unit. I am so proud that I am in this Brigade. I almost feel prouder to be representing [the] North Carolina [Guard] than our nation (although I am proud of that too). Be forewarned if I start sounding like a convert when speaking about our beautiful state.

I believe that what we are doing is a historically significant thing. This is the largest call up of citizen soldiers since WWII. I feel like we are the modern day minutemen. We are beginning to look and act like soldiers. You would be proud. . . .

For those [in the church] who like to sew, I am looking for someone who could make me a desert camouflage stole. It could be the size of a regular stole except in desert camo. At the ends it would be great to have a black embroidered cross. . . . The only difficulty with all this is finding the correct camouflage fabric. It would have to be exactly like the desert pattern that the Army uses . . . if someone would be interested in making it. I, of course, would pay for the supplies.

I worry I am sounding bossy. Hope I am not. As always, am missing Josh and Heather. At least four or five times a day I go through a "slide show" of my favorite pictures of my family. I miss you all.

CH Kevin Wainwright
Grace, Mercy, and Peace

11

April 2, 2004

Frank: My husband Lt. Col. Clark R Lethin, USMC, (age 44) wrote this letter to his sons while he was on the way to Afghanistan. He was the operations officer for Task Force 58.

Wendy Lethin

October 22, 2001

Subject: FOR THE MEN
Jake, Mack, Cullen: Dad here. . . .

I sure miss every one of you and wish I could be there to help [you] do homework or just have fun.

Please understand that when I'm gone I think of you boys often and think about all the fun things we have done and still need to do. In the mean time, I want you to know a couple of things.

Throughout our country's history, men and women fought for our right to be free. . . . You guys have not traveled the world, yet. Your mom and I have. I've probably seen the most. There is not a place on this earth like the USA. Most people live in poverty, are oppressed, can't say what they would like to say, and don't know where their next meal will come from. There are many reasons for this. The biggest reason is that a few people in [many] countries [get] power and abuse it. They don't think of the people and their happiness. They feel that people exist to serve them.

In our country, we have a system that gives people confidence to live and work together. . . . Of course there is a cost. The cost is we are prepared to defend our way of life. That means we have a military that will defend our country, our citizens around the world and a military that will help other countries if they ask. Since I'm in the military, I have to be ready to go and do what is asked of me. It's a sacrifice, I know now it's a sacrifice for the families more than the military person told to go off and fight our country's battles. . . .

Your sacrifice is that I can't be there with you. . . . Your sacrifice is you have to keep your chins up and not feel sorry for yourselves. Your sacrifice is you have to work together to keep our family strong. That means caring for each other and helping your mom. . . .

I don't want you to worry about me. . . . I don't want you to worry too much about the world. Let me and your mom do that. Just like I have a mission, you have to have a mission. Your mission is to grow up strong, caring, loving, honest, knowing that God, Mom and I love you.

Know that I miss you and love you dearly. I don't know exactly when I'll be home, but when I find out, I'll let you know. So men, go forth and conquer.

Love,
Dad
Lt. Col. Clark R Lethin, USMC

Lt. Col. Clark R. Lethin, USMC, just returned from his second deployment to Iraq, which lasted five months. His deployment to Afghanistan also lasted five months.—FS

March 5, 2004

Hi Frank,

My name is Angela Borgmann and my husband Chad, age 23, is a Marine and served in the Iraq war. He wrote me this letter last year while in Kuwait waiting to go into Iraq.

Our son Logan has just turned 7 months. Chad got back from his deployment to Iraq a month and a half before Logan was born. Now Chad is back in Iraq a second time. Chad is now 24 and I'm 25. I'm expecting our second baby Sept. 2004. I don't know if Chad will be back for the birth. I don't think he will. Chad is in Fallujah right now in a big fight there.

Angela Borgmann

March 10, 2003

From LCpl. Chad Borgmann, USMC (Infantry)

Thoughts to Angela and Logan from Kuwait. . . .

War is all around us here. I can hear it, I can see it, and I can feel it. Sitting outside of my tent I see piles of debris and wreckage from the first time we were here. . . . All day and night the sounds of fully loaded combat aircraft fill the sky. The jets fly over us low enough that we can see hell bent objects of destruction hanging from their wings. Sometimes the [pilots] will wave at us by rocking their wings back and forth. There are many moments like that here, brief moments of joy separated by hours of boredom.

The faces of the men do not reflect the possible horror in front of us. That is partly because the young men that make up the majority of the USMC refuse to accept our mortality. They will believe themselves to be indestructible until death slams face first into us or into the guy next to us. The first sight of death and blood will send us spiraling into reality.

The other reason is the weaknesses of our enemy. A recon patrol close to the Kuwait and Iraq border witnessed an enemy observation post on the Iraq side waving a white flag. We haven't even made movements toward them yet. The enemy defensive positions have been built facing the wrong way so that we won't attack them and they can surrender as soon as we get there.

Marine artillery was being fired at a range about 15 miles from the border. The Iraqis, mistaking the sounds of the artillery for the beginning of the war, began walking toward the border to surrender to us. The majority of them don't want to fight us, the rest are unprepared.

They are forced to serve in a war they don't believe in and for a leader they don't trust. They fear us. They are told that we must kill a member of our immediate family in order to enlist in the USMC. So not only are we better trained and have better equipment but we are "bloodthirsty murderers" as well.

All of the men here want to do one of two things: move north into Iraq, or get back on ship. The entertainment of the dessert has worn thin. Many feel that if we don't go to combat then our time spent here has been a total waste. I happen to disagree. By sitting in this wasteland doing nothing I am saving lives. The show of force we are displaying is going to be the reason that war is averted, if it is averted. If there is no war then there are no lives lost by means of violence, as necessary as that violence may be.

My sitting here means that other young men from around the country don't have to leave their families. I sacrifice so they don't have to. I will sacrifice to the point of death . . . and to honor those who have done the same before me.

As I sit here outside of my tent I care about nothing but my God, my wife, and my child. In a matter of hours I may be asked to risk it all in defense of them. I will do it gladly to ensure that my wife and child can live safely for the rest of their lives, with or without me.

I am a United States Marine. That is my job. It goes unappreciated by most of the country but I don't mind. I seek only the approval and love of my wife. . . .

I will come home. I will remain one of the few and the one of the proud.

LCpl. Chad Borgmann, USMC (Infantry)

LCpl. Chad Borgmann is now patrolling the streets of Fallujah in Iraq.—FS

February 21, 2004

Frank:

You and I are quite different in background but so much alike in many ways. Similarly, my son Sean U.S. Navy, (HT2C on the USS *John C. Stennis*) and your boy are also different, but probably more similar in their gentle ways, work ethic and dedication to our country. Sean is my hero.

I had the good fortune to experience a "Tiger Cruise," joining him and his shipmates in Hawaii as they returned from an eight month deployment off the coast of Afghanistan and sailing back to San Diego on the ship. I slept in a bunk in his berthing area . . . followed him on a couple of welding jobs he was assigned to do (helping carry the tools and torches), met his friends, and generally got a good understanding of [my son's] life at sea as a sailor in the Navy.

I think very few Americans understand the tremendous sacrifice our young men and women make to serve in the armed forces. The thing that impressed me most is the wonderful spirit that permeated that ship. The spirit of oneness and purpose was awesome to me.

Sean and I had our tensions [during] his last months before his going off to Great Lakes Navy Training Station. Sean had an opportunity to get out on medical problems. . . . Sean will be the first to admit that Navy boot camp was not even close to what [your son] John went through [in the USMC]. Still, I think my boy would have gotten through [Marine Corps boot camp] too. Like John, he's lean and hard. . . .

Here are some emails that I have received from my son, HT2C Sean Wyman, who proudly serves on the USS *John C. Stennis*. Sean spent over 100 days off the coast of Afghanistan. . . .

Charlie Wyman

Sean Wyman wrote this letter when he was twenty years old from the USS *John C. Stennis.*—FS

Wednesday, November 5, 2003

Yeah, sounds to me like a long, LONG deployment is in store for us. I hear people I work with already trying to figure out a way to weasel out of it. I think that a 10 month deployment will definitely be stressful but if 5,700 other sailors can do it then why can't I do it?

. . . . I would love to return to East Coast next summer more than anything to join you in the father-son activities we have talked about; however we would not be able to enjoy those freedoms if our "boys" didn't volunteer a piece of their life and sacrifice their time to defend our freedom and to support democracy around the world. . . . I will not hesitate to sail another mission if I am considered mission critical to my battle group.

Love . . .
Sean
HT2C Sean Wyman, U.S. Navy

June 14, 2003

My father . . . It seems like such a long time ago that we started this rough journey of you raising me to be a man. . . . On [this] Father's Day I get to show you all of my appreciation. . . . You gave me the kind of guidance that every son needs, but at the time it was a pain in the ass to me. Well you know something; it seemed to work pretty well because I'm on my feet. . . .

One thing I couldn't figure out until recently was why on earth you would want to wake up at four in the damn morning on a -10 degrees day to stand in an ice rink. Now that I think back on it playing hockey was like playing life; you have to be there on time, in the right state of mind, and do your best. . . . I got the message.

I guess you helped me turn out all right for someone who grew up . . . with the wrong crowd. Even when I was all fucked up, covered in blood in the middle of the waterfront, I had nothing to worry about because of my hero named Dad. . . .

Now that you are retiring in a happy place I will be happy to return the favor that you did for me. I have to finish my military thing first because someone taught me never to back out of a contract. . . .

Happy Father's Day Dad, I think you're the best, and for anyone who thinks less, "fuck 'em."

HT2C Sean Wyman, U.S. Navy

HT2C Sean Wyman, U.S. Navy, is now a petty officer 2nd Class, Hull Technician.—FS

March 11, 2004

Frank:

My name is Chantal and I have a few e-mails that my boyfriend, now husband, LCpl. David W. Bryant, USMC, sent me while on his way to and from the war last year. My husband just went back over to Iraq so if you have any questions, please contact me. . . . Thank you,

Chantal Bryant

Thursday January 9, 2003

Hey babe how's it going. Man I miss you soooo much. I've been staring at that picture that you gave me it makes me feel closer to you. . . .

Babe, don't worry too much about me. I'm in God's hands even more than before and He will look over me. A scripture that helps me a lot is: "I will not put more weight on your shoulders than you can bear." It's not an exact quote but you know it.

Every time I get the feeling like I can't go on any more I think of that scripture and I feel a 100X's better. . . .

Signing out with LOVE,
David
LCpl. David W. Bryant, USMC

May 6, 2003

. . . . What do I expect when I come home? That's a good question! I don't expect anything cause I know things are constantly changing so if I was to expect something and it wasn't like I had thought, I'd be disappointed. I would just like to see you, hold you and forget everything around me. I know that I've been sending confusing messages here lately, and they are soon to halt because everyday that goes by I straighten myself out and figure out a little something that has to change or stay the same. So don't worry, in a little while I'll be completely settled down and know exactly what to say.

While I was working out tonight I thought the whole time (an hour) about what I was going to say in this email, and the only big thing that I could come up with is that to say I'm sorry. I'm sorry for not saying the three words that I needed to say when I talked to you and when I first emailed you—I LOVE YOU! I LOVE YOU! I LOVE YOU!

I know they are just words but they say so much, and they should tell you exactly what my feelings are for you. They haven't changed. Do you still have that message that I put on your answering machine before I left? If you ever doubt my feelings for you play the message and remember how I was sitting right next to you and looking at you when I left it there. . . . David

LCpl. David W. Bryant, USMC

LCpl. David W. Bryant is currently deployed in Fallujah, Iraq. He has been in Iraq since February 29, 2004, and is supposed to return in October 2004.—FS

12

This letter was written from Brandon Bailey (we heard from him earlier in the book), from his base in South Korea.—FS

May 2003

Dear Sarah,

I actually don't know how to even start this letter because I'm missing you so bad. I don't know the words to say what I'm feeling right now. How about, I love you tremendously and I miss you terribly. . . .

There is no way that I will ever re-enlist no matter what. You mean too much to me and I never want to have to be away from you again, it's killing me. It's kind of selfish but I really don't care. In the back of my mind I always thought it would be easy to retire from the Air Force but I would way rather work hard my entire life and always get to come home to you at night than to have to go through time without [you]. . . . I tried calling you Friday night but the phone was busy and there were people waiting to use the phone.

Ok, so this is the next day because I was so tired last night that I fell asleep while writing to you. . . . I can't wait for this year to be over; it's not going by fast enough.

All my love sent to you,
Brandon Bailey, USAF

June 21, 2003

Yobosaeyo, Yobo. There's my Korean for the night. That's how I say hi honey . . . I know I'm spending more money right now than what I should, but really most of it is just moving in stuff that we have had to get. I'll really try to check myself and not spend as much. It's hard to remember that I am now not just spending money for myself but that I have someone else that will be using some of it also and when you combine both spending rates it can add up. I'm not used to that, I'm just used to spending money as I want as long as there is money there to spend. . . .

You just kind of threw me off this afternoon [on the phone] when right away you started in about how much I've been spending. It's been a long week, and though I am working hard now, I still miss you a ton and miss you every second of every day and the whole money thing is really not what I was wanting [to hear] about. . . .

I hope you know that if it wasn't punishable under law to be [there] right now there would be nothing keeping me from you. I really hope you understand the depth of my love for you. I would do anything you ever ask of me just ask. I love you so much.

Will you please forgive me for being short with you? I'm so sorry, I hate having to apologize over the internet but again, it's all I've got right now. I LOVE YOU!!!!

Brandon
Brandon Bailey, USAF

July 17, 2003

Hello my love,

. . . . I am so glad that we didn't wait to get married, I can't imagine going through my time here without you in my life. . . . I am so glad that each night when everyone else is gearing up for going downtown and watching the dancers I am gearing up for coming back to my room, calling you, my only love, and then taking a shower and winding down so I can go to sleep. [It] always thrills me and sends butterflies through my stomach hearing your voice on the other end of the line.

You know those realistic dreams I said I have had about you here with me but when I wake up you aren't? The great thing about those is the fact that they don't disappoint me when I realize that my life with you isn't just a realistic dream, that it is my reality and I get to live with that the rest of my life. . . .

I love having the candle that smells like your perfume, I still have that piece of cloth that you sent me during basic with your perfume on it. . . .

Your Husband
Brandon Bailey, USAF

13

This Marine (who requested that his name be withheld) wrote these letters when he was twenty-one.—FS

Feburary 28, 2003
Kuwait

Dear Mom & Dad,

We finally got the tractors here, about a week or two ago. The first few days we spent going over them to make sure we took care of all the mechanical problems that we could. Of course, logistics out there is a nightmare (all the high ranking mechanics have been VERY grouchy) so we really can't rely on getting any spare parts. And, unfortunately, yesterday we were out practicing a battalion size movement (or, a company of AAV's with grunts, and a bunch of Hummers driving around in a column, one after the other) when my generator exploded (not quite literally). So now my vehicle can't move until it gets replaced.

The grunts that have been assigned to my tractor (2nd Squad 3rd(r) Plt KCo 3/5) are a class A bunch of loonies. We should work very well together.

The day before yesterday we finally went to the range to test fire our weapons, sort of. We didn't get to fire our 40s at all and we only got 50 rounds for our .50 cals. I shot off all my rounds in one minute. But at least now I can rest a little easier because I did manage to kill the bush that I was aiming at.

And, yes, they do have bushes out here, and BIG trees, too. I don't know where the heck they came from. But every once in a while you'll see this big ol' tree right there surrounded by hundreds of miles of sand. And I saw my first wild camels yesterday! We drove by a family of them. Speaking of animals, we are still waiting to be issued our *COMBAT CHICKENS. [*To be expanded later—FS]

Anyway, I really look forward to hearing from you guys. All your prayers are greatly appreciated. Please pray especially for my Lieutenant, our leaders, my crew, and my grunts (they really are nuts). Please send some black socks, baby wipes, and maybe any other useful goodies. I love you guys a lot and I miss you very much. Please send lots of news about what's going on back there. Bye for now.

Your son,
Cpl., USMC

March 10, 2003
Kuwait
Day 38/4th pair of socks/2nd pair of underwear

Dear Mom & Dad,

Well, if you've been getting all these letters in the same order that I've been writing them, a remote possibility, then you will recall that the last letter was to be my "last letter." [Before combat was to begin—FS] Of course, being familiar, as you are, with how they run this circus, you probably thought, "I'll bet this ISN'T the last letter for a while." You were right, of course, to think that.

They told us today that the schedule has been pushed back. This is actually good news for me, because I still haven't gotten a generator to replace the exploded one. But they did come today, while I was in the middle of praying for, among other things, a new generator, and took the old generator away. They said that they would take it to another camp tomorrow and hopefully get it traded out for a new one.

Speaking of praying, I've been thinking a lot about it lately. One issue I've been bothered by is the generator issue—you see, if they split up my crew to different vehicles, I will probably end up driving. I really don't want that, though. I want to be in the turret (my office) with the guns. Being with the guns means you are the guy blowing people up. So, it just sounds weird to me to say "Lord, please get me a generator so I can ride in my turret and blow people up." I'm sure you see my point. I guess I'm just not sure if it's a good thing that I should be so eager to go out and kill bad guys. I can't help but get worked up about it, kind of like a football game. I know that Saddam and his buddies DESERVE to be put to death, but is it good to want to be the guy to do it?

Well, at least writing this down and getting it off my chest helped to make me feel better. Please don't think I'm going crazy or anything. I've just been sitting out in the desert too long with nothing to do but think, I guess. Well, if I still haven't settled the issue with myself, if it comes down to it, I'll just shoot first and ask questions later. Usually, I just pray that God's will be done—that should cover it. . . .

Your son,
Cpl., USMC

March 5, 2003
Kuwait

Dear Mom & Dad,

Hello! Greetings from the sandbox. I finally got my first mail from you guys a few days ago.

Well it's been business as usual with ol' Uncle Sam's Misguided Children [USMC]. The combat chickens we were supposed to get all died. No, not from chemical weapons, though. Apparently they'd never left the barn before and going outside sent them all into shock. All this would definitely explain all the chicken we've been fed out here!

[The military issued chickens to test the air for chemical gas attack.—FS]

Right now we are living at Camp Coyote (yes the one with absolutely NO amenities). But to make room for all of the personnel here we are still living in our vehicles, which is fine with me anyway. Speaking of my vehicle, it is still broken. They actually took good parts off of my vehicle and traded them out with bad parts from another vehicle since mine was down anyway. All I've gotta say is somebody's gonna pay through the nose if I end up stuck HERE, while everybody else has all the fun!

Meanwhile we are still waiting for the go-ahead. They told us today that we've been bombing the heck out of Iraq lately. You guys probably know more from CNN than I do, actually. But tell me this. I heard the other day that Congress is SUING the President. I'm not quite sure what to make of that. Of course, I realize that this could be some wacky, off-the-wall rumor. In this day and age, though, it is believable. Please let me know what's going on back there.

Anyway, popular opinion among the old guys is that this ought to be a short war, if they call it a war. They all seem to think that we should be coming home in about 7 to 8 months, and they say maybe not even that long. Of course, nobody really knows, but all there is to do around here is wonder about it. . . .

Your son,
Cpl., USMC

April 13, 2003
Baghdad

Dear Mom & Dad,

Hey, how's it goin'? We made it into Baghdad about two days ago. Right now I'm sitting in my Amtrac in an empty lot in the city.

The Iraqi people couldn't be happier to see us. When we drove into the city they all lined the streets and waved at us. I felt more like I was in a parade than a war zone. Dad was right about the Iraqi army. For the most part they have been surrendering (with a little persuasion from air strikes and artillery bombardment). The ones that do try and fight aren't very effective. Some of the other units have gotten pretty heavily engaged, but so far we have been skating by (at least in my optinion).

As far as I know there isn't much resistance left. The only group giving us trouble is the Islamic Jihad guys. During the day here things have been mostly quiet. At night, though, when they send out foot patrols, they usually get shot at. The night before last a patrol from 3rd Plt K Co (who ride on our AAV's) got ambushed by a guy with an AK-47 while they were coming back in friendly lines. The guy had his wife and daughter with him. When the Marines got close enough he pushed them both down and started shooting. He killed two guys before they could take care of him. There were other guys with him. I think they were engaged from three sides. I was on radio watch in the driver's station and I saw the tracers flying around. Some stray rounds actually hit one of our vehicles, and I heard a few go whizzing by. So far, though, nobody in our platoon has gotten hurt and K Co has only taken three casualties. Compared to some of the other units we have been pretty lucky. I still feel bad for those three guys though.

Thanks a lot for sending me the baby wipes and stuff. They

are really appreciated. I haven't had a shower in over a month now. I reek.

Please keep writing letters and praying. Tell everybody back home that I say hello. I love and miss you guys very much. When I get home I'm taking you guys out for a BIG dinner (and for that matter, some beer,* too)! Well, bye for now.

Your son,
Cpl., USMC
P.S. Happy Easter

———

April 23, 2003
Iraq

Dear Mom & Dad,

Hey, how's it goin'! Thanks a lot for the baby wipes and toothpaste! In response to your questions about my NBC [nuclear, biological, chemical warfare] chicken, well, I didn't get one. Instead we got one (1) NBC pigeon. His wings are clipped so he can't fly and thankfully he is still alive. I did get a picture, but unfortunately my camera has now been claimed as a confirmed kill of the desert. I've still got it, but it doesn't work.

The war is pretty much over now (I think) at least it looks that way for us. The day before yesterday we dropped our grunts off in some town so they could maintain law & order while the community gets back on its feet. If I was a mayor in that town I don't think I'd really want those loonies running around my town, though. At any rate, we are now detached from them and now we belong to 2nd AABN again.

Thanks again for the letters and packages. Please keep them

* This Marine had celebrated his twenty-first birthday earlier that week.—FS

coming. If you could, please send some jelly beans. Also keep praying for us. I am absolutely positive that that is the only reason that our company hasn't had one casualty yet (I say "yet" because we aren't home yet).

Yesterday in formation our Master Sergeant said that we should all reflect on why we were "spared." He told us to keep in mind that we all made it through OK, not because we were "lucky" or "bad asses," but because we were spared. I think he was right.

Well I'm out of stuff to yap about at the moment. I hope you guys are all doing well. Tell everyone that I know that I said hello. I miss you guys.

Bye for now,
Cpl., USMC

This Marine was in the USMC for four years. As of June 2004 he is about to join the Navy and try out for the Navy SEALS.—FS

14

Dear Mr. Schaeffer,

I have three sons who are presently serving in the armed forces, Jeremy Lussi age 22, is with the 10th Mountain Division and Aaron Lussi, age 18 is in the Marine Corps plus my husband Emory C. Lussi, age 48 is a Navy chaplain. I have tried to pick letters that tell how things have affected [us]. This is [the] 2nd deployment to Afghanistan for my son Jeremy. . . .

Our oldest son, Matthew, age 25 was the first to enter the military. He joined the Wyoming Army National Guard when he graduated from high school in 1997 and left for basic training at Fort Sill, OK, in August of '97. He was the first and he inspired his brothers. [Matthew Lussi has been reactivated and may now going back to Iraq.—FS]

I was one person that was clueless about what the American military family was like or what they went through. My husband did not become a Navy chaplain until April, 2001, at the age of 45, not the age most people go into the military! With our sons having gone into the military and then my husband going in, my eyes were opened to what many face daily with having loved ones serving and fighting for our country.

Freedom.
Blessings, Beverly Lussi

PS. Here are a few emails sent to different members of our family from my husband, Emory, right after 9/11 and while he was deployed during Operation Enduring Freedom.

His first tour of duty was aboard the USS John F. Kennedy (aircraft carrier). His first day out to sea was on Sept. 11, 2001. They were headed out for training exercise, but were re-routed to New York to . . . provide [air cover] security after the [attacks on the World Trade Center]. I received these [two] emails from him the next [two] day[s].

Freedom.
Blessings, Beverly Lussi

Lt. Emory C. Lussi, chaplain, USS JFK
September 12, 2001

Beverly

Well it was an exciting first day at sea to say the least! [I can't] say anything about what we're doing. You can probably get that from . . . CNN. [Do] have some shipmates with family that worked at the World Trade Center. . . .

The food is good, the shower cold the first morning but nice today, and the feeling for me is like being at camp. You get up early, go to bed late, and run around all day. . . . Got to do my first counseling session last night.

It is cool being on the ship and realizing you're out at sea, with planes landing on a moving target. Tell everyone I'm fine but to pray.

Check your email often as we may lose [email privileges] at some point. . . . Was wondering if our friend in Wyoming is okay since she is an American [Airlines] stewardess.

[American Airlines planes were used in the terrorist attacks of 9/11.—FS]

Sleeping isn't too bad, just have to get used to trusting a new clock. Also, have to get into a routine of [shipboard] exercise.

Well, better go, love you bunches. Tell the kids the same. . . .

EM

Lt. Emory C. Lussi, chaplain, USS JFK
September 12, 2001 19:24

Hey,

. . . . We're still headed to our destination and our job is just to help people feel safer [in New York City]. Other vessels will be involved in the actual rescue efforts.

We'll see what transpires over the next few days. We do have a mass casualty drill tonight. The chaplains are to be there for the dead and dying. Hopefully I can get to bed a little early tonight. Tell the kids I'm well and they would like to see the ocean this far out. It really is something! You can see a long way. . . . We may be here for such a time as this. Got to go, have a counselee that just came in.

Bye,
EM

Emails sent to Aaron Lussi (at the time sixteen-years-old) and Bethany Lussi (at the time 8 yrs. old) from their dad Lt. Emory C. Lussi, chaplain, USS *JFK*, while still out to sea after 9/11.—FS

Lt. Emory C. Lussi, chaplain, USS JFK
September 30, 2001

Aaron

Yes, your message came through. I'm doing fine. Today I kind of took it easy, washed clothes, etc. It was an easy day for most people on the ship. We still have lots to do so the tempo will pick back up in a couple of days. Mom said you and Josh went and played football. Did you like it? What is this about you and the heat? You have to drink lots of water and watch yourself. How was the Jaguars' game? I'm sure Mom had a great time. She is so into that you know. Pass this next bit on to Bethany.

Bethany,

I bet I miss you more. Right now the ship is making a turn I think because my chair was trying to roll across the floor, and it feels like they increased the speed the way the ship is vibrating. It is really jiggling. I can't tell you when I'm coming home. . . . You just keep busy with school and all that other stuff you do and before you know it I'll be there. Then we'll have some fun. You and Aaron keep helping Mama and be sweet, okay?

Love you
Daddy

This letter was from Sgt. Jeremy Lussi, 10th Mtn. Div./Army, while in Uzbekistan, starting his first tour, on his way to Afghanistan in 2001. Jeremy was twenty.—FS

October 18, 2001

Dear Fam,

Well, I've been here, still cannot tell you where, for 1 week and 2 days. It seems more like a month, what with the little sleep we get. . . . I can't tell you exactly where I am, but I can tell you that life in this desert is NOT swell. It's usually pretty dang hot during the day, and all but freezing at night. The first night really shocked me. I nearly froze, especially my poor, little toes. We, or at least I, didn't get hardly a wink of sleep the first couple of nights here.

A whole lot has changed from when I first arrived. The greatest improvement is the latrines. When first arriving all there was, was a slit trench in the middle of camp to pee in, and only 2 crappers. There are now latrines, or outhouses, everywhere, and they smell, oh so good! Ha, Ha. 6 more outhouses just rolled in. They got showers about 4 nights ago, and the chow hall opened up 2 nights ago. Till then all we've been eating is MREs [meals ready to eat]. We still eat them for breakfast and lunch. That first soybean burger was a lovely treat.

Rumor has it that we'll be here 6 to 8 months, but the truth is nobody, not even the big dogs, really know for sure. At first I was all about it, and wanted to stay a full year. But now, seeing how slow time ticks away, and doing the stuff, stupid stuff, we do, 6 months won't come soon enough.

The days are getting more of a routine to them, so time has started going a little faster, but there's just not much to do. . . . They don't want us telling anyone too much. This is definitely not a typical war, and don't worry—your son, and brother, is quite safe and will probably remain that way because I don't think "Stanly" is going to try anything here. (Stanly is what we call the terrorists, Taliban, or bad guys. The reason is because every country around here ends in . . . stan.) On that note, I named my .50 cal. "Taliblaster." Pretty good, huh? Our truck is called "Warmonger."

About mail, letters are fine, just don't put my rank on them, and you can send packages. However they can be no larger than a shoebox. And, they are going to get a form of P.X. so you can send money for my B-day and Christmas.

If you send a package don't send too much stuff that I have to bring back. Send things such as snacks, candy, AA batteries, disposable camera, and pictures of the family, stamps and envelopes, notepads about the same size as this one, and maybe a pen or two.

. . . . Not much else going on, so I guess I'll wind this letter to an end. I hope everything in Florida is good and you all are doing fine. I keep you in my prayers. Keep me in yours because we never know when the enemy might try something.

Sorry I won't be home for any holidays this time around again, but I can't wait to see ya'll and will as soon as I can. For now duty calls and I must answer. I love you all very much and will write again soon. Love,

> Your soldier boy,
> Jeremy Lussi
> Sgt. Jeremy Lussi, 10th Mtn. Div./Army

P.S. Please send grandma and grandpa Branch's address.

The following e-mails were sent from Emory while on deployment aboard the USS *JFK* from February 7 to August 17, 2002, during Operation Enduring Freedom.—FS

> *Lt. Emory C. Lussi, chaplain, USS* JFK
> *February 7, 2002*

Hey there,

Well I guess we're off to see the wizard. It was tough watching ya'll waving good-bye. Before we left the pier you could hear a kid hollering, "Daddy," over and over. That wasn't too great for the emotions either. There you are trying to be the tough sailor with tears running down your face. One girl said on her last trip she finally saw her Chief cry when they pulled in and he spotted his wife on the pier. She said "He really was normal." Well I must be normal.

. . . I got to thinking how many men have done the same thing down through history and I'm now one of them. Kind of a pump-you-up thought. I went down to the flight deck and stood on the end and watched the lights get farther away. Then walked to the front and faced into the wind, looked at the water (as far as I could with the rain and clouds), and thought well now it's time to do the job. Then realized I can't. So I said a quick prayer for God to enable me to do what He's given me to do.

Squared away my gear . . . so mostly am settled in. . . .

Squeeze the kids.

I love you.
EM

Letter from Sgt. Jeremy Lussi, 10th Mtn. Div./Army in Afghanistan.—FS

January 24, 2002

Dear Fam,

Well, I finally got my wish and got to go down south to the "real" stan [Afghanistan]. It's a lot colder here and we are surrounded by mountains, many of which look like the Tetons. There are tiny little villages all along the bases of the mountains. . . . We stay/live in old half blown up, shot-up buildings. . . . It's not too bad.

Gone are the modern conveniences. No running water, nasty old wooden smelly outhouses. Not so good chow and MRE's. There are showers, but no one uses them cause they're so chlorinated. We just have baby-wipe "showers."

This place is also a mine-fest, so we have to stick to certain paths. Several guys have already been blown up. . . . Every so often, the EOD guys blow up more mines, and it shakes the whole building. It's pretty cool. It's funny when they don't warn us cause everyone jumps. But, even all that doesn't make me want to go back where I was or even back home. You know me, this is what I like to do, even if it sucks, but really it doesn't. It's also very, very, extremely, horribly dusty here. . . .

Some other cool stuff has happened here, but I don't believe I should tell you in a letter. . . .

Well, that's all for now. Thanks for the pictures, and I was able to watch the DVD's from Circuit City. [Circuit City invited military families to record messages and then sent them to the soldiers.—FS] They were great and all my buds said the family acts just like me. I guess they could tell we're related. Some want to come home with me and meet the Thompson girls. Ha, ha.

Ta, ta for now.

Love, Jeremy Lussi
Sgt. Jeremy Lussi, 10th Mtn. Div./Army

E-mail sent to daughter, Bethany, after she e-mailed and asked Emory what a hiccup was.—FS

Lt. Emory C. Lussi, chaplain, USS JFK
February 13, 2002

Bethany,

A hiccup is a spasmodic movement of the diaphragm involuntarily checked by a sudden closure of the glottis that produces a characteristic sound. What that means is that sometimes when you breathe in, the air is kind of jerked in and the back of your throat closes real quickly and makes that funny noise. I hope that will help you with one of life's dilemmas! It can be tough trying to discover the meaning of life when all these other profound questions keep popping up and demanding answers. . . .

Now to some fun stuff: I found a little-bitty crab the other day on the flight deck. He was dead but there he was in a little puddle of water. Saw two birds flying around the ship yesterday. We must not be too far from land. There were also a bunch of ships around us this morning, probably 7 or 8 of them of all kinds. Everything else is going well. You just keep those cheekies soft so you can rub yours on mine when I get home. Love you a bushel and a peck and a hug around the neck.

Daddy

This letter is from Sgt. Jeremy Lussi, 10th Mtn. Div./Army, in Afghanistan.—FS

February 5, 2002

Dear Fam,

Well life goes on and so do the rumors. They flock by the truck loads, but no matter what I heard or hear, I hold true to my belief that we're not going home for a while longer and maybe, just maybe we'll do something hooah, dangerous, exciting, or even something that will get one's adrenaline pumping.

I've gotten several souvenirs and keepsakes for myself and you guys. I've also gone looking around this place to see more of it (at least the trails we're allowed to use; the ones cleared of land mines). The little kids here will maul you with things to buy, and they'll all try to out-bid each other. If you look at them or slow down, they got you. The only way to get out is to say "no money" and keep walking. They still will put things in your arms yelling prices. . . .

We actually have some entertainment now besides games. They got a DVD player down here now and guess what we watched? "Lord of the Rings"! Yep, the Army can get that, but not [the military equipment] we need — huh? Also, Sanyo sent a whole bunch of world wide radios for the unit. They're awesome. We can get radio stations all over the world. It plays all day long. . . .

Well, another day of guard. Oh, and HAPPY VALENTINES DAY. (Just one more holiday spent overseas.) I'm probably going to call you tonight, so probably everything in this letter you will already have heard. Oh, well. I just thought of something I'd really like if you guys send another package. Some form of Reese's Peanut Butter Cup. Yeah, baby, Yeah!

. . . I got pinned [promoted when a new rank is pinned on the soldiers uniform—FS] on the 7th, finally. They pinned me in Dec., but made me take it off because the paperwork got jacked up. Then, we didn't get any waivers in January, so now; I finally have it [E-4 specialist]. I'll boost up $200 more a month.

Grandma is trying to hook me up with some good southern belles, so she's doing a great service to her fellow soldier, ha, ha. She's doing her part. (Can you tell I'm a wee-bit girl crazy? Not really, it's just there's nothing else to talk about. . . .)

So, I was talking to a Navy man the other day and he said the JFK [the ship his father is on] failed another trial run, so they're not going out, another ship is. Is that true? I also read that they had an accident involving a re-fueler. I hope everything's fine, and even though it'll suck for you, Mom, I really want Dad to go on deployment so I can go with him to the VFW. Everyone else there with their dads will be sharing stories of different wars. Me and Dad will be talking about the same one.

It's kinda funny, yet something I think only a soldier experiences:

You pull guard with some guy in the middle of the night. He tells you more personal stuff than you might want to know, and then, when your guard shift is over, you know all about him, his last name, but you never see his face and you don't even know what he looks like. Perhaps that's why he tells you so much about himself and his problems.

(Feb. 17)

Yes, the days have slipped away. Yesterday I had to help put up tents. It rained and everything got muddy, yet we continued to build. Then to get out of that I got on a detail to gather up sandbags. I got to mud bog all over in this British Toyota. It was a ball, then we hot-rodded an M-hator (a 6 wheeler). I was very muddy, needless to say.

I went to church today, first time in a while. Our battalion is split [to different places] so the chaplain has to bounce back and forth. He'd been gone a while.

Not much else to say, so I'll mail this thing. I guess I didn't call either.

Love,
Jeremy Lussi
Sgt. Jeremy Lussi, 10th Mtn. Div./Army

Lt. Emory C. Lussi, chaplain, USS JFK
July 8, 2002 16:16

Well is anybody home?

We just got through with our port visit and are back on station doing our thing. The port visit was good. There were some improvements to the place plus (Chaplain) Kim and I had several things planned. The best was the Coffee House we had on Friday night. It was a blast. We hauled all the equipment out, set it up, and our worship team sang a few songs, then the Gospel Choir sang a few and back and forth a couple of times, after which we had open mic time where folks could get up and testify or sing and quite a few did. . . . Two others and myself sang Amazing Grace accapella (had the crowd join us on the last part), the choir's band joined in and whoooeee it was gooooddd!

. . . People are getting pretty excited about coming home. 40 days left. For the first time, last Monday to be exact, I really wanted to go home. Not that I haven't missed it, but just had the desire to go home. Happened again Thurs, or Fri. I'm tired, that's not exactly it, either. Not sure how to describe how it is. I think part of it is learning where I get my strength. . . .

Well hopefully, barring any world catastrophe, we'll be home in little over a month. It will be a strange thing I think, coming back I mean and getting into a new way of life. . . .

Love you lavishly,
EM

COMBAT
AFGHANISTAN

15

Sgt. Jeremy Lussi, 10th Mtn. Division, U.S. Army, sent this letter to Emory, Beverly, and Bethany Lussi (parents and sibling). He was writing from Afghanistan and was twenty-one at the time.—FS

July 22, 2003

Dear Fam,

Well, I'm at the fire base now. . . . It looks and reminds me of the Alamo. However there's not much that I can tell you about how it is or what I do. They watch and listen to everything. We can use a satellite phone once a week on Tuesday. They also weren't lying when they said this was the "hot spot." It's kinda weird knowing someone tried to kill you, and if their timing [had been] better they might have succeeded. . . .

It's amazing how much parts of this country look like Wyoming and surrounding states, besides all the clay huts and Afghan people, of course. That brings me to something amazing. The chopper ride over was one of the awesomest things my eyes have ever seen. We had to sling-load some pallets so I sat right over the hole in the chopper so I could see out. . . .

So far this tour has been [a] much different [deployment to Afghanistan than] the last one. . . . We are actually being used properly. We can actually do our job. We will be pushed though, cause of course there aren't many of us. We'll be doing lots and lots of missions—some [good], some horrible. Sorry I can't think of much more to fill up this page with, except keep praying and I miss you guys. It's time to eat, and then off on a mission so I got to get hoppin'. Write later. Love,

SGT. Lussi
Sgt. Jeremy Lussi, 10th Mtn. Div., U.S. Army

Letter sent from Sgt. Jeremy Lussi 10th Mtn. Div./Army at fire base Shkin in Afghanistan.—FS

August 23, 2003

Dear fam,

Well, this is good news, but may be a little concerning. It's only by a miracle that all my buddies are still here and alive. One of my SSG's and my buddy Dickey, the one from Utah who I went to basic with, hit a land mine. The explosion lifted the whole 12,000 lbs armor humvee in the air. It blew the engine area up and blew the right front tire to bits. Parts of which flew 800 meters. Neither were injured severely, just banged up from the landing. Dickey hurt his ribs in the back, and the SSG hurt his neck, back, and foot. The explosion launched a rock backwards that hit the windshield of the cargo humvee behind it which was driven by one of our new guys. The rock hit right at esophagus level, but miraculously stopped and didn't go through the window.

My section was QRF, quick reaction force. On the way out to help our buddies because there was still enemy in the area and they were shooting at us, my other buddy rolled a humvee onto its side. The .50 cal kept it from rolling onto its roof and crushing the gunner.

Another SSG who was in the back got his knee broken or sprained; we're not sure, by some ammo cans and the other guy in the back. I don't think I've ever had so many adrenaline rushes or run so much on a mountain ridge. We decided to lift the blown-up humvee by chopper. The engineers had to blow a tree that was next to it so the chopper could get low enough. It was quite possibly the coolest explosion my eyes have ever witnessed. That tree flew into a billion pieces.

They hooked up the sling legs wrong so me and a buddy had to sprint back to the truck and fix it. Just as we reached the hummer, sucking wind and all, the chopper showed up kicking up more debris and dirt and everything else imaginable. We could barely see, and wouldn't have been able to without my goggles. Plus it made breathing really tough. One rock pegged me right in the throat and didn't feel too swell. The chopper took off and things calmed down a bit.

Supposedly we killed a few and wounded a few. Not for sure on numbers. In the end everyone was pretty much all right. The guy that hurt his knee got a free ticket home I think or at least out of here. Just one example of how an ordinary day can turn unordinary and quite exciting. In fact, I love days like this one.

About a week ago I got to do a mission where I got to interact with a bunch of kids. It was fun and they wanted everything I had. Camera, especially that, knife, pen, lighter, glasses, and anything else. One kid actually succeeded in pick pocketing me for my lighter. Little punk. I got it back though. Some of these boys are so cute and funny. The girls never get to come over to us. There were probably 15-20 boys, and a couple of men. They ranged from 4-18.

Yesterday we got to chill out with the AMF (Afghan Military Force) for a while. We drank chi and ate hajji bread for breakfast. I learned how to spell my name in Arabic and got the whole alphabet. It was pretty fun. Those guys are funny and made fun of each other constantly. Also, I guess every country tells mama jokes.

That place dad was talking about, Bramel, where some police

chiefs got killed and the mayor or governor or whatever they call him and a few locals. Well, that's pretty close to me and the day after it happened we were sent out to get the dead but they had already been buried. I believe 8 died altogether. We could hear the battle going on at night. . . .

As of today I still have received no mail from Sue,* which really creates a vacuum, a dirt devil even. You guys will probably be moving or moved when you get this. Other than the no mail from my girl, I'm doing swell. The food isn't the greatest here. It's not that it's bad, it's just the same thing all the time. . . . There's still a billion flies during the day, but none at night. It's funny, at night a ton of frogs come out. Some get stepped on cause you can't see them till they hop. I think the boat with the rest of our equipment finally got to country. So maybe in a while we'll get it way out here. . . . Hope ya'll are doing swell or sweller than I. Hope you like Camp Lejeune and the Marines. Dad, you'll probably see more of what my lifestyle is like if you work with the infantry. Well, running out of room. Better go. Love and miss you guys.

Love,
SGT. Jeremy Lussi
Sgt. Jeremy Lussi, 10th Mtn. Div., U.S. Army

Note of explanation from Beverly Lussi:

Frank:

* Sue, not her real name, was Jeremy's girlfriend. He had plans to ask her to marry him after he returned home from Afghanistan. He looked at the deployment as a test to see whether the relationship would survive the separations that military life affords. Unfortunately, Sue found the separation unbearable and ended the relationship in late

fall of that year. Receiving a "Dear John" letter, even when it may be the best decision in the long run, is extremely hard for the soldier in the field. He does not have the privilege to sit down and talk through the situation or even talk on the phone for an extended period of time. Basically, he just has to deal with it while at the same time trying to keep focused on the task at hand—going after the enemy—not an easy thing to do.

Letter sent to recruit Aaron Lussi, USMC, while at boot camp at Parris Island, South Carolina, from his ten-year-old sister, Bethany.—FS

September 4, 2003

Dear Aaron,

I have a pot on my head. I'm a good art person now. Know why? You know your [art] note book? I have it now and that's why. What's a pit? Are you bald? Is it hot? Is the food good? What's the diddies? Are you dumb? I miss you and hope you're ok. Take care of my art. Guess what? Mom squirted a lot of brown mustard on her sandwich. It looked like poop. I lost a tooth.

Love,
Bethany

P.S. I'm praying for you.

Letter from Jeremy's younger brother Aaron Lussi, now eighteen, from Marine boot camp at Parris Island, South Carolina. The last time we heard from Jeremy he was age sixteen and at home getting letters from his dad, who was on an aircraft carrier after 9/11. At this point all the Lussi brothers are or have been in the military and so is their father.—FS

September 11, 2003
Wednesday? (don't know the day; hint, hint; send me a small calendar)
Hey Mom and Dad,

How ya doin'? Good I hope and all tucked and squared away at the new home (or at least getting it tucked and squared away).

We did initial drill today. It's the 1st real competition between the platoons. We got 5th out of six. Yeah, we really sucked! (Sorry Mom).

. . . We also got our desert utilities today and they are being taken to be made "bullet-proof" (that means your name and "U.S. Marines" will be sewn on). We will wear them on grass week (the week we do all the shooting and stuff like that).

Swim week is next week. Pray for me, cause I'm a little nervous about it. I'm not much at swimming with stuff dragging me down.

I've been reading my Bible as much as possible. I'm about to finish Genesis. Well, I'm in the middle of a pre-pre-test and I can't think of anything else to write so tonight I'll write Beth-alee [his little sister, now age ten] on the back and answer all her questions. Bye.

With love,
PVT Lussi Yo! Yo! Yo!

Beth-Beth,

Thanks for the pictures. My rack-mate (the guy that sleeps on the bunk below me) got some pictures from his little cousin at the same time.

Okay, you asked what the pit was. It's a big sand filled area where the drill instructors make us do lots of pushups, sit-ups, jumping-jacks, and other exercises and makes us real tired and sandy.

Next question. Am I bald? No, not completely, but I'm pretty darn close, and it hurts like a booger when we get our haircut. OUCH!

You also asked if it was hot. Right now it's actually kinda cool and nice most of the time cause it's cloudy a lot. The food is good or at least I think so.

"Diddies" are things we all yell out when we are marching to remind us what to do. Like if we are at port arms (get Dad to show you) and we get the command "Left Shoulder" we say "Stick it!" and then he'll say "Arms" and as we move our rifle we'll say "Stick pause Rip!"

Last question, no I am not dumb. Your hiney is though. Bye, Bye. Write again.

With love,
PVT Lussi

Letter from Aaron Lussi at Marine boot camp at Parris Island, South Carolina.—FS

September 29-30, 2003

Hey Mommy, Daddy, and Beth-alee,

DAY 1: Hope you're all doin' well. Sorry I haven't written in so long, but someone took all my envelopes and stamps when the DI's made us dump our footlockers. Soooo, if ya'd like to send some more of both (and 2 or 3 power bars) that would be nice. I shot two possibles today. A possible is when you hit the bull's eye 10 outta 10 times on rapid fire. I did it both times at the 200 yd. line. Ya, I rock. This week is gonna go by fast. Well, not much time left so I'll pick it up tomorrow. Keep prayin' that the whole platoon will qualify [on the rifle range] and we'll get to call home. G'night.

DAY 2: Well, it's Tuesday now. . . . Well, too bad. I got one possible today and all the others were only one off. Had to dump footlockers again today, twice in a row, but I'm quick and got all my stuff back. I got a letter from Jeremy [from Afghanistan] today. Soooey, I don't know what all he can or did tell you but since I'm in the military now he can tell me everything . . . I guess. Man he's got some goodn's. Pray for his protection. He always sends me Bible verses just like you, Mom. Well, gonna go over my data book (for the rifle range) and read my Bible now. G'night.

SAT: Well, pooey. I didn't get to write the rest of the week cause Wed. we had absolutely no time, Thurs. we packed up everything, and Fri. we were fixing everything. Just to let ya know, your son/brother is a master. I qualified EXPERT! [on the rifle range]. Oh, yeah! And on top of that I was the only one in the whole company that got possibles at the 200 and 300 yard line. So our SDI gave me a Pepsi.

. . . Yeah, you can just call me Bullseye now. Ha! Ha! We also went on a six mile hike this morning. Wooo, it was a walk. It wouldn't have been so bad, but I was a road guard, and road guards have to stay in front of the company and practically run the whole time to get to the roads.

[The road guard makes sure traffic stops so the platoon can march safely.—FS]

Well, I'm gonna read my Bible now, so I'll write tomorrow morning. Luv ya! G'night . . . again.

SUN: Well, I've decided I'll go to Catholic service this morning, just to see what it's like. One of the guys said they sing hymns so that'll be good. I finished 1st Samuel this morning. Oh and Mom, I think you were confused on how fast I was reading the Bible. I started in Genesis then skipped over to Judges and continued on from there. I don't get that much time. From now on when you send a letter put a power bar, oatmeal cookie, or something in there. Unless of course I'm not worth an extra stamp! Ha, ha, that would be kinda nice though. Well gonna let ya go now. Love ya bunches. Bye, bye.

With love,
PVT Lussi

For Beth's eye only
Hey Beth-beth,

Doin' good? I hope so. Have ya got a lot of friends yet? I bet ya do. Well, I've got to ask a couple of favors from ya. First off, when you guys come down for graduation get my cool CD. The yellow and red one, ya know. And bring my CD player and all the stuff so I can listen to it in the car. It's all in my underwear drawer in my dresser. Thanks. Love ya, bye, bye. Don't forget.

April 17, 2004

Frank:

Here are two letters written by Bethany to her brother, Sgt. Jeremy Lussi, 10th Mountain Div./Army, while he was deployed to Afghanistan from July 2003 to April 2004. What you can't see is all the "extras" that she draws on her letters. She draws hearts with "Jeremy" written in the center, flowers, happy sunshine faces, angels, double explanation points with a smile or frown drawn under them depending on what she's written, etc. She also would make up fun pages with mazes, dot to dot pictures, and code messages for him to figure out. Bethany was 10 years old when she wrote these letters.

Freedom.
Blessings, Beverly Lussi

September 12, 2003

Dear Jerm, [this is not a typo]

I got your letter this week. I hope your finger and hand is better. I bet it is better because it's been a month.

Ya, it feels really weird being the only kid at home. It is really quiet sometimes. I'm not getting old!! Your getting old!! Ha Ha Ha Ha! I gave ya 6 pens for six kids. The different pen is for you. I met some girls. They're fun. One of them is called the horrible bus driver because we were playing that some one is a school bus driver and she didn't stop at stop sign and she sped and that kind of stuff.

I know some one is having a birthday soon. YOU!! So what do ya want for your B-day?

When we went to church on Wed [I learned these verses]. I know what John 3:36 says. "He who believes in the Son has everlasting life; and He who does not believe in the Son shall not see life, but the wrath of God abides in him." And I know Acts 16:31: "Believe on the Lord Jesus Christ, and you will be saved. . . ." And I know some more verses. Well I better go, Mom keeps saying "Come on so I can mail this." I'll talk to ya later.

Love your sis,
Bethany
I MISS YOU

Letter from Sgt. Jeremy Lussi, age twenty-one, 10th Mtn. Div./Army, previously based at fire base Shkin in Afghanistan, had just moved to fire base Orgun-e in Afghanistan, but writing from Kandahar, where he had gone to reenlist.—FS

September 30, 2003

Dear Fam,

Well, it's been 1 month since the death of the 2 scout/snipers. What's worse is that just yesterday another scout/sniper got hit in the shoulder. One of the line guys got shrapnel in the face and one was killed in action. I didn't know the 2 line guys, but I knew the scout. The worst is this all happened [back] at [my own fire base] Shkin and I'm stuck here in Kandahar for reenlistment. It's really horrible hearing all that and knowing you can't do a bloody thing about it.

Good news is that on Sunday I got to go to church. Here in Kandahar, they actually have a big wooden church. It was really great, especially the worship service. It was awesome. Next Sunday I might even play the drums for them if I'm still here.

On the 26th of Sep my section moved to the fire base Orgun-e. The other section will move down later. It's a little bigger, and there's better food and colder and more drinks.

It's not quite as hot in Kandahar as it was when we first arrived, but it's still hotter and dustier than the smaller bases. It's also funny listening to everyone complain how it sucks here. We come here for R&R! There is so much to eat here. It's nice.

I've lost a little weight. I got here on Saturday the 27th and that night Lee Greenwood did a concert. It was kinda cool, although it's been a while since I've seen someone wear a full denim outfit. A Canadian tuxedo as we call it. Ha, ha.

Some people here have actually heard of us [his unit and fire base] and know where we've been and what we've done. It's rewarding and feels pretty good to know that someone knows we're in the hell-hole getting blasted regularly, but are blasting back.

I got the box with the Cheetos in it. Thanks. I bought several things at a bazaar, so when I get a chance I'll mail them to you.

The higher-ups left today to go pick up the body. Tomorrow

we'll have the ceremony here, then put him on a bird back to the States. I never thought I'd be in a battalion that lost men in combat. Last time [during his first deployment to Afghanistan—FS] we had lots of casualties, but no one was killed. It's definitely real, and now I finally know how all soldiers in war before me felt.

You can't describe it in words or on paper, so I won't try. The only thing that gets me is how no one in my platoon has died. Because, while all these line platoons rotate patrols, we go on all of them. So a few squads have been in 1 contact, but my platoon has been in every single one. We also have 4 [very tall] guys whose bodies stick half-way out of the turret. God must be with us.

Also, the last 2 contacts my truck was in, we were in our truck from Ft. Drum, which has no armor. It doesn't even have doors. My driver doesn't like that too much, but he does his job.

I tell you what, there is nothing like rounds cracking right over your head, especially when you don't know where they're coming from. A lot of things go through your mind, super fast when that happens, probably cause you realize that you were almost killed.

God is so amazing. I had a good long talk with a buddy of mine [about] how some of these guys don't and won't believe in God after what happened.

Not much going on. Just got back from the ceremony practice [for the killed soldiers]. Also, I've got my name down for the Airborne unit in Alaska. It would be fun to jump again. However, there is no opening right now. I just don't know. Well, I'm gonna go for now. Love and miss you all.

Love, Jeremy
Sgt. Jeremy Lussi, 10th Mtn. Div., U.S. Army

Romans 12:19-20 "Do not take revenge, my friends, but leave room for God's wrath, for it is written: 'It is mine to avenge; I will repay,' says the Lord. On the contrary: 'If your enemy is hungry, feed him;

if he is thirsty, give him something to drink. In doing this, you will heap burning coals on his head.' "

This is a hard one to obey.

Letter from Sgt. Jeremy Lussi, 10th Mtn. Div./Army, from fire base Orgun-e in Afghanistan.—FS

December 6, 2003

Dear Fam,

Well, yes I'm still alive. Sorry it's been so long since my last letter. I'm at that point where I don't really feel like writing. Plus, we have less free time now, so I just don't make myself write anymore. However, I'll try and keep you guys updated. Tons of the soldiers here were griping about the phone and computer situation, so they changed it, and all it did was make it worse. Stupid people never realize that it's not that bad and any other way would be worse. Now there are hours and days for the phones, so Dad probably won't ever be home when I call, at least until late January when my platoon hopefully goes back to Shkin.

The point of this letter is to wish all of you a Merry Christmas and Happy New Year. I hope you all have a great one and get what you wanted for X-mas. I got [you] some gifts, but you'll have to wait till I return home.

It's weird sometimes when I realize that this is my second Christmas over here. Sometimes it saddens me that I can't be there with all you being loud and crazy . . . and making up off the wall songs. Then, sometimes I can't think of anywhere else that I'd rather be than here.

Being with my buds who have fought next to me in over 9 fire-fights: the bond that forms is like nothing else. Also, driving around and seeing all the little kids run to the road to wave and hopefully get some candy or a pen, and then to see the joy it brings when you throw them something is far [more] gratifying than most things I've done. I could move here and be a permanent "candy man." To know that I'm making a difference, not only for America, but for Afghanistan and the people is so rewarding.

You know how I always wanted to be famous, well, not anymore, this is better. I'm doing and living what famous people can only make movies or songs about. So, I pray that your Christmas will be as blessed as mine and everyone please eat a piece of pecan pie for me.

A little about what's been going on. We did that 4 day mission and it was kinda funny. The town that was our main focus wound up being a ghost town. Not a soul there. All we found was a building full of "weed." We stayed in an old British fort. It was really old. An MP [accidentally] shot himself in the foot with his 9mm in his sleeping bag. Mainly all we did was a ton of driving. We drove over 200 kilometers in 4 days. It gets you a little sore riding with all your gear on, but it was awesome seeing so much of the countryside.

I don't remember if I told you, but I did get Alaska. [He reenlisted and volunteered to go to a special "jump" parachute training base.—FS] Report in April, but I deferred my orders until August so I could finish out the deployment [here], go on leave, go to Pathfinder school, then head up to Alaska.

They rocketed us 2 days ago. Only now it's on a whole new level. They used "willie peet" or white phosphorus which burns roughly with the surface temperature of the sun. If they actually hit us with that stuff it won't be good. They were way off, but they hit some local compounds. I believe they killed a few innocent people also.

We're launched to go chase them as soon as the rockets start coming in, so we were actually pretty close to the impact zone. We went back the next day to check it out. Oxygen makes this stuff burn, so when the line guys walked through the impact zone it flared up a little. Nasty stuff.

Been throwing lots of candy. Not too much else going on. Merry X-mas again. Miss ya'll lots.

Love, Jeremy

Sgt. Jeremy Lussi, 10th Mtn. Div., U.S. Army

Philippians 1:20 "I eagerly expect and hope that I will in no way be ashamed, but will have sufficient courage so that now as always Christ will be exalted in my body, whether by life or by death."

———————

Letter from Jeremy Lussi, 10th Mtn. Div./Army (to his sister, Bethany just turned eleven), from firebase Orgun-e.—FS

January 10, 2004

Dear Beth-a-lee,

Well, I'm sorry you won't get this till a while after your birthday. But, I hope you had a wonderful one, anyways.

We had to get rid of our puppy cause it kept peeing and pooping in the tent and my platoon sergeant didn't like that very much. We still see him running around outside, though. It's still cold, and snows from time to time. Today we left on a 3 day mission, but 2 trucks broke down, so my platoon had to bring them back to base. We will go back out tomorrow.

I'm still throwing lots of candy to kids. Actually I threw some gum to 4 girls today on the way back.

I love my new video camera I got for Christmas. However sometimes it's hard to film stuff I want because I usually have to help, so then I can't film. I got some good stuff, though.

Not much else is going on. I hope you did have a great B-day and I'll think of you tomorrow. Wish I could be there. Miss you lots and lots.

Love, Jeremy
Sgt. Jeremy Lussi, 10th Mtn. Div., U.S. Army

Today is your Birthday
you're turning eleven,
But also today
January turns eleven.
You're growing up so quick and so fast.
Where has the time gone
it's been such a blast.
I remember when you were a baby
so cute and so small
I need to put a brick on your head
cause you're getting too tall.
You're the best sister
a boy could ever have,
cause you like to make poot noises,
and act like a spazz.
I wish I could be there,
but I can not be.
So, have a Happy Birthday
From your brother across the sea.

SGT Jeremy Lussi
Orgun-e Afghanistan
Sgt. Jeremy Lussi, 10th Mtn. Div., U.S. Army

February 22, 2004

Dear Jeremy,

I miss you so much!! I can't wait for when you come home!! I will be so happy!! !! Gizzy [the dog] and Gunny [the bunny] are so funny when they play. It makes me and Mom laugh. I've been doing well in school. Mom is doing well too. I miss you so much. You and your buds are in my prayers!!

Luv, your sis,
Bethany

As of May 2004 Emory Lussi (chaplain in the Navy) is in Afghanistan, as is PFC Aaron Lussi, USMC. Sgt Jeremy Lussi 10th Mtn. Div. is in Ft. Drum, New York. Bethany and her mom, Beverly, are at home in North Carolina, and Matthew (National Guard) is in Atlanta and thinking of going active duty full time in the Army. At the end of this book we will meet the Lussis again.—FS

16

Frank:

Here is one of the letters from our son Jason Thomas Bohrer. It was
written Dec. 7, 2001 at Forward Operating Base Rhino, Afghanistan.
Jason was a lance corporal at the time, serving with the 15th Marine
Expeditionary Unit, 1/1, A. Co., 1st Plt. He was his company's radio
operator and one of the first Marines to reach Afghanistan. The 15th
MEU was in port at Darwin, Australia on Sept. 11, 2001.

Dave & Martha Bohrer

Jason was twenty-two yeas old when he wrote these letters.—FS

December 7, 2001

Mom & Dad,

I don't know what you have seen on the news, but from the little
news that we do get out here, the reports are fairly accurate. I've had
a good past few days here, with the exception of last night's attack.

I definitely have the company clerk's job. I start training as soon
as I get back on ship.

I was, also, photographed by Newsweek. Maybe Dad has already seen the photo of me from Reuters. I'm hoping to be in newspapers and Newsweek. . . . Although I thought they [the reporters and photographer] were bad omens, because that night [after they took pictures] I had to go out and provide security for a helo [helicopter] that crashed not far from here.

I guess you're eager to know what my days are like here. It's pretty much the same thing every day, living in our fighting holes, waiting and watching for anything, literally. The Taliban and al Qaeda have sent in "camel bombs" at us, along with trying to infiltrate our lines at night.

The days are pretty much the same every day. The only thing that changes is the wind. If there's no wind like today, it's pretty hot out here. But when the wind comes, it gets fairly cool. The wind kicks up a lot of sand.

At night, it gets pretty cold, at least for what I'm used to. Weather reports say with wind chill, the temps drop below freezing. I have plenty of gear to keep me warm, though. Don't worry.

We do get time off every day. I monitor the radio, though, so the only time I have off is when the radio isn't busy. I've been reading a lot, writing a little, and singing all the time to keep spirits up.

Yours is the only address I have, so make sure you pass on the news to everyone. I can't write about a lot of stuff here, and I don't particularly care to share many of my experiences so far here in Afghanistan. I'm proud to be one of the few Americans here. Thinking back on Sept. 11, and before, I'd never dreamt in my wildest dreams that I'd be living out of a fighting hole in the middle of the desert in the "Stan."

Emotionally, it's rough out here. Actually any which way you look at it, it's rough out here, but especially emotionally. Not only from the absolute isolation, both geographically and communications-wise, but from the rigors of war itself.

This isn't anything like Vietnam, or even Desert Storm, but just sitting here, watching and waiting, not knowing what's next. Like last night, Dec. 6, the crap hit the fan at the other side of our base, but we were lucky. All we really lost was sleep. Speaking of which, I haven't been sleeping very well lately, but I'm sure I'll pull out of this soon.

We don't know when we're getting out of here yet, but I'm hoping to be home around the same time that I last told you. . . .

Well, I guess that's all for now, I'll write again in a week or two; envelopes are very scarce, so if you get some cardboard postcards, don't be too upset, it's about all I have out here. I love you both with all my heart, and you are constantly in my thoughts and prayers.

Love always,
Jason
Cpl. Jason Thomas Bohrer USMC

As of June 2004 Cpl. Jason Bohrer, USMC, got out of the Corps and is headed back to college.—FS

Marine Colonel Matthew Bogdanos, a New York City homicide prosecutor, was recalled to active duty days after losing his apartment near the World Trade Center on September 11, 2001 as a result of the terrorist attack. He received the Bronze Star for classified counter-terrorism operations in Afghanistan, later deploying to Iraq in March 2003 and again in June 2004.—FS

May 22, 2004

Sir,

My name is Matthew Bogdanos, colonel, USMCR. I was recalled on September 11 and served in both Afghanistan and Iraq as the head of a Special Forces interagency team. While in Iraq, I also headed the investigation into the looting of the Iraqi antiquities. . . .

The attached is a group e-mail I sent to some friends right before Operation Anaconda. . . .

Semper Fi,
Matthew Bogdanos, colonel, USMCR

Greeting from Afghanistan
March 2002

. . . . Things here are xoub hastam (fine). Here, for now, in Bagram. Apparently, I can now tell you that because the media is reporting that combat operations in Afghanistan are being run out of Bagram (just in case al-Qaida wanted to know where to find any good targets—thank you very much). So our location is no longer classified. I obviously cannot go into details about what we do or how we do it (except to say how talented and dedicated the people here are), but I can offer some limited observations and reflections in no particular order and with no particular method. "If this be madness, there is indeed a method to it" Act II or III? Someone help me out here. . . .

British General Sir William Slim said that the dominant feeling on the battlefield is loneliness. He knew what he was speaking about. (Yes, I ended that sentence in a preposition, and I still remember that when Churchill was chastised for doing the same, he replied that it is this type of errant pedantry "up with which I shall not put." But I digress.) Though people surround you, the overwhelming feeling is loneliness or, better, isolation. The other emotions are fear and exhaustion. Simply put, you are always afraid and you are always tired. It must have something to do with the constant flow of adrenaline. Each of us is convinced, quite regardless of probabilities, that the next mortar round or bullet or RPG [rocket-propelled grenade] is coming directly at him personally. It does not matter that you can tell by the sound that the mortars are well beyond range. Somehow, through some freak atmospheric occurrence, it is going to hit you (and only you).

Interestingly enough, what keeps you going despite the fear and exhaustion are not abstractions like freedom and honor and discipline (though those are the most important). No, what really keeps you going is the guy next to you. The one counting on you to do your job, just as you are counting on him to do his.

You have his "6" (his six o'clock, his back) and he has yours. It is a refusal to let your buddies down. In writing of his experiences as a Marine on Okinawa, William Manchester observed that any man in combat who lacks comrades who will die for him, or for whom he is willing to die, is not a man at all. He is truly damned. Exactly. And that guy's race, skin color, religion, gender, or sexual orientation are not even close to being relevant. Public opinion polls and politicians notwithstanding, we (that is, those with the rifles in our hands) do not care. On the other hand, I hope that the guy (or girl) watching my back earned his or her stripes and did not get in on some type of quota or to satisfy some social agenda. The simple reality is that all those other notions may have meaning in chic cafes, on college campuses, or among well-fed pundits posturing over a glass of wine, but they mean absolutely nothing in the hills of Afghanistan.

Then what is relevant? Easy. Can he do his job, can he carry his own pack, and can he hit what he shoots at? How does he react under pressure? Will he choke and panic or rise to the occasion? Can he save your ass when it needs saving? Can you trust him to do the right thing? And does he do what he says he is going to do? Like I said, easy. Nor does it matter if you just met that guy a week ago or that you will never see each other again back in the world. (In a classic case of life imitating art, the "world" is what we call you guys. We also imagine that you guys back in the world eat eggs benedict and pommes frites for breakfast every morning, poached salmon with a light dill sauce for lunch, and a thick prime rib—end cut, of course—with a good bottle of Montepulciano every night for dinner. You do, right?)

So, what is it like? On a good day, you get a hot meal—of course, calling it a "meal" is somewhat misleading. In a good week, you get a hot shower—hot water is decidedly not overrated. And a good month? That is when you still have all your body parts. I have lost count of how many good kids have not had a good month. Every one of them is a hero. Me? Just another guy doing his job the best he can. Nothing more, nothing less. Those details that I can give you are mundane: you wake up in the morning with a sore throat and one of a dozen, albeit minor, eye or ear infections. You get dressed quickly before the warmth of the sleeping bag wears off, pack everything up, and then dump out your piss bottle. I know that is crude and more information than you might want, but it gives you an idea of the conditions: you do not go around in the dark looking for a place to relieve yourself. Not if you want to have a good month. See above re: body parts. You carry a bottle for that purpose and empty it in the daylight.

I will give you another silly example. About a week ago, we got a box of pears for breakfast. I am not sure where they came from because I could not read the writing on the outside. When we opened the box, the pears were all brown and black and covered with small holes where some member of the insect or (and?) animal kingdom had nibbled. Definitely not the kind of pear you would pick at the corner bodega. If it were the last one left, you would go to the peaches. If you saw it in your refrigerator, you would throw it away. I ate it. It was the best pear I have ever had.

Now up, you do what you have to do to get through the day. Every bend in the road is a potential ambush site. Every shadow hides an Arab or Chechen fighter. Every person you meet is suspect until proven otherwise. Competing against this necessary paranoia (remember, just because you are paranoid does not mean they are not out to get you) is the overwhelming affection you cannot help feeling for the Afghan people. They are all (Pashtun, Tajik, Hezari, and Uzbek) warm and (when not trying to kill you) very friendly people.

I am invited at least once a day for the traditional tea, almonds, and raisins. To refuse this invitation in such a guest culture is an unforgivable insult. Nor does it matter if the tea is being served in the only room with a roof, where the remainder of the mud-brick house is bombed-out rubble. Most of the houses I have seen outside of Kabul are mud-brick, but every one has a guestroom with their best carpet and, sometimes, pillows.

I have a terrific interpreter and the conversations over tea are priceless. Many Afghans have blue eyes, which they attribute to Sikander the Great. We call him Alexander the Great, but Afghans like Persians could not pronounce his name, so they call him Sikander. He is still revered. We argue about the routes Sikander traveled, his use of cavalry, and whether he ever conquered the Afghans. They always ask why President Clinton abandoned them when the Taliban took over and if we are going to do the same. I tell them that I hope not, but that I am low on the food chain. Actually, what I told Matobwadeen (a 23-year-old Tajik with a heart of gold and an artificial right leg) is "I'm not the Madam, just one of the whores." It translates well and now he repeats it in English half-a-dozen times a day.

It is during tea you hear about the real horrors, things done by the Taliban and al-Qaida you find impossible to believe—until you walk outside and see how many people are maimed or missing body parts. Matobwadeen is not alone. You also see the despair, the hunger, and the poverty, and you know they are telling you the truth without embellishment or exaggeration. You feel uncontrollable rage, softened only by the sight of the children laughing and playing. Even if they are playing across the road from a minefield. That is my favorite part—the children, not the minefield. They love chocolate the best, so I always make sure to carry around enough in my pockets, along with some more proper food as well. I show them the chocolate first and then make them eat the other stuff (delicious MRE's) before I give them the chocolate.

As I said, you do what you have to do to get through the day. I think the psychologists call it "accommodation." You make the necessary ones, internally mostly. You hope these accommodations are temporary and that you will become "normal" again when you are back home. Of course, you are never sure. In this regard, we are very proud of the steps we take to minimize civilian casualties—always to our tactical disadvantage. Yet there are still things that must be done that you hope will fade from your memory. Someone once said that the real tragedy of war is not that its atrocities are committed by abnormal men, but by normal men in abnormal circumstances. No, that does not mean we are committing atrocities; we are not. In fact, we scrupulously avoid "collateral damage," again, to our disadvantage. But there is a lot of death. Everywhere. That takes something out of you no matter how justified or "righteous" the target was.

Yes, I have heard the drivel from sincere but mind-numbingly ignorant people who look for reasons al-Qaida and Taliban hate us, thinking we must have done something to cause the murders of September 11. Of course, they ignore that al-Qaida and Taliban have committed unimaginable atrocities against their own people that make September 11 look like a minor traffic accident. I wonder what they (the Hezaras, Kurds, Uzbeks, Tajiks, etc.) did to "deserve" it. Those same people, upon pain of self-hypocrisy, I guess, also wonder what Jews did to cause Hitler's hatred or what the rape victim did to cause the rapist to attack her. They must have done something. I have come to accept there is nothing anyone can do to teach such fools. I take solace in John Stuart Mill's observation that it is better to be Socrates dissatisfied than a fool satisfied.

I told you already about a good day. There have also been some bad ones. Michael's first day of school in January. I was supposed to be the one to pack his Clifford lunch box. I wanted to be the one he told about what dinosaur he drew (bet it was a T-Rex) and whether he cried after he was dropped off (probably). That was a bad day. Another was the day Jason was born in November. I wish I had been there. Others will be Diana's 2d birthday next week and Michael's 4th this summer. I will not be there for them. I have missed every single significant event of their lives since my recall to active duty.

Of course, whenever I start to feel sorry for myself, I think of all those children whose mothers and fathers did not come home on 11 September. . . .

. . . This is where I belong for now. I have no doubts about that at all. Nor about the fact that I cannot wait to be done and come home. It has been five months; every second is one second too long. And you never get them back. Not ever. I do not know our schedule, but I am sure we will be returning to U.S. Central Command Head-quarters (Tampa, Florida) before redeploying to another country. I do not know what country that will be, but I can guess as well as anyone. I am guessing hot with a lot of sand. On a brighter note, I hope to get some leave while in Tampa to go home for four or five days before the next deployment. Insha'Allah (God willing).

Semper Fi,
Matthew Bogdanos, colonel, USMCR

Matthew Bogdanos, colonel, USMCR, is now in Iraq. His wife, Claudia, is in New York City with their three children, ages five, four and two.—FS

COMBAT
IRAQ

17

Major General J. N. Mattis, U.S. Marines
March 2003

1st Marine Division (REIN) Commanding General's Message to All Hands

For decades, Saddam Hussein has tortured, imprisoned, raped, and murdered the Iraqi people; invaded neighboring countries without provocation; and threatened the world with weapons of mass destruction. The time has come to end his reign of terror. On your young shoulders rest the hopes of mankind. When I give you the word, together we will cross the Line of Departure, close with those forces that choose to fight, and destroy them. Our fight is not with the Iraqi people, nor is it with members of the Iraqi army who choose to surrender. While we will move swiftly and aggressively against those who resist, we will treat all others with decency, demonstrating chivalry and soldierly compassion for people who have endured a lifetime under Saddam's oppression.

Chemical attack, treachery, and use of the innocent as human shields can be expected, as can other unethical tactics. Take it all in stride. Be the hunter, not the hunted: never allow your unit to be caught with its guard down. Use good judgment and act in the best interests of our Nation. You are part of the world's most feared and trusted force. Engage your brain before you engage your weapon. Share your courage with each other as we enter the uncertain terrain north of the Line of Departure. Keep faith in your comrades on your left and right and Marine Air overhead. Fight with a happy heart and strong spirit. For the mission's sake, our country's sake, and the sake of the men who carried the Division's colors in past battles—who fought for life and never lost their nerve—carry out your mission and keep your honor clean. Demonstrate to the world there is "No Better Friend, No Worse Enemy" than a U.S. Marine.

Major General J. N. Mattis, U.S. Marines
Commanding

This letter was written by Amatangelo, an eighteen-year-old Marine.—FS

February 7, 2003
To my family, Mom:

Here I sit another lonesome night. . . . Full of sorrow and longing for what was. Days seem to dwindle by, slowly wasting away. . . . Lessons, I've learned a few. Friends, I've lost them too. Growing up, needless to say has already happened. . . . Deserts, I've crossed. Life, I'm ready to live it. I know now in hindsight what this war was for. Yesterday an old man approached me as I was patrolling through the city of Diwaniyah. . . . As he drew closer, he opened his arms speaking to me and grabbed me. I drew back, alarmed and angry because he touched me. As I stepped back I saw him sobbing. He then grabbed me and practically fell into my arms hugging me.

My translator quickly ran to my side to see what was going on. As the man continued to sob words into my shoulder the translator processed the words and then he started to cry. He said the man was so happy to see us. He said he'd been waiting for us for so long. "We were his saviors." As the translator told me this, I started to cry because I had finally realized what good we did. It hit me like one huge wave. . . . So there we were, three men on a busy street in a war-torn country, crying. The simple look on a hungry child's face is enough to make you lose your bearing and burst into tears. . . . Soon, children will not have to worry about hunger. We've done good. And I couldn't be prouder. . . . I DID IT. . . .

But I can't help feeling greedy for what I've gotten out of this. If I could sum it up all in one word it would be Appreciation. My life will never be the same. War is not all bad. Well, let me re-phrase: War is hell, I've been through it. But when wars are fought out of need and righteousness the outcome is immeasurable. My only hope is that someday Americans will realize this. We have to endure hardships to reach happiness and good. . . . I'm out of words. My thoughts are on paper and I feel good. Another day is done. You could look at it as another day closer to home. But I don't. . . . Soon I hope . . . soon.

> With all my love,
> Amatangelo
> LCpl. Amatangelo Pasciuti, USMC

LCpl. Amatangelo Pasciuti, USMC, is currently in 29 Palms, California getting ready to redeploy to Iraq.—FS

18

Cameron was twenty-two when he wrote this letter.—FS

Jan 30, 2003

Mom,

Well, we arrived in Kuwait on Sunday, and moved to our encampment Monday morning around 3:00 AM. We took buses from the airport, and the Kuwaiti driver was very tired and kept dozing at the wheel. Since I was the security guard, or what we call guardian angel, I sat in the front seat opposite the driver. Every time he would start to get heavy in the eyes, I would shake my rifle.

When we first got here there wasn't much, but now it is . . . becoming livable. We just got showers, and hear that soon we will get a chow hall. We have been eating MRE's since we left.

The desert out here is nothing like 29 Palms [Marine base in California]. 29 Palms has mountains and such, this place looks like North Dakota, only with sand. You can see for miles in any direction. I cannot say how far, but we are very close to the Iraqi Border.

I just heard today that some Special Forces guys caught some Iraqis trying to take pictures and spy on us. Also at Camp Commando some Marines got sick. They traced it to the chow, which was made by Kuwaiti civilians. So the British run it now.

Just to give you an example of how tense it is around here, some grunts went outside the camp to do some training, and we were all working on the tanks on the edge of camp. Well the grunts were coming back from their training, and since the majority of people on the vehicles didn't know who they were, someone yelled "get down," and pretty soon everyone had a weapon drawn.

I'm doing ok. I miss good food, friends and being able to keep myself clean.

Gunny GySGT [Gunnery Sergeant] B—, our head mechanic and maintenance chief is driving everyone nuts. I can honestly say that if something happened to him out here, I wouldn't care. . . .

Write me. Hopefully we will still be here when your letters arrive. I miss you and love you.

> Your son,
> Cameron
> SUPPORT OUR TROOPS!
> LCpl. Cameron White, USMC

March 30, 2003

Mom—

It is Sunday. We are sitting in a regiment size defensive position in Iraq.

The past two weeks have been quite crazy. We were led into an Iraqi artillery battery, after it was secured, and there was unexploded ordnance everywhere. (This was Day 2 of the war.) We lost 2 Marines and 2 Docs who stepped on either anti-personal mines or ordnance. No one was killed, but they were seriously injured.

After we progressed towards An Nasiriyah, it was intense fighting. There was a U.S. servicemen captured and assassinated and many casualties. We got shot at while driving through. . . . It has been like that in every city.

These Iraqis are ruthless. They use civilians as human shields and wear civilian clothing, so that we will not engage them. This caused many innocent people to die.

I hope Ethan, Duncan [his brothers] and my own children (if I ever have any) do not have to witness the things we do in war. Dead bodies of Iraqi soldiers mixed in with women and children.

Iraqis use civilian buses, cars, trucks and such to transport troops, so it is very hard to decipher friend from foe.

Up until now, I have not had to take someone's life, and for that I am grateful, however that will probably change when we reach Baghdad it will be an all out battle.

War is ugly.

Just remember we are here so that our future doesn't have to be filled with power-hungry dictators selling weapons and toxins to terrorists who will use them to kill innocent civilians. The Saddam's of the world cannot be allowed to run free. Freedom is not free.

Give everyone my love,

Your Son,
Cameron St. John
LCpl. Cameron White, USMC

PS: Hang the "Serving our country" banner in the window of your clinic. Let people know.

LCpl. Cameron White, USMC, is presently in California at March Air force Base doing special training before returning to Iraq with his company in late September 2004. He just returned from his second deployment to Iraq in April 2004.—FS

March 10, 2004

Frank:

I received this letter from my husband, Captain Sean Riddell, USMCR, written while he was in Iraq fighting in the war (he was there from 2/2003-6/2003). Tonya Riddell

---

March 2003

Dear Tonya,

There are times when this all seems routine.

There are times when I wonder how I got here.

There are times when it is all so surreal I have trouble thinking it is not a dream.

There are times when I just want to freeze the moment; dissect it; study it; cherish its uniqueness and oddity.

We just had a company formation so Col. Matchut could speak with us. In the middle of it we received news that Cpl. Wooden's wife gave birth to a baby girl. At the end of the formation Mark read out the baby's measurements. The Marines all yelled out encouragement and congrats. The proud father soon left with the 1st Sgt. to call home and speak to his wife.

Standing in the sun on a hot day in Kuwait, this young man found out he has another child. In Oregon, a woman holds a baby while her husband is half way around the world getting ready to fight in a war. For a day—for a moment he is the most popular Marine in the Company. For a while we all wish we were him. Not because we want children or daughters. Not because he is famous for a day. Not because he gets a phone call home. We wish we were him because for a moment, a brief moment, he is invincible. He does not feel the heat from the sun, the dirt that surrounds us, the hunger of our bodies, or the distance from home. For a brief moment he is lost in the news from home and nothing else matters. There are times when words cannot express the world we live in or our current existence. There are times when for a moment, we all are fathers to a new baby girl. . . .

Sean
Captain Sean J. Riddell USMCR

Captain Sean J. Riddell, USMC, was thirty-one years old while he was in Iraq and has now returned to his job as a district attorney in Multnomah County (Portland), Oregon. He is the commanding officer of the same reserve unit he went over to Iraq with, the 6th Engineer Support Battalion, Company A, out of Eugene, Oregon.—FS

19

Frank—

I am attaching [my son] Matt's Webster's letters from Operation Iraqi Freedom. One of the letters is the letter he wrote to his family and friends, the night before he shipped out and the rest are ones he sent from Kuwait and Iraq.

Cyndy Calkins

Matt was a nineteen-year-old lance corporal in Alpha Company, 1/5, 2nd Platoon, when he wrote these letters during his first deployment to Iraq.—FS

February 16, 2003 Kuwait

Dear Mom, Dad & Timmy Toes,

. . . . I've been really busy lately. I've been here [in Kuwait] two weeks and I finally took my first shower today. I can't describe how good it felt. It was like coming across an oasis in the desert. It was great.

The MEF (Marine Expeditionary Force) Commander came and talked to our whole Regiment today. Basically, he just said we were going to kick some ass and said some bad jokes and motivating words. But when it came to the part when he was talking about all the air support we've got, two F-15 Hornets (fighter planes) flew about 50 feet over our heads followed by 4 AH-10 Cobras (attack choppers). It just all of a sudden got loud as hell and the ground started shaking when the jets flew over. Scared the shit out of me— I thought I would have to change my undies!

I got a new weapon today, an M16-A4. It's a newer model of what I've already got, but it has a scope attached and a few other differences. I got it because I'm the Designated Marksman for my squad—that's kind of like a sniper but I get to stay with my unit. Anyway tomorrow I have to leave at 5 a.m. to go shoot and check it out. Should be pretty cool. . . .

Besides that, did I mention how much I absolutely hate this place? I hate the sand, I hate the sun, I hate the wind, I hate it all. Sorry, just had to get that off my chest.

I got out of the field yesterday and I had a few letters waiting for me—two from you Mom, two from Awnie and one from Gene. Thanks. My favorite part is getting mail. It feels like boot camp all over again. Damn what I wouldn't do for a supreme pizza, with chicken kickers and a large Mountain Dew, a Big Mac, a Whopper with cheese, anything. I'm going nuts.

Well enough of my problems. Hope all is well at home. Toes I hope you're not getting into too much trouble. . . . Hey Pops I know you're looking after my house, right? Momma, I miss you and hope you're doing all right. Tell everyone thanks for their letters. Tell everyone I miss them and love them. Hope to see you soon.

Yours truly, Matt
LCpl. Matthew W. Webster, USMC

––––––––––––––

February 19, 2002

Hey Guys,

. . . . Yesterday a camera crew from MTV came out and spent the day with us. It was that guy who always does the MTV News Breaks. They interviewed me and a few of my buddies. He said that the show would probably air in about a week and a half. So you should try to catch that if you can.

It rained last night, again. How does it rain in the desert? I don't understand. They say that the annual rain fall is 5 inches. If that's true then I must have been here for 3 or 4 years. . . .

I just can't wait for this thing to start and get over with, because even in crappy California I can get a cheeseburger. And I don't have to knock the sand out my eyes every five minutes.

I miss you all. . . .

Yours truly, Matt
LCpl. Matthew W. Webster, USMC

P.S. I haven't gotten any packages. Hopefully I will get one soon.

February 23, 2003

Hey Guys,

What's going on everyone? It's Sunday, which means we have church and pretty much just kick back the rest of the day. So, I'm listening to some DMB and cleaning my rifle. I finally got a hair cut and shower yesterday. So I reckon I don't look and smell too bad right now. We even started getting hot chow every night. So things haven't been too horrible here.

When they give us hot chow out here it's all from Kuwait. So like the juice, milk and yogurt have Arabic written all over it. The eggs are powdered and the bacon and meat definitely doesn't taste like pork or beef.

The PX truck comes about once a week and since there are around six thousand Marines in my camp, the line is at least 5 hours long. No joke. So I haven't had the opportunity to get anything yet.

No word yet on when we're leaving. Y'all probably have a better idea of the situation than I do. I'm hoping that it starts soon, because the sooner it starts the sooner it ends and the sooner I get back home.

Yours truly, Matthew Wayne
LCpl. Matthew W. Webster, USMC

March 5, 2003

Dear Family,

. . . . Today is Ash Wednesday and I went to Mass this morning. It was pretty crowded but the sermon was really good. I've decided to give up swearing and belittling people for Lent. It seemed like the only thing I could give up out here that would make me a better man. . . .

Matt
LCpl. Matthew W. Webster, USMC

March 28, 2003

Hey Guys,

I know I haven't written in a while, I'm sorry. But I've been kind of busy lately. You probably know why. Well I'm sure the question on your mind is how am I doing. Well, pretty good considering the circumstances. Right now I'm in Iraq, but by the time you get this letter, I don't know where I'll be. Home, hopefully. . . .

In these past days I've really learned a lot about myself and everyone around. You can read every book on war there is to read. And talk to vets about their experiences. But nothing can prepare you for what you see.

Our company has taken two casualties so far. A machine gunner stepped on a mine and took some shrapnel in the foot and leg. He's alright though. The other one was our lieutenant—Lt Childers.[*] He got shot in the gut in our first fight. I was standing right next to him when he got hit and it didn't look too bad at first. But he died before the Medivac chopper even got here. He was the first American to die in the war.

I've never seen anyone die before, especially someone as close to me as him. I don't know if I ever talked about him before, but he was probably one of the best Marines and men I've ever known. Without him pushing us and teaching us I'm not sure if any of my platoon would be half as good as it is.

I'd never been so scared in my entire life. I've never felt so all alone. One minute he was there fighting, the next he was gone.

But we've pushed on and I hate to say this but I think we've grown stronger. We have a new form of motivation. Instead of "let's win this so we can go home," it's "let's win this so the Lt. didn't die for naught." Still it's the worst thing I've ever seen in my life. And I've seen a lot of other stuff that gives me nightmares. But I'm sick of writing about bad stuff.

I'm trying to think of something funny to say. If it's not too funny, I'm sorry but we look for humor everywhere we can. The other morning at around 5 a.m. we were all standing post and we heard something moving in front of us. Normally I would just say

[*] [Second Lieutenant (Therrel) Shane Childers, 1st Battalion, 5th Marines, killed serving his country on March 21, 2003.—FS]

shoot, but there are a lot of Marines and civilians around so we want to be careful what we shoot. It was too dark to see with our eyes and there wasn't enough illumination for us to use our night vision. So naturally we were scared shitless. So for about thirty minutes there we are, all in our fighting hole, tired-ass as hell, itching to shoot and scared out of our minds, waiting for the sun to come out or for it to start shooting at us.

After about thirty minutes we were told to get back on our Amtracks (armored vehicles). And everyone turned and ran to the Amtrack as fast as we could, hoping we didn't get shot in the back. As I reached the Amtrack, Sonny and I turned back to see if we had to shoot whoever it was. And there he was—a little baby camel looking for his mommy. Just imagine, 30 rough, tough grunt Marines running for their lives from a little baby camel. I hope y'all got a smile out of that one.

We haven't got mail for a while, so I hope all is well. Don't know when I'll be coming home. But I hope it's soon. I miss and love y'all so much. Don't worry about me, because you know somehow this little, skinny Mick always lands on his feet.

Love you.
Yours truly, Matthew Wayne Webster
LCpl. Matthew W. Webster, USMC

LCpl. Matthew Webster, USMC, is now a corporal, still in Alpha Co. and serving his second deployment in Iraq, where Alpha was involved in the fight in Fallujah. He is currently based outside that city.—FS

20

March 14, 2004

Dear Mr. Schaeffer,

Enclosed you will find several letters. . . . The first letter describes to Grandpa and Grandma our son's heroic act. For this . . . he was awarded the Navy and Marine Corps Commendation Medal with a Combat V device. We are very proud of him for this and his many other accomplishments in the USMC. The second letter goes hand-and-hand with the first letter. The third letter describes the feelings he had in the loss of the one and only member of his unit.

Sincerely,
LF
Proud Marine Mom of a LCpl., USMC

This letter was sent to a certain Marine corporal's grandparents. He requested that his name be withheld. He did not feel it was appropriate to boast about his actions, other than to his grandparents. So these letters are included anonymously herein, although, as editor, I do know who the Marine Corporal author is and can vouch for the authenticity of his letters.—FS

March 30, 2003

Grandpa & Grandma,

Hello from the Middle East. How are you guys doing? How is everything in Wisconsin? Everything here is going the best it can. Although I am stuck in the middle of a war, everything is on the up and up. I couldn't ask for a better group of guys to be working with in a situation like this. The following information I am about to tell you, I would appreciate if you would not tell Mom and Dad. Especially Mom! You know how she can be.

Well, me and three other guys got attached to an infantry unit support communications. It was a last minute thing for us to go with them. The day we got attached to them we were sent out on our first mission. We were instructed to secure the city so we could re-supply vehicles to re-supply other units. The unit I am attached to was the first one in country. So I was one of the first [Marines] in country.

I'm getting sidetracked. We got to the city and they welcomed us with a boom. They started sending everything they could throw at us in our direction. We took cover and the war began. We secured the south side of the city and we started pushing forward. We got to the central part with no resistance. We got a new order saying go east and make sure everything was good on that side. . . .

One of our vehicles got stuck and then it happened. We were being ambushed. Rounds were coming from every angle possible. With our convoy of vehicles spread across the whole east side, we thought we were done for. Everyone got out of their vehicles and took cover. The infantry swept through that half of the city forcing the Iraqis out towards us or they killed them. I was watching the whole raid. One of the infantrymen, the last one, got stuck in a mud hole up to his armpits. He couldn't move. The rest of his squad pushed forward not knowing about him. I was the only one that saw this Marine in trouble. At that time I got a rush of courage. All I remember is saying, "Cover me, I'm going in." I ran to that mud hole, while taking fire, and pulled that Marine out. In the process of running to this Marine, I killed two Iraqi soldiers and wounded a third that crawled into a building. He was soon killed shortly after.

When I returned to my fighting position to take cover, the guys I was with looked at me in shock. They finally grasped the concept of what I just did. They never thought in a lifetime I would ever do such a thing. One guy said, "I'm proud of you. You showed your true colors." That made me feel like I was king of the world.

Shortly after that we secured the east side which we call "Ambush Alley." We pushed a little further north to our new position, that's where I am sitting now.

Now the whole city, the city has 300,000 people living in it or did, is secured. Now we are waiting to get this war over with so we can come home. Well Grandpa and Grandma, I hope you like my story of what happened to me in my first and last war experience. . . .

Other than what I have told you, that's all that has been going on. There are a few other things I would like to tell you, but it's hard for me to even stomach them. I will tell you later. . . .

That is my quick rundown on what is going on so far. I have been told that I am not going to see anymore combat. We have completed our mission, now its time for other units to push forward and complete theirs so we can go home. The way things are going, I should be home by June. I'm going to cross my fingers and pray. . . . Well, I just wanted to write and let you know about my adventure. I hope all is well back home. I love and miss you guys very much.

Love,
Cpl., USMC

April 24, 2003

Mom,

. . . . Just wanted to write and tell you something that I couldn't tell you last night on the phone. Well for starters I want to clarify something. You sounded upset when I told you that I rescued a guy in a fire fight. Well, it wasn't me trying to be a hero. It was a reflex. I saw him; I ran to him and then brought him to safety. I didn't even think about it. It was God telling me that it was my time to shine. God was with me. . . . After all this, I am now more faithful in the Lord than I ever was before. He has rewarded me with good health, and allowing me to come home in one piece. The Marine Corps is also rewarding me. They are giving me a combat promotion and they nominated me for the Bronze Star. The combat promotion is for being an outstanding Marine in the time of war.

The Bronze star is for bravery and valor in time of war. The Bronze star is the 4th highest award given in all branches of the military. So it is an honor and a privilege to wear such an award. Not many people wear such an award, plus, it may make me the highest honored Marine in 8th Com BN. So I am just waiting to see if I get it. So that is my quick rundown of that situation.

On April 22nd was a sad day for Alpha Company. One of my fellow Marines was killed in a routine firing exercise. They were disposing of Iraqi ammo when an RPG, rocket propelled grenade, backfired and blew up. It killed him and another Marine from another unit. Today we have a religious service for him. It was a real reality check for a lot of people. I've included the service program along with this letter. It was real hard because he was the only Marine to be killed out of A Co. plus we are getting out of this hell hole soon. We all planned to come out here together, and go home together. But, that's not the case anymore.

Moving on now. I just found out that I was "voluntold" [Marinespeak for a combination of volunteered and told—FS] to stay back for a working party. I won't be riding back on the ship so I won't be hitting any libo [liberty] ports. It's alright though. I'm flying back so I will be back before everyone else. I will get plenty of R&R when I get back to the States. The bonus is I will be getting more money. It will be nice when I get back. I have a lot of future plans for when I get back, and a lot of things to prepare for. . . . Just a lot of things on my mind right now.

I mentioned that me and Kari, the girl form Dennis' wedding, have been talking a lot. We started writing around Sept. of last year and have continued since. We like each other a lot so who knows what may happen in a couple of months. . . . I think she is a great person and really pretty. So I am hoping. . . .

Love and miss you very much.

Bye for now.
Love,
Cpl., USMC

The Corporal is back home and out of the USMC.—FS

21

Frank,

I heard through the mommy network you're looking for letters from Iraq. . . . My son was 18 and newly married to his high school sweetheart when he shipped out to Kuwait in early Feb 03. I'm not a fan of early marriage but these two kids are going to make it. I'm convinced my daughter in law is the reason my son is still alive and sane.

Will is a machine gunner in the 3/5 Marines. His sgt called me after returning stateside and told me Will rode on top of the humvee guarding his back all during the war. He saw a lot of action and did a lot of growing up. Every time the return date was changed the morale sunk lower and lower. The battalion finally returned the first week of September. They were home less than a month when they were told they'll be going back—at this point it looks like late summer but that could change depending on what happens over there.

This first letter describes action that resulted in three Silver Stars and a Navy Cross for members of Will's platoon. The letter was written to my daughter-in-law who gave me a copy last year.

Susan Porter

LCpl. Porter was eighteen when he wrote this letter.—FS

March 30, 2003

Hey Babe,

What's up? Well, I haven't written for awhile. I haven't had too much time. We crossed the border into Iraq on the 20th. We left at about 12 AM that night. We drove about 30 miles into Iraq and took over 1 of our division's 4 main objectives.

We had to case and cordon a GOSP (gas, oil separation plant). We took the northernmost GOSP. It was scary as fuck! We didn't have any real problem doing it though. We got there as the sun came up and the guys guarding it were freaked out. They tried running away. We drove after them for awhile and they all surrendered. We captured 20 something guys and just as many weapons.

That night we set up a defense and left to push north again the next day. Half of our group got into some shit on the way to our next staging area. They only ended up shooting 1 dude in the foot. The next day we drove farther north and saw a lot of the country. Everyone and their cousin was lined up alongside the road begging us for food and smokes. We barely had enough food for us so we didn't give them any. We don't have anymore damn cigs either. That makes for some seriously butt hurt Marines.

We waited around for everyone else to catch up for two days. We were all kind of paranoid. Once everybody caught up to us we started moving with the entire regiment (5th Marines). We drove about 4 klicks (km) ahead of the column and got ambushed real bad. The first two trucks had .50 cals on top, and they passed the kill zone before they started. The rest of us got pimpslapped by the little bastards. They were up on a berm to our right, w/a trench behind it, and one in front of it. The berm was about 10-15 feet. A bunch of the little fucks jumped up, and shot RPGs at us. The rest opened up w/AKs and machine guns. That was the scariest thing I've ever heard.

We took two casualties. Doc Johnson died when an RPG went through his truck. It hit Cpl. Quinntero on the hip and blew up on Doc. Q's in the hospital. He's going home soon. Doc wasn't as lucky.

The rest of our platoon drove into the ambush to break it up. Half of us dismounted the humvees to clear the trenches while the others provided fire to the guys on the berm. We wasted those bastards. We regrouped when they were all dead and set up another little defense. That evening we had to go down the same road to establish another position. We went about 5 klicks farther. I was the most scared I've been in my life. I told myself that if I lived through that night I'd come home for sure. Ha! I did.

There was a dust storm while we moved out. It was just after noon and it was almost dark. The sky was completely orange— you couldn't see more than 30 feet in front of you. It was insane. They brought up 4 tanks to help us clear the road. They blasted a few trucks. Everything on fire had a weird white glow to it. It was like a movie. We got in another little engagement on the way there.

I sit on top of the truck w/my gunner. I have my M-16, he's got a MK-19 (automatic grenade launcher) I saw a dude jump out of a ditch and try to run up the berm. I opened up on him and then every truck did too. We probably fired over 2,000 rounds at some dumb ass who was too stupid to keep his ass down. Better him than me, right?

It got crazier when some psycho drove down the road at 50 mph in his little white truck screaming some wierd shit. I only got 1 shot off at him before he was gone (found out later I hit 'em). Then it started to rain when we got there. It was just a crazy night.

The last couple days we've just been sitting as a blockade on the freeway. Iraqi highway 1 and 17. There is a big clover leaf here that we don't let anyone through. The fuckers keep dressing like civilians so it's really hard to distinguish who's who. We should move soon, we just have to wait for the Army to get their shit together. This thing should be done by the end of April and add another month, month & 1/2 of humanitarian shit. Should be home soon. Tell everyone I said hi and keep writing me. We haven't got mail for over two weeks. Know that I love you and I pray every night that I'll come home to you safe, so we can start our life together. . . .

LCpl. William B. Porter USMC

This next letter is to LCpl Porter's family.—FS

April 13, 2003

What's up everyone?

Well right now I'm sitting in the middle of Baghdad drinking a 7-Up and having a smoke. Never thought I'd see this day. Shit couldn't be any weirder. I honestly don't know what to write. So much has happened in the last three weeks I don't know what to say. I got mail last night for the first time in a couple of weeks.

Hilary, I'll start with some of your ?s. 1. Yes, we've had tons of people surrender to us. The first day, just our section of our platoon had over 40 surrenders. That was southern Iraq. They didn't want to be there. Two weeks ago when we were moving towards Saddam City, we started encountering Republican Guard troops. They fought for a few hours, and then the ones that were still alive gave up. Some tried to change into civilian clothes, but they had no shoes other than boots. If they were barefoot, we knew who they were. (No civilian in his right mind would stay around a firefight, especially a military aged male.)

2. The Iraqi people all seem to love us. The streets look like Mardi Gras. Everyone cheers and honks their horns. There are so many little kids. I've never seen so many people! They can't make up their fuckin' minds though. We'll have kids that no shit, shook our hands the day before dead on the street 5 hours later with an AK 47 next to 'em. They piss me off!

3. As for dramatizations on TV, no, everything I've seen is real. These people hate Saddam's regime. Now I'll explain what I do. In CAAT plt. we have 12 humvees. We are supposed to be anti-armor (tanks) but the only people we've been fighting are infantry. (Now there are more terrorists here from Saudi and Syria than Iraqis.) Anyway, before the battalion moves we lead with tanks up to wherever the battalion plans on moving next. Going first sucks. You're guaranteed to get into some kind of fight. We have 4 TOW missile trucks, 4MK-19 grenade trucks and 4 .50 cal machine gun trucks. We usually split in 2 groups to cover a lot of ground. It works. We do a lot of patrols through cities. Those are the worst. You have nowhere to hide when motherfuckers on rooftops start shooting.

My favorite missions are raids. We do a lot of stuff that normal infantry units should do but since we're mobile, we're faster at it. We raid lots of govt officials houses. We roll up real fast and hop out and storm the buildings. That's fun cuz you're the aggressor, not them. Makes shit a lot easier. *Now* we're all good at what we do. I'll put it lightly, we've *all* earned our combat action ribbon.

Oh yeah, I got promoted to Lance Corporal two weeks ago. That's another $200 a month. What else did you ask? Oh yeah, am I still a gun crazy nut case? Answer—of course.

4. And that brings us to your next one Hilly. Yes, I have had to kill people and no, it doesn't feel different than I thought it would. We don't do it for fun, we do it because if we don't, then they'll shoot us. Your perspective on life changes with a blink of an eye when some pussy behind a wall has the audacity to shoot an RPG at you. FUCK THAT!

It's pretty hard to explain so I won't go into it any further. It's not going to change me. Whatever happens here I'm determined to leave here. I'm not letting anyone get in my way when it comes to going home.

So the situation now is this. We took Baghdad w/little resistance. (Moving up was hard.) Now the battalion commander is moving us north 1 more time to take 2 smaller cities. 1 is Saddam's hometown. There is where we expect the last resistance. As of today, Sunday the 13th of April, he says 1 more week of combat operations. Then the Army should take over and begin humanitarian ops. Their goal (USMC) is to have us home by June. It seems like I've already been gone for years. I haven't taken a shower since the beginning of March. Everyone's so dirty we can't even smell ourselves. That's sad.

I gotta sleep. I've had about 1 hour in 2 days. Tell everyone thanks for the mail, it means a lot to me. Thank you guys for thinking about us. . . .

Love ya lots,
Will
LCpl. William B. Porter, USMC

April 27, 2003

Well it's been a while since I've written you guys. Last time I wrote I was in Baghdad. We moved north to Samarra. They thought that was going to be the last big fight, but I didn't fire 1 round. We stayed there for a couple of days to make sure no shit went down. I got to see Saddam's entire air force all in pieces (literally). He had tons of jets and helos, but they either had no nose or tailfin or engine. He stashed them in people's backyards and other weird places. I got a pic of me in front of one of his full intact helos. It still had rockets in it. Now we moved south to Diwaniya. It's a pretty awkward city for us, because when we first pushed up here, it was the first time we engaged enemy, and it's where Doc Johnson was killed. That seems like a year ago. I think it was just around 1 month ago. Cpl. Quintero is doing alright. He's in Germany right now (I think). He got hit by the same RPG that hit Doc.

Pres Bush gave Q his Purple Heart in person. I think it was

televised because he was one of the first no-shit casualties. Anyway, this city is really annoying. We have to help the fuckin' Duneleoons [a slang name combining "loons" and "sand dunes"—FS] establish a govt and police force here. They don't really need us here and that's the Army's job. They're here too.

We do night patrols all over the city. We established a police force already and sometimes we take them with us. It's really strange looking down at a guy w/green on and an AK 47 in his hand 2 feet below you that most likely was shooting at you 2 weeks ago. . . .

People still shoot all over the city at night but I haven't had a round fly my way in about 2 weeks. I've got tons of mail since I've been here. We got all the packages they couldn't give to us on the front lines. I haven't really gotten any letter mail though. The last letter was from Nik and dated April 5.

We're staying at a compound right next to a hospital. The majority of 3/5 is here and it's lame because they're treating us like we're at Pendleton. . . .

It sucks, and I'm really wanting a phone call! The place we're staying at is like a college. It's pretty nice. A brand new building. A bunch of guys are going home from my platoon. They were the stop loss guys [those kept in for special emergencies after their service contract is over—FS] who were supposed to get out in Jan/Feb who got stuck coming here. One of them will call you when they get back for me. I gotta go. It's getting dark and my schedule = 12 hrs on reaction force/patrol and 6 hrs rest. It blows. I'm thinking about you guys. I'll be home soon enough. I love you all and I'll see you soon.

Love ya,
Will
LCpl. William B. Porter, USMC

The following is an excerpt from a letter to LCpl. Porter's sister.—FS

June 10, 2003

. . . . I hate this country . . . ! I hate the people, the landscape, the annoying dude who prays over a loudspeaker at 3 in the morning, the heat, the mosquitoes—I think it's safe to say I hate everything here. I've slept on the ground since Feb (the ground or in my humvee) and the worst thing is, there's no one left to shoot!

LCpl. William B. Porter, USMC

June 23, 2003

What's up family?

Still in the epicenter of ass. I'm finally convinced that I'm going to become a permanent resident here. You know a place sucks when everything in it smells like human waste. I have A/C for the first time in over 4 months. Only problem is the power in this country is worthless and it's usually only on when you don't need it.

What's new at home? How is everyone? All I want to do is go home and be w/Nik and you guys. That's it. I've (along w/ everyone else here) considered many ways to get home early. Most would only end up w/brig time. I HATE THIS PLACE!!!!!

The Iraqi people are the most annoying I have ever met. They all think that Americans owe them something. I don't owe [them] shit. You guys can't even begin to comprehend how horrible this place is.

I should be home later, how about fall. I will have been in this shithole for every season of an entire year! OK, I'm done bitching for now. I need AT&T phone cards. We now have a phone but it can only use those cards. 200 minutes on card gets us 15 minutes overseas so get a big card. I love you guys. I'll see you whenever.

Your butt hurt baby—
LCpl. William B. Porter, USMC

July 29, 2003

Hey guys,

Taking part in Task Force Scorpion. Sorry I haven't written. Still getting shot at. Coming home by Sept 1. . . . See you.

Love ya,
Will
LCpl. William B. Porter, USMC

LCpl. William Porter, USMC, is back in the States and will deploy to Iraq again in September 2004. He married Nicole on January 20, 2003, just before he deployed to Iraq the first time.—FS

22

This letter was submitted by Melissa Carter and was written to her by her husband.—FS

March 28, 2003
13:22 Zulu
(8:22 your time)

Melissa,

Hi baby. I don't know when you'll receive this letter, but I want you to know that as of now I'm alive and well. Don't worry too much and don't pay too close attention to the news, as they tend to exaggerate. I wish I could have called you before we attacked, but it was all of a sudden. I know that the big news stations are probably reporting bad things. Don't let it stress you out. Keep charging hard in school and we'll be together by August in time for our anniversary. I know it probably seems like doom and gloom back home.

For the last couple days the log train and I have been camped out somewhere in Iraq. Other Marine elements have encountered opposition, but we haven't. Our only problem was this—3 or 4 days ago we crossed the Tigris River at about 0300. There were so many Marine vehicles that it caused a grid-locked traffic jam. (Picture the 5 during the rush hour near LA or San Diego.) The truck

I was in was parked on the side of the road while me and the driver waited for the rest of our group. Since I had been awake for 2 days and there were so many Marines, I felt it safe to sleep. Sniper fire woke me up. I jumped out of the truck and assumed a defensive position ready to fire; however, I couldn't find a target. Someone from 5th Marines (who happened to be there the same time as us) opened fire with a SAW and someone else shot off a 203 (grenade launcher). I thought no one found the sniper, but rumor has it there were 2 men, one was killed, the other escaped. That is the only action you can say I've seen. I've heard bad stories, but nothing has come our way.

Right now we're in the middle of nowhere with nothing to do. I can't wait to come home, but I try not to think about it. I just take it day to day, of course; because of a couple night moves I'm not sure how long I've actually been here. If in case I don't come back, which I'm afraid is a real possibility, I want you to know how much I love you.

I've always been head over heels for you. All the times I've driven to Youngstown to spend my last dollar on gas is a good show of that. I've always tried to spend as much time with you as I could because I needed you. . . . I've never before met someone who I connected with so well. When I started dating you it was as if my lonely days were over. I don't feel alone anymore. . . .

I know that in life you will do well, should it be without me. . . . I really don't know what to write as a last letter. I still believe I'll be coming home, which may be why this letter seems a little dry. As far as the kids are concerned, we've already talked about them. Just raise them the best you can, the way I would. It's hard for me to say anything about what I think you should do. I totally trust in your judgment. Don't get too worked up over that sniper thing. I just want you to know I have [kept] my wits in danger, and I want you to know a couple gunshots in the night is all the danger I've seen. I don't have much more to say so I'll go.

I love you, I always have, and I always will.

> Your Husband,
> Bill
> Corporal William Carter, USMC

I was not able to learn the whereabouts of Corporal William Carter USMC at this time.—FS

March 12, 2003

This is the text of a letter my daughter in law Rachel received from my son, Sgt. Ian Leavy, USMC, while he was on his way into Baghdad last spring.

> Benita Leavy

Ian was twenty-three when he wrote this letter.—FS

April 12, 2003

Hey Honey,

Oh-My-God! Have I got some stories for you! I'll probably wait to give you the long version until I get home but I'll give you the down & dirty right now. Remember I told you we had only been in small fire-fights? Well all that changed about five days ago. At least I think it was 5 days ago, the days have been running together. Anyway, about five days ago we got the order to move into and secure Saddam City, which is a little city about 15 miles south of Baghdad. (It's really ghetto, not nice like Baghdad.) So we move into the city and make contact with the enemy. (That's just a fancy military way of saying that we started getting shot at.) This was our first real fire fight. One of the vehicles in my platoon got shot with an RPG. Fortunately no one died. One of the Grunts got hit in the lip with some shrapnel, but he's o.k.

So after we cleared the town (that's just a fancy military way of saying we whooped everyone's ass) and secured all of our objectives we come to find out that one of the objectives we cleared was a prison for children. I guess Saddam was holding thousands of children hostages so that their parents would do what he told them to. Isn't that horrible?! Anyway we liberated that prison and destroyed a couple of military bases. It was amazing! Afterward we were rolling through the city and the people of the city were everywhere, clapping and cheering and saying that they loved us and that "Bush good! Saddam no good!" It was a really good feeling, like we were celebrities or something. I was actually signing autographs for little kids. Isn't that funny!

So anyway we stayed in the defense at Saddam City for about two days and word was that we might not be leaving Saddam City until the end of the war. Then on the evening of the 9th we heard different. The lieutenant came to our trak [Amtrak armored vehicle] and told us we would be moving out that night to go into the heart of Baghdad and raid Saddam Hussein's main palace! I couldn't believe it! I didn't think we were going to get to go into Baghdad (when I say "we," I mean 5th Marines) let alone to Saddam's main palace! Needless to say I was pretty excited and scared too, I'll admit, because urban warfare is the most dangerous because it's such close quarters (like in "Black Hawk Down").

So basically the plan was to haul ass up the freeway (AAV's, tanks, LAV's and all) and punch straight in downtown at about dawn. So we drive all night up to Baghdad and stop for a minute right outside the city. Everything was quiet except the sound of the vehicles and the sound of my heart pounding like a goddamn kettle drum in my chest! We knew right up the road there were Republican Guard waiting for us.

(Above)
Robert Mark Neno, Jr., USMC, left,
with his mother, sister and father

(Right)
Jonathan Fox

(Right)
Kelley L. Chambers, USN

[Not all the letters writers are shown in
these photographs.—FS]

(Above)
David Sandifer, USMC and wife Katie

(Right)
Joseph Giardino, USMC

(Below)
Nate Nemitz, USMC

(Above)
Brandon Scott Bailey,
Airman 1st Class, USAF

(Above)
Cody M. Harkins, USMC

(Right)
Andy Kaplan,
USMC, with
mother Gaye
Lowe-Kaplan
and father,
Frank Kaplan

(Top of opposite page)
Jason D. Grose, USMC, and family

(Bottom left of opposite page)
David W. Bryant, USMC
and wife, Chantal

(Bottom right of opposite page)
Sean Wyman, USN

(Right)
Aaron Lussi, USMC

(Right)
Chaplain Emory Lussi, USN

(Right)
Jeremy S. Lussi, 10th Mtn.
Division, U.S. Army

(Above clockwise from bottom left)
Jeremy, Matthew, Bethany, Aaron, Emory and Beverly Lussi

(Below)
Matthew Lussi, Wyoming Army
National Guard

(Below)
Amatangelo Pasciuti, USMC

(Right)
Jason Bohrer, USMC

(Below)
Matthew Bogdanos,
USMC (far right)

(Above on left)

Sean J. Riddell, USMC

(Below)

Cameron White, USMC

(Below)

Matthew W. Webster, USMC

(Above)
Clayton Colman,
USMC, center, with
mother and fiancé

(Right)
William B. Porter,
USMC

(Above)
Aaron White, USMC and daughter, Brianna

(Left)
Aaron White, USMC and wife, Michele

(Below)
Sgts. Warren G. Hardy and Janelle R. Hardy, USMC (with son, William)

(above)
Colin A. Smith, USMC
(back row, right), with family,
including brother Scott, USMC
(back row, left)

(Right)
Clint Turnbull, Iowa Army National
Guard in his Iraqi corn field

(Below)
Jason A. Climer, USMC with
children, Cailin and Cameron

(Above left)
Michael Jernigan, USMC,
and wife, Drew

(Above right)
Matthew Mertz, USMC *(right)*
and father

(Left)
Army Reservist Stephen
McDowell

(Right)
Cory R. Mracek, 82nd
Airborne, U.S. Army
(upper right), with
family, including
mother, Pat *(far left)*

(Bottom right)
Jack Wilder, U.S. Army
and wife, Susan

(Above)

William Joseph Fiack, USN, SEAL Team II

(Right)

Joe DePew, USMC

(Below)

Family of Joe DePew, including mother Tina, and his three sisters

(Above)

Josh Davey, USMC, with family, including father, Rob

(Below)

John J. Thomas, USAF, and family

(Above)
Mike Strobl, USMC and wife, Stacey

(Right)
Jane (Vizzi) Blair, USMC and Peter
Blair, USMC at their wedding

(Below)
Jane (Vizzi) Blair, USMC and Peter Blair,
USMC in Iraq

But we also knew we had them out manned and out gunned. So finally they come over the radio and we get the word that we're moving and we just start barreling down the freeway like a bat out 'a hell! Me and a bunch of the grunts in the back are hanging out the cargo hatches with our rifles, machine guns, and 203's (grenade launchers). Needless to say the adrenaline was flowing pretty good by now. I hadn't slept all night, but I wasn't one bit tired. Then all of a sudden shit started going off like it was the 4th of July. There were muzzle flashes on both sides of the road from AK-47's and RPG's were whistling past us like it was cool. All of the turrets on the AAV's were lighting shit up, as were all of us in the back of the vehicles. Tanks were just nailing bunkers left and right and, don't forget, this is while flying down the freeway at about 40 mph.

This lasted about 5 minutes and then we were in the city streets. So they tell us we are no longer going to Saddam's palace because he escaped and that we're going to go building to building through the city to look for him. Anyway, that is a whole other story. . . . I'll just say I never imagined myself seeing anything like it in my whole life! And even though I was scared, I've gotta admit, I loved it!

I guess it's just the adrenaline or something, it's like a drug. But I think I had enough, don't worry, I'm still getting out. I must say I was thinking of reenlisting during the battle downtown, though. It was really motivating with the combat and everyone doing such a good job and all the moving parts of the Marine Corps coming together and kicking so much ass! Anyway we cleared the area and took the palace. Oh yeah! Guess where we are staying right now as I write this? Saddam's palace! It's huge! We are actually sleeping on the vehicles right outside but we can go inside during the day. I got some really cool stuff to show you. I got good pic's too.

Anyway enough about me. How are you doing? How is that big *one year old* boy doing? And how 'bout his big brother? I sure miss you guys. It sounds like we are getting pretty close to getting to go home, and we are getting pretty anxious.

Oh Yeah, I forgot to tell you, the people in Baghdad (which is a lot more modern than Saddam City) love us too. They are cheering and clapping when they drive by us. It's like we are heroes already and we haven't even come home yet!

Well I'd better get some sleep. Go ahead and let everyone back home know what I said in this letter because I don't have time to write ten copies of this OK? Anyway, I love you and the boys and can't wait to see you again! Hopefully pretty soon now!

Love, Ian
Sgt. Ian Leavy, USMC

Sgt. Ian Leavy, USMC, is back in the States and is out of the Corps and going to college. He and his wife, Rachel, have two children, with a third on the way.—FS

—————————

March 4, 2004

Frank:

Our son is a Marine Lance Corporal with 1/7 Charlie Company Stationed in Twenty Nine Palms, California. Here is a letter he wrote to us while stationed in Iraq. Our son was only 19 years old when he went to Iraq. He was a certified nanny when he graduated from high school. He has a real love for children as you can see from his letter.

Kenda Colman

—————————

April 14, 2003

Hey There,

How are you guys doing? We are doing great. Sorry I haven't wrote in a while, but I've been pretty busy blowing off safe doors in Saddam's Palace, yah that's right Saddam's Palace.

The War is over so we are chillin in Saddam's Palaces right now waiting to get relieved by the 4th Armor ID. We are not exactly sure how long we are going to be here, but rumor has it that we should be home hopefully late May.

Let me fill you in on what has been going on so far.

1. Took over a torture camp of Saddam's, found two bodies, one decapitated the other mutilated.
2. Blew up some tanks.
3. Secured a town.
4. Took over Saddam's Palace.
5. Ransacked the hell out of the prime minister's house.

The entire time we have been here, we haven't been shot at once. The people here are very happy to see us though. The other day I was standing post, and the children in the area came over to me and brought me flowers and water (bottled). They sat and talked to us for a while. They are so cute. A little boy walked up to me and held his arms up like he wanted to be picked up so I unslung my weapon and picked him up. He laid his head on my shoulder and kissed my cheek. Right then and there I knew why God wanted me here.

As far as Saddam's belongings we have taken them and we are giving them back to the people. So that has been my last 2 1/2 months.

Well I love you guys and I miss you. Hopefully I will be home soon.

Love,
LCpl. Clayton D. Colman, USMC

LCpl. Clayton D. Colman got back from Iraq in October 2003. He is still in the USMC and is stationed at 29 Palms, Califorina. He will be getting married to Jessica in July and then is being sent back to Iraq in August 2004 as a demolition expert with Charlie Company, 1st Marine Expeditionary Force.—FS

23

Some readers will remember Michele Linn (White) from the description of my meeting with her found in *Faith of Our Sons*. She and her daughter Brianna—to whom this book is dedicated—live in Oceanside, California.—FS

February 24, 2004

Frank,

This month has actually been very depressing for me. Aaron left last Feb. [2003] for Kuwait, so it's been a year since I've seen him. My birthday was the 13th, the first in 10 years he's not around. His is the 29th. Of course reading these letters made me cry! I suffer from occasional nightmares about the crash.

I am still in school. Brianna [age 2] is growing like a weed. Nothing has really been going on around here. I'm sorry to say that I didn't save many of Aaron's letters. It never occurred to me that I would need to keep them. . . . I hope you and your family are well.

Michele
Michele Linn (White)

Staff Sergeant Aaron White, USMC Medium Helicopter Squadron 364 MAG 39 3rd MAW Purple Foxes, was killed in a helicopter crash on May 19, 2003, in Ah Hillah, Iraq. These are his last letters home to his wife, Michele, and to his baby daughter Brianna.—FS

February 24, 2003

Dear Michele & Brianna,

You have no idea how much your Valentines Day card and letter meant to me. I was really getting pretty down with all the work and more work going on, not to mention not hearing from anyone for a couple weeks. I couldn't stop smiling all day. I grew teary eyed when I saw the pictures of Brianna. I miss her so much. I'd give anything to just leave here to be with you two. Hold you both in a huge long hug. Just to sit with you and watch her play. I am so sorry to have left you all alone. I know this is harder on you because you know so few people there. What I would give to make this all go away, so I can be with you again.

I'll try tomorrow to get you a POA [power of attorney] for the taxes. I really am having hard time writing a will. It bothers me to think that hard about actually dying. I guess I'm just trying to not face the fact it could happen.

I have to tell you, as we grow closer to war, I really have some strong fears. Fear of dying, of being crippled, burned, gassed, and of never seeing my two beautiful women again. What keeps me up at night is thinking you may never know what you mean to me. I can't explain it [in] my words just how much a part of me you have become. I'll do my best to show you when I come home. If I don't come home, please tell Brianna that her daddy loves her more than life and that I am so proud to be her daddy. She's the best thing that we've ever done Michele, a little ball of happiness. I can never help myself from smiling when I see her face. She's always been such a sweet baby. I hope it bodes well for her future happiness. I know we'll do anything to keep her smile going.

I don't know what I did to deserve you two in my life, but I hope I can make both of you as happy as you've made me.

Believe me I am not having a good time here. This is an ugly hasty land. I hope these people appreciate the blood we are soon to spill, both Iraqis and our own. To any anti-war people you've seen just tell them we can still see the bullet holes on the walls from the firing squads the Iraqis used to kill Kuwaitis. This needs to be done and it will be. Soon I hope.

Pray for this guy [Saddam] to give up. But it won't happen. Please write often babe. It's what keeps me going. I love you and miss you.

Hug our daughter tight, always,
Aaron
SSgt. Aaron White, USMC

P.S. Tell people to send foot powder!

Birthday card from Aaron to Brianna.—FS

Dear Brianna,

It breaks my heart to have to miss your first birthday. I hope that you will forgive me. Please know that I would be there if at all possible. We are doing a good thing here so that little boys and girls can enjoy the freedoms that are your birthright.

I carry several pictures of you and miss you constantly. I know you are in the capable care of your loving mother and are no doubt growing like a weed. You have brought so much joy and happiness into our lives. I hope to bring the same to you in the coming years. I fall asleep every night with visions of you and your mommy in my head, reminding me of all I have been blessed with. I will be with you every day, if not in body, then in spirit. I love more than my words could ever say.

Happy first birthday. I love you and miss your sweet smile.

Hugs to my little girl,
Love,
Daddy

SSgt. Aaron White was killed two days after Brianna turned one. The next letter was written for Brianna's baby book and sent to Michele for Brianna.—FS

Ali Al Salem Air Base
Kuwait
March 5, 2003

Dear Brianna,

Hello this is your daddy. I am writing you from far away in a country called Kuwait. I am here because I am a U.S. Marine and have been called upon, with several thousand other people, to possibly remove a very bad man from power in a country called Iraq. I know that by the time you read this that you will have heard about the events leading up to this so I will spare you the history lesson.

I have been away from you for over a month now and I miss you terribly. No matter how sad I ever am your smile always cheered me up. You've been such a happy baby and I hope it has carried on throughout your childhood.

Your mommy and I have loved you from the time we knew you were on the way. We planned and hoped for you when we lived in Japan. When you were born on May 17, 2002 in Camp Pendleton hospital you were so tiny and stayed in the hospital for a few days. This scared us very much but you've since been so healthy and have grown so fast. We both love to get you to giggle and smile. Your happiness is infectious. When I left home you were sitting up pretty well and playing with some of your toys. You have a tiny piano you play with a Pooh bear that you are scared of. It's so cute when you get upset. Your bottom lip sticks out and you try so hard not to cry. We have to try very hard not to laugh, when we know you aren't hurt, and you make that face!

Your mom takes such good care of you. She never ignores you and seems to know what you need simply by instinct. I am constantly amazed at how she knows what you need. I can tell when you need your diaper changed and maybe when you're hungry, but mommy has me beat when it comes to knowing what you need.

My favorite game right now is to hold you up so you can stand a little. Not quite on your own yet, but you seem so happy and really enjoy just standing up. You laugh constantly.

I hope to be home long before you can read this. In any case, I want you to know how happy you made me. I am so proud of you and know you will be a wonderful person.

Bad things happen in life. Sometimes you'll wonder what the point of it all is. For me it has been loving you and your mommy. Of all things in life loving someone so much is the greatest joy I've known. Seeing you and your mom together gives me the warmest feeling and a purpose in life.

I'll be home soon and will hug you so much. You are the greatest thing to happen to your mom and I. We both would do anything for you and will endeavor to bring you happiness and love in your life.

> All my love to you Brianna. I will be home soon,
> Daddy
> SSgt. Aaron White, USMC

Michele has gone back to school. Times are tough. When an American in uniform is killed his or her family receives a one-time "Death Gratuity" of

$6000. (In 2004 this number was increased to $12,000.) The surviving family may also qualify for "Survivors Benefit Plan" (SBP) paid up to age 62 or until the widow remarries. SBP amounts to a mere 55% of the soldier's retirement pay, which itself is calculated against a percentage of pay so low it already qualifies many military families for food stamps. Michele did not qualify for this because Aaron was in the Corps *just under ten years* service. Several further benefits, such as the income-based Dependency and Indemnity Compensation (DIC) run by the VA, *may or may not* pay out about $800 per month and $200 per child depending on the case. Michele also did not qualify. Medical benefits end after three years.—FS

24

April 2, 2004

Mr. Schaeffer:

. . . . In today's media, we seem to get overlooked. We sacrifice many things, some more than others, sacrifices that most civilians do not experience. Thank you for giving us a voice. Here are some letters that I have found dating from spring 2003. They are between my husband, Sgt Hardy and me. I hope they help. . . .

Here is our brief history. Sgt. Warren "Geoff" Hardy, USMC and I, Cpl. Janelle R. Hardy, USMC became friends in March 1999. We started dating in May 1999 and were engaged by May 28, 1999. After a short long distance engagement, we were sealed in the San Diego Temple on 24 Nov 1999.

Two months after our wedding, we rec'd news that we were expecting our first in late Sept 2000. In May 2000, I finally got stationed with my husband. My orders were for Marine Corps Forces, Atlantic (MarForLant), Norfolk, Virginia. With Geoff stationed across town as an instructor with Marine Security Forces, Cadre NAB Little Creek, Virginia Beach, Virginia. This was a nice change from 3-4 hour drives to Cherry Point each way every weekend. William Grant Hardy rec'd his commission [was born] into our family on 26 Sep 2000. In the spring 2001, Geoff re-enlisted for orders to 2/1, Fox Co at Camp Pendleton. Facing the end of my contract at the time Geoff was to execute his orders, I decided to extend for a year in order for me to get orders to 1st Force Service Support Group (1st FSSG) G-3 Plans. Family is very important to both of us and keeping us together has always been a priority, God and Corps willing. We knew that if I did not extend, I would be getting out in Oct 2002. Geoff would have been in California for 6 months by himself and in the middle of deployment workups when I would arrive with William, which would be followed by Geoff's departure on 6 Jan 2003. . . .

Deployment was completely new to us. . . . With war coming upon us and Geoff already deployed and William now 2 . . . my command, Lt. Col. Burke and others, decided that in the best interest of the Corps and troop welfare . . . there was no point in sending me, when there were other single Marines with no "baggage" just as capable to go first. They left me as RBE (remain behind element). Now we, my family and I, knew that there might be a time when and if one of my Marines got wounded or KIA, [killed in action] I was next to go. In fact, the Marine part of me was longing to go and be over there, doing what we have been trained to do. The mommy part was relieved that I was chosen to be RBE for the time being. . . . Being a Marine and with the nature of my job; I was never too worried about Geoff. . . . I was able to stay focused on things here and not worry about what was going on there. . . . I had the inside scope, unlike being just a Marine wife where all you have is Fox News. . . . That is the difference between being just a wife and being a Marine with a really cool job and a [Marine's] wife. Since getting out in Sept, I have had several opportunities to come back and serve. Do I miss the Corps? Yes. But right now would not trade it for the opportunity that I have to be just a mom to our handsome 3 year old and new baby on the way. . . . Thanks

Semper Fi
Janelle Hardy
Cpl. Janelle R. Hardy, USMC

P.S. Here are our letters.

February 28, 2003

Dear Geoff

. . . . You probably want to know who delivered this package. Maj Rovira works with me in the G-3. He asked if I would like to give him a package to send to you. So here it is. He is pretty cool.

I've enclosed some of your favorites along w/batteries, gum, & last month's ensign. Also I have enclosed & laminated a picture that Little Man made all by him self. He colored it, picked out the picture and then glued it together. I love the one he picked out of the dad holding the baby.

You should have seen him last night. We got a couple of your letters. Two were for Willie & one for me. We got your picture. . . . Boy, you look sexy! I just want to jump you! Man, I can't wait to get you home. The song you wrote me had me in tears. When I showed Will your picture & started to read, he said as clear as day "Daddy." He got a huge smile and then took the picture & letter, folded it back up and put it in the envelope & held on to it. It was the cutest thing ever.

Oh he is 97% in height & 94% in weight.

Tomorrow Will & I are going house looking w/ Jennifer (Dan's Associate). Don't worry I don't plan on buying anything. I thought it would be good to see the area & just do some looking. I promise I won't do anything you didn't give me a SPOA [spousal power of attorney] for. Just kidding! However it would be nice to move into a place by April, since our lease will be up. . . .

We miss you. Only 129 days left! We are very proud of you & what you are going. I tell Willie every day that you love him.

Love,
Nel
Cpl. Janelle R. Hardy, USMC

March 1, 2003

Hi Baby,

Not much new has happened. We have had a lot of windy days lately. The nights have been cold and I wish I had you to cuddle with. I hope Willie is doing fine. I miss you both so much. I can't wait to be home and spend time with both of you.

Out here the days are starting to become routine. I received the Valentines Day cards that you two made for me. I hope I receive a letter from you soon. I'll try to write you every couple of days. We don't know if or when we'll move from the spot. I hope we have a change soon before the boredom sets in. We would all like to get back on ship.

I don't know what kind of memories I'll have from this experience but I know at least I'll have some good ones. The other day some [British] Royal Marines came over to trade stuff. We ended up talking with them for a little while. It seems life for them in their camp is just like ours.

The worst part over here is the constant blowing of sand. You can never be clean no matter how much you try. A mobile PX came through today. I was able to get a couple of candy bars for a change. Right now we have one MRE for noon chow. . . .

Sometimes I wish you would get deployed just for the whole experience. . . . At times I definitely want to get out of the Marine Corps and other times I don't. I'm just rambling on so I'll let you go. Remember to take the cars to a quick lube and get them serviced. I hope you were able to file the taxes. If the truck needs tires then we can use some of the tax [refund] money. Hopefully between the tax [refund] and my tax free [combat] paychecks, we'll be able to put a dent into our debt. . . . I love you and all you do for me and Willie.

Love,
Geoff
Sgt. Warren "Geoff" Hardy, USMC

March 10, 2003

Hey Sweetie,

How are you doing? You're probably pretty busy at work. I guess by the time you get this I may be pretty busy also. There are a lot of signs that time is getting close. Certain equipment that we've been waiting on has finally gotten here. We got our combat issue of ammo; training and rehearsals have also been stepped up. I know you'll be worried. . . .

I also received a couple photos for my Kevlar.* You two make me so happy. . . .

Love,
Geoff
Sgt. Warren "Geoff" Hardy, USMC

March 20, 2003

Dear Geoff,

Well as I write this letter, the war has been going on for about 18 hours. We just saw on CNN that 1MarDiv has crossed the borders. Our prayers are with you. I want you to know that I did mail pictures to you awhile back. It was one of you and Will and then one of us together. . . .

Today, Andrea left for Sacramento for a week. She took William. It was so sad. They are talking about putting us into Threatcon Delta. So this may be the last time I see Will for a while. He was so sweet. He just hugged me as I held him and told him that you and I

*His Kevlar helmet in which, like many Marines, he kept his family pictures.—FS

love him very much and that we are trying to protect his freedom, that we love him and that he needs to remember that.

As I put him in his car seat, He said, "I love you, Mom" so clearly that I started to tear up. And he then said again "Mom, I love you, bye." Man that was hard. It made me realize how you felt when you left both of us. The one thing we remember and I tell William everyday, is that you love us and you are doing this for us. . . .

I got to go to the temple this past Tuesday. It was nice . . . I put your name on the prayer roll along with Willie's and mine. I figure we all need as much help as we can get. . . . Just the thought of you, brings a smile to my face and I long to hold you. I can't wait until you get back and we can go on with our lives together with each other. . . .

Have you shaved your head since 4 March? Your dad sent me a picture of a Marine with the 15th MEU with his gas mask on trying to drink from his canteen. The Marine's blouse was off and just wearing a green-T. I couldn't see any tattoos on his left side and it didn't look like he had a "hickie" either. I told your dad that I didn't think it was you b/c your letter I got that was dated Mar 4th, said that you had a full head of hair.

Sometimes my body yearns for you. To be held by you. . . . I love you forever. I am glad that you are my Best Friend and that we have a Temple marriage. This is so reassuring to me to know that we have this blessing in our lives, not to mention our little guy. Speaking of which [he] needs a little brother. He will make a good big brother. That is for sure.

WE LOVE YOU FOREVER!
Nel and your little man, WILLIE.
Cpl. Janelle R. Hardy, USMC

March 25, 2003

Dear Geoff,

Hello, cutie pie. As I write, there are civilian Iraqi's in Basra who are uprising against Saddam's Army. I bet you are all hoping that this happens. The weather out there where you are is raining and sand storm. Water plus sand equals a bunch of crap. I have seen a couple of photos of you and your guys. I have enclosed them. I also enclosed some new ones that Will and I have taken since you have been gone.

By the time you get this, I hope this whole war thing is done with. . . . I don't know if you heard that the Saddam has 7 POW's, all of which are Army, 6 guys, 1 girl. There is a lot of talk about the POW's and how the previous Desert Storm POW's were treated. . . .

I rec'd your letter last night that was dated 6 Mar 03.

I love you
Nel
Janelle R. Hardy, USMC

March 28, 2003

Dear Sweeties

Hey. Everything is fine. We've been in Iraq for about a week. The section is great. We did some illum missions the other night. Not a whole lot to tell you. Believe it or not we've had some really boring moments. I don't know what to say or what to tell you. I only want to let you know I Love you both and miss you a lot. I can't wait to be home and hold you in my arms. I Love you both with all my heart.

Love,
Geoff/Daddy

P.S. I got the hand-delivered box the morning we went in. I Love you. Thank you for being my wife.

Sgt. Warren "Geoff" Hardy, USMC

April 11, 2003

Hey Sweetie,

How are you? We've been on float [deployed] for 3 months now. I guess we're half way done. Man I really miss you and your body. We are now in a defense and conducting patrol. We hear Baghdad has fallen. Hopefully we'll be leaving soon. I can't really think of anything to say right now.

By the time you get this it will probably be close to Mother's Day. I want to send you a little message. This is what you have to do. Get some cash from my account and go to the music store. . . . pick up a *Lone Star* CD. The title of the CD is "Lonely Grill."

. . . Make sure you play track #3 & 5 from the CD. And I hope you have a good Mothers Day. . . .

Tell Will that I say hi and let him know how much I love him. I can't wait to come home to the both of you. I hope our relationship has really grown stronger and our love for one another grown deeper since we've been apart.

I Love Forever and Always,
Geoff
Sgt. Warren "Geoff" Hardy, USMC

Currently Sgt. Warren "Geoff" Hardy is in Iraq with his unit, 1st Marines. Janelle Hardy is expecting her second child and will start school again in the fall of 2004.—FS

May 22, 2004

You can take a boy out of the country, but you can't take the country out of the boy, even in Iraq. [My husband] Spc. Clint Turnbull, Iowa Army National Guard, recently brought a little bit of the Midwest to the central Iraq, harvesting over 350 ears of sweet corn for a Thanksgiving feast.

Stacie Turnbull

Spc. Clint Turnbull, Iowa Army National Guard currently stationed in Iraq, is a graduate student in agronomy at Iowa State University. Called to active duty in February 2003, Turnbull was disheartened by the thought of missing a planting season and hungry for a bit of home cooking.—FS

July 21, 2003

We're getting ready to convoy up [from Kuwait to Balad] on Thursday. A little nervous, but ready. Hope you don't worry too much. Just pray for our safety.

Love, Clint
Spc. Clint Turnbull, Iowa Army National Guard

August 6, 2003

I just took a shower from the showers we built out of wood, hoses, and sprinklers. It felt great—so hot, dirty and stinky. . . .

Spc. Clint Turnbull, Iowa Army National Guard

August 14, 2003

Sitting on our "patio"; made on one end of our tent. We made shade with camo netting and ponchos and laid cement squares on the ground. Also have folding chairs and a make-shift table. Sitting in the shade with my back drenched in sweat!

I want to inform you, without worrying you, if that's possible. Early this morning, we had the biggest mortar attack since we've been here. It woke me up about 4 a.m. and lasted for about 20 minutes. I said a prayer right away to protect us all. The good Lord has been watching over me/us.

Have the day off because it's my birthday. Not much to do on a day off though, so this morning we filled and stacked sandbags around our tent out again. . . .

Spc. Clint Turnbull, Iowa Army National Guard

September 5, 2003

Another guy and I were chosen as escorts for a group of Iraqi contractors and their workers. What we do is pick the crew up at the gate and sign them in after they've been searched. Bring them to our area to start work. Then we would go with them to make estimates and make arrangements for the different jobs.

Received the sweet corn seed today. Yesterday, I dug some trial irrigation ditches. Already identified some improvements and planning out how to water my crops. It's going to be quite a large garden.

Spc. Clint Turnbull, Iowa Army National Guard

September 6, 2003

Got a mortar attack for the last three nights and in the afternoon today and yesterday.

Spc. Clint Turnbull, Iowa Army National Guard

September 9, 2003

Another guy and I planted more sweet corn yesterday. This morning, I worked about three hours, working up more ground and digging more furrows in the garden. . . . Finally came up with planters for the flower seeds you sent—sandbags! They should blend right in our tent.

Worked this afternoon in flight ops. No flights this afternoon. I updated the map with restricted operating zones, no fly zones, etc. It was also my duty today to maintain the shit trenches. That involves shoveling dirt into the hole to cover it, pouring some diesel into the hole to kill the flies and help the odor, then wiping down the seats.

Fun. Otherwise, life as usual in Iraq.

Spc. Clint Turnbull, Iowa Army National Guard

September 9, 2003

Dear Rebekah [six-year-old daughter],

Did mom tell you that the Army keeps changing their mind and I don't know when I can come home? Remember that no-matter how long I'm gone, I love you and miss you.

Love, Dad
Spc. Clint Turnbull, Iowa Army National Guard

September 21, 2003

Just finished church. . . . It's in a tent. Thankful we have it.

Spc. Clint Turnbull, Iowa Army National Guard

October 16, 2003

Although I may be disappointed that I'm gone for so long, I do not regret enlisting. It is not for me, or any other soldier for that matter, to decide if being deployed was right or wrong. We took an oath to uphold the constitution and obey the orders of the Commander-in-Chief, President Bush. And that is that. It is up to the voting citizens and government to elect the officials who make those decisions about war, etc. . . . I am not disappointed and am proud to serve here in the Army . . . I am still proud to be serving as a soldier here and it really doesn't matter if I think this whole thing is being run correctly or not. That's not my job and I have to trust those whose job it is, though it is tough at times.

I'm only witnessing a tiny portion of life in Iraq and I really don't know all the ins and outs. What I do know is that . . . this is not the time to just wrap it up and come home. When we do come home, there need to be units to replace us. Our presence alone is sending a message to anti-coalitionists, Iraqis or otherwise, about our commitment to remain until order and government is re-instituted. It is also giving hope and confidence to the pro-American/Coalition Iraqis that do want a better country and way of life for themselves.

In the first Gulf War, thousands of deserters and supporters of the U.S./Coalition were killed or threatened or put into submission. If we left now, there would be a) total return of power to Saddam or his party/followers and a similar situation or b) total anarchy until someone with an iron-fist took control.

There is indeed huge progress being made . . . a police force is being trained and implemented in Baghdad (where they are *learning* to not torture those picked up for questioning). Baghdad is not the only city or place of population, but it is the biggest city with the most influence on the rest of the country and it is the most populated with more than 1 million people.

When we drove through Baghdad on the convoy, didn't have time to take photos—I was more concerned with someone shooting us, it was filthy. It looked as if no one had taken care of it for years. Trash was piled up on the side of the roads, buildings were grafitied and some falling down/apart. And then there were other parts that were well taken care of and apparently rich areas. I don't think it had—the entire city I mean—consistent electricity, water, sewer, phones or trash removal for some time. Maybe never a reliable public works system. So, I think we're making definite leaps and bounds. . . .

The moral of the story is . . . the Army is here for an overall worth-while purpose. I am proud to be a part—even miniscule as I am—of our great forces here and I hope you are proud of me. Thanks for your continued support and encouragement.

Spc. Clint Turnbull, Iowa Army National Guard

December 1, 2003

Temps during the day are now in the 70s, getting down to the 35 degrees at night. Mice are the new big problem—we've caught well over 50 to date. Send more mouse traps!

The sweet corn crop is ready! Fed 150 members of the unit on Sunday! Planned to harvest it for Thanksgiving, but we got rain. . . . Fired up the grills again for the corn. Everyone had a good time, I think. Boy, did it taste amazing. Grilled the corn on the husk—soaked it in water first, grilled it, then put it in a cooler to finish cooking. . . .

Spc. Clint Turnbull, Iowa Army National Guard

Spc. Clint Turnbull, Iowa Army National Guard, is still in Iraq.—FS

25

LCpl. Colin Smith was nineteen when he wrote this letter.—FS

April 18, 2003

Hey Mom and Dad,

. . . . We were chosen to actually go up past Baghdad, we drove through Baghdad on the outskirts as we couldn't make a mad dash to the center cause there was too much risk, even on the outskirts we received some gunshot fire, some stupid ragheads popping up out of their cars firing their AK's at us and whatnot, we couldn't really identify who or where it was coming from because the roads were way too crowded so we couldn't return fire because innocent people might get hit.

All we could do is duck and cover and hope that was all they were going to do, was shoot a couple of rounds at us then run away. You should have seen the Iraqi's faces though when we racked those 50 cals and mark 19's, oh man, we whipped out our M 16's they hit the deck faster than you would imagine. They were falling backwards, forward, saying "no, no please don't shoot" "love Americans, love Americans" "Saddam bad" that is pretty much all they would say, they don't know much English, but they know how to say "George Bush good, Saddam bad."

So, here I am in the birthplace and hometown of Saddam Hussein, we came up here to try to confirm whether he is dead or alive.

Haven't gotten much word on whether he is dead or alive, just rumors.

Wow, the war is pretty much over now, it went by faster than I thought it would, which is a good thing and your prayers were answered and so were mine. It has been a fast moving war but slow at the same time, a lot of action and a whole lot of down time.

I really never knew what to expect in a war. I have talked to a lot of the guys I am with right now who were here in the first Gulf War or know people from Vietnam and they all say the same thing, "war is about 10% heart stopping action and 90% boredom," although even in the down times we are still on guard, and don't get much sleep. . . .

On the 3rd night into Iraq, at the 19th RRP, we got there and it was real hazy and pitch black, we couldn't see our own hands waving in front of our faces and even with night vision we couldn't see very well, maybe 15 feet in front of us. . . . That night we received lots of mortar fire, and contact from enemy soldiers and combatants. We opened up online, we laid down a barrage of fire, it was pretty exciting, and got my adrenaline going.

I was up on the top of the turret on a hardback humvee with the 50 cal and ready to fire, but I couldn't engage because it was too dark and I wouldn't take the chance of accidentally shooting a fellow Marine, because there was no way to tell whose gunfire was whose and all I could see was tracers flying by, mark 19 rounds blowing up, mortars going off, it was pretty exciting, what a way to start the war!

Things slowed down after that, most Iraqi's we run into don't want to fight us, imagine that. . . . They wave their little white flags around and throw down their weapons, which is good for us. Although this was the first time I have ever seen dead people, since I have never been to a funeral. It was surreal. I know it is part of war but I guess I never thought about that. . . .

There are a lot of civilians here, they love Americans and hate Saddam, I am not sure if they are just saying that or not but I think they are sincere. Saddam has been persecuting them for years and keeping them in the dark ages. On the drive up Iraq, it felt like I went back in time to when Jesus was around, you know people walk around in sandals and white garments herding their sheep with staffs, I thought, man, this is what is was like when Jesus walked the earth.

I also almost hit a crazy camel that decided to jump in front of my humvee. My buddies thought it was pretty crazy. The cities are higher tech, they have running water, electricity. There are some rich people and we assume they have ties with Saddam, since they have the money and they have some really nice houses.

Right now we are staying at a huge ranch that has enough stables (made of marble!) to house over 60 horses. We suspect the horses were very valuable Arabian's (They are gone now). The people don't even live as nicely as these horses did. We think it belonged to Saddam or his followers, whatever the heck they are called.

We have handed out lots of water and MREs to the kids on our way, that's so cool to do that, it reminds me of when I [was deployed to] Honduras. The kids look at you with their sad eyes and you give them anything you can. Unfortunately the Marine Corps isn't set up to do that right now, we are not supposed to give up our own rations and water, our command doesn't like us to do it. The Army is supposed to be setting up to help the people in need.

We had a little down time up here just gathering up looters and stupid people who have AK's in their cars trying to ambush Marines. We are just taking in the last little pockets of resistance. . . .

Oh man, I had some fun a few days ago! I went hunting, for the very first time. (You know how I have always wanted to go hunting.) Well, here on the ranch there is a lot of wide open space and lots of gazelles, (they are a little smaller than an American white tailed dear) and they travel in families.

Anyway, I actually caught this gazelle—that travels at 50-60 mph—with my bare hands. How I did it is kind of fun, the stupid gazelle moved away from me toward the fence (there are fences here to keep the horses in) instead of out into the open land and with a couple of Marines helping as I was chasing it down I got it near the fence and it jumped trying to jump over about a 6 1/2 or 7 foot high fence, it didn't quite make it over the fence, flipped over onto its back then its side and tried to kick its legs as hard as it could to get back up but before it could, I jumped on it and had my Kbar [knife] stuck in its neck. It's interesting, I have never killed any animal much less one that size, it makes a strange gargling sound as it chokes on its own blood, it is kind of disturbing. That was my first confirmed kill in Iraq. . . .

I came back dragging this gazelle with its guts hanging out and my buddies and my Sgts were pretty amazed, actually my Lt. told me he was going to have my head examined when we got back. But I know I am fine, I . . . have always wanted to go hunting so I got my chance, besides, it was really good eating and everyone enjoyed it.

I love and miss you guys so much and can't wait to be home with you. Tell everyone Hi from me and thanks to everyone who has sent me packages, I love getting all of the goodies. Goldfish, beef jerky and M&M's are the best, I think I have enough baby wipes, and Kleenex now.

Colin
LCpl. Colin Smith, USMC

LCpl. Colin Smith is headed back to Iraq with the 11th Marine Expeditionary Unit.—FS

26

.... I hopped a flight to Baghdad today via KC-130 in order to hear Secretary of Defense Rumsfeld address some troops at the Saddam International Airport. The secretary spoke for about 10 min. and took some questions. In his remarks, he mentioned that this was the fastest time a modern army took a capital. He praised our efforts and our sacrifices (those of our families as well). He was flanked on the stage by the CG of IMEF, V Corps, and CFLCC (Combined Forces Land Component Commander). After his speech and responding to questions from the crowd the Secretary moved down into the mass of Soldiers, Sailors, Airmen, and Marines and shook every hand offered and posed for countless pictures. I could not even get close.

My group and I moved onto our truck for the trip across the airfield and to our KC-130 cargo plane. After we got off the truck I saw the Rumsfeld motorcade begin to wind around near our location on the runway. The motorcade approached us and drove right past us ... and stopped. Out stepped the secretary. . . . There were about 12 Seabees, 5 Marines, and myself. We were about 3 meters from the Secretary. The Seabees crowded around and began to take pictures and shake hands. I produced an Iraqi 250 dinar note (with portrait of Saddam Hussein) and patiently waited for an opportunity. A Secret Service agent recognized my intentions and ushered me close to the Secretary. I said "Your signature, Mr. Secretary?" He responded with "This guy again?" He took my book, dinar note, and pen and signed his name across the portrait of Hussein. . . .

Within a few days I received my orders to return to Kuwait to wait for transportation home. I made it back to the United States on 17 May 2003, 12 weeks after I left home.

Major Jason A. Climer, USMC

Major Jason A. Climer, USMC, is back in the United States.—FS

March 5, 2004

Mr. Schaeffer,

I wrote this letter for my father and his employees who had sent me a care package, because I wanted to share with them what I considered a significant experience. . . .

Sgt. Carl J. Ronhaar, USMC

Carl was twenty-three when he wrote this letter.—FS

April 16, 2003
Baghdad, Iraq

I recently had the opportunity to travel with one of our Battle Damage Assessment and Recovery Teams (BDAR) to the heart of Baghdad to retrieve a deadlined Amphibious Assault Vehicle (AAV). While most of the fighting in Baghdad had stopped, I was along for the ride to provide security while the mechanics worked to recover the broken vehicle. Just two nights prior one of the BDAR teams had to return to camp because they were receiving fire, so I was unsure of what to expect.

As we traveled into the city what we found was not a hostile group of people, but a people overcome with joy celebrating on the streets. I turned from security Marine to an instant celebrity as everyone was waving, clapping or whistling. Little kids would hear the tracks rolling down the street and come running out of their houses screaming and waving as we drove by. A simple wave in their direction would fill them with so much joy and excitement you would have thought it was Christmas morning. Everywhere we went we were greeted by people who shared the same enthusiasm.

Once we reached our location, one of Saddam's palaces, we set up security outside the gates as the BDAR team went in to recover the vehicle. It was hard to remain vigilant when everyone that passed was happy and generally thrilled with our presence. However, we had been told of Iraqis approaching Marines looking for food and then shooting them with AK-47's so we were cautious. . . .

Not long after arriving a young Iraqi man on a bicycle approached and asked us in very good English what we thought of the war, and our presence in Iraq. One of the other Sergeants responded that it was the desire of our President to free the Iraqi people from Saddam and give the government back to the people. The man responded that he did not live in the area, but had come quite a ways to say "Thank you." We wouldn't understand the significance of the length of his journey until later.

He began to tell us how "If you did not say yes to him (Saddam), he would kill you." Over three million Iraqis died at the hand of Saddam according to this man. For over twenty years he tortured, raped and killed innocent Iraqis. We knew all of this, yet it was so much more powerful hearing a first hand account.

He continued saying that he appreciated us coming, but that it was too late. The Iraqi people would never fully recover from

Saddam. Another Marine responded by saying "At least you're alive and still have your health." This seemed to anger the Iraqi who began telling us how he wasn't fine. He couldn't run and could barely walk. He told us how one of Saddam's sons had shot him in the legs for no reason. As he pulled up his pant leg you could see gunshots in both sides of his leg, his foot, and that he was missing his big toe. It was obvious by the nature of the wounds that they were not meant to kill him, but rather cripple him for life to serve as a living warning to those who dare cross Saddam's regime.

I don't know why but I was overcome with guilt. He was right; we should have taken care of Saddam 12 years ago. Perhaps there would have been hope for this young man and the countless others who must have suffered similar torture or worse. It seemed of little comfort that I was in the fifth grade during the Gulf War and had no influence over the situation.

I wasn't sure how to respond, but I asked him if he had a son. He did not and I told him that when he did, he would grow up in a free Iraq and never have to worry about the cruelty of Saddam and his regime. He smiled and seemed comforted by the idea. I also explained that he would be free to come and go as he pleased and that he should visit America. He said he would like that very much and seemed especially intrigued by the description of California. We talked a while longer before he left. As he left, it became apparent that he had not ridden his bicycle the great distance he had traveled to thank us, but rather used it as a rolling crutch as he hobbled down the street.

Despite what protesters may say, and what the media portrays back home, this war was a huge success. Weapons of mass destruction aside we have done a truly remarkable thing by liberating the Iraqi people. I have seen their joy with my own eyes, and as I look at the children who line the streets to greet us, I can't help but think that I have been part of something historic. We went when nobody else would and did what nobody else could, and it is a testament to the greatness of our county and the American people.

Sgt. Carl J. Ronhaar, USMC

Sgt. Carl J. Ronhaar, USMC, is back in Camp Pendleton, California. Two of the companies from his unit are back in Iraq.—FS

May 28, 2004

Frank here is an email I received from my son, 1 Lt. Scott Wicklund, 3rd ACR U.S. Army out of Fort Carson, CO, on the Syrian border.

Roy Wicklund

Scott was twenty-five when he wrote this letter.—FS

December 8, 2003

Hello Pops,

Just got pinned to 1LT [promoted]. Nice pay raise. Get a little more respect also, which is a big plus. Today was a good day. Got to relax for a change. We were doing QRF, escort detail, and "perimeter patrol." Busy. Not fun.

Have an interesting story about one night. We had to escort the body of a dead Iraqi general in the back of my Bradley to the hospital. Not really sure how much I can say, but you probably would understand the humor once I tell the story. We go through ruts out here morale wise. Right now we're starting to go up a little, so I enjoy it again. Overall I actually do like this place . . .

too much some days. Can do whatever we want. We took in a little puppy the other day. We were going through a town and this kid kicks this cute little puppy, so I stop and tell the kid to give it to me. I put the puppy in my jacket and he rode on the turret the rest of the time. The kid was asking for him back . . . but, I didn't like the way he was treating the dog, so I kept it. He likes to run around the tent. We already had a troop dog, but this one was too cute to pass up. . . .

Don't really have much to talk about. The mission up north was long. Took my first shower yesterday in about 45 days. Ran over a lot of land mines and got wet. There's a couple Bradley crews that hit IED's [improvised explosive devices] three different times in one day. We could hear the explosion and the radio call on all three and on the third one you could hear the frustration in his voice. I've seen no one who is afraid to do their jobs. One of the Bradley drivers in my 1/4 troop ran over [a mine] everyday for 3 days. He is a little nervous about driving, but is not afraid.

Very good soldiers and NCO's here. We'll be driving through an area and have no doubt in our mind that we'll hit something and everyone is cool. Even the times we have been shot at with RPG's and machine guns, everyone has reacted perfectly. I'm very safe with these guys. Love going out with them. Everyone here is pretty close and gets along great. Makes it a little better during the holiday season. Right now the computer is down so I hope this letter gets to you.

"They" say that were going to start leaving here by April 4th. We'll see. Our equipment won't be home until July. That means nothing to do once we get home. Collect all my weekends that I missed. I wish. Once in awhile I catch some nice grammatical errors in here. Feel like I'm getting dumber by the day. Well, I'm going to send this off. . . . Tell the family back home I say hi and to send me nothing for Christmas.

Don't really need much. Take care and happy holidays. I'll call you as soon as possible. Don't worry about me over here. I know, I know, that's a hard thing to ask, but try. Scott

1st Lt. Scott Wicklund, 3rd ACR, U.S. Army

1st Lt. Scott Wicklund is in Fort Carson, Colorado. He returned from Iraq in April 2004.—FS

27

March 7, 2004

Dear Mr. Schaeffer,

Attached is a letter from me to my husband Michael during the war. My husband Major Michael Jernigan was the Executive Officer 1st Combat Engineer Battalion, 1st Marine Division (Camp Pendleton Marine Corps Base) before, during and after the war in Iraq. . . .

I am a homemaker. During the war I was very involved in our wives network helping families cope while their spouse was at war. We have two children, our son Brady (7) and our daughter Hunter Grace (4). . . .

I am very pleased that you are doing this. In fact, I am reading "War Letters" by Andrew Carroll right now. It gives a great perspective and sense of reality to the people who go to war and the loved ones who send them off. Thank you again,

Drew Jernigan

Certain names have been omitted from Drew Jernigan's letters at her request.—FS

April 6, 2003

Letter to Major Michael Jernigan Executive Officer 1st Combat Engineer Battalion, 1st Marine Division (Camp Pendleton Marine Corps Base)—FS

From: Drew Jernigan

Dear Michael,

I hardly know where to begin, there's so much that has gone on here. It has been very difficult for me to write to you. I think that it's just that there are so many aspects of my life right now that are going full tilt that I can barely keep up with myself. I had wanted to keep a journal but that quickly fell by the wayside. I've been doing pretty well. In fact, I told Wendy today that I feel a little strange about how detached I've been about all of the things going on. I definitely feel something—just can't express it right now. It's like someone else is dealing with everything and the part of me that feels emotions is just in the background somewhere. I have only cried two times since you left—the day you left and the night the war started. Since then we've had two 1st CEB KIA [1st Combat Engineer Battalion killed in action] reports with all of the emotion and turmoil that has gone along with it and I just can't cry right now. I was able to vent and process a little with Wendy tonight. It helped.

The CACO* call for Sgt. —— was a disaster. I know you probably know the details by now, but it was an absolute embarrassment for the Marine Corps. All of the times they told the families that CACO calls would be done right and handled with utmost care and dignity seem like a cruel lie. [The wife] was NEVER notified by a HQMC [headquarters Marine Corps] CACO—no one ever showed up. Seven hours after she got a call from [her husband's] brother in

---

* Casualty assistance calls officer, the person who notifies families of casualties—through a phone call for injuries and in person when a soldier or Marine is killed.—FS

Indiana saying CACO had come to his house and four hours after another CACO team went to another family member's house to notify them, Top —— and (new) Lt. —— went. (She was listed as the first next of kin on the red card.)

They were delayed because Lieutenant —— had to get his "CACO training" over the phone from HQMC and they had to wait for a chaplain. It was disgraceful.

I called —— and notified Top—— and Col. ——. I sure do hope someone is held accountable for the way this was handled.

[The wife] said to [my friend] several times that she felt it was a huge slap in the face. Francis said that none of the CACO calls have gone as planned. What really makes me angry is that there have only been 80 total American deaths and maybe half of them are Marines. Surely the Marine Corps has the ability to give each of these the utmost care and attention. I'm really disappointed. I am going to write an e-mail to Top —— and ask him if Col. —— or someone higher is planning to apologize on behalf of the Marine Corps. . . .

I am still incredibly busy with Key Volunteer stuff. There's always something going on. I think we're working together well and most of the ladies are happy. We can't make everyone happy though. I have an average of 20-30 e-mails a day and at least 15 phone calls. Most things are fairly quickly resolved but there are things like today with Sgt. ——that really take all of the wind out of your sails.

I am missing you very much. It doesn't seem right sleeping in our bed with all of the sheets intact in the morning! No one there to pull them out from the end of the bed. I read the articles about you guys sleeping on roads, in holes and who knows where and I know you are ready to come home.

I have been hoping that things are going well for you spiritually there. I think I'm doing well. The prayer group has been good for me. Also, seeing the live TV helps me pray while things are happening— sometimes I feel like I've been there. I'm concerned about the things you're seeing and the things you're going through. I just have to hold on to hope that God will keep you intact and strong in every area of your life. Plenty of people come home from war and lead normal lives and I have no doubt that you will too.

I am so sorry that you have to go through this time. I can't imagine anything more frightening. Even though I know you have trained for this, I also know you, as you, my Michael. I know your heart is soft. I know you are not reveling in the thought of being in combat. I think it's terrifying. I think that's most of the reason that I haven't been good at writing about life here—it seems so trivial: Laundry, finger-painting, tearing my hair out with the kids.

I feel so much like we need to debrief. There's so much I want to hear about what you're going through and there are so many emotions that neither of us can feel right now because they are just too overwhelming.

I want you to know how immensely proud I am to be your wife. You are everything I ever hoped for when I was a little girl dreaming. You make me feel complete in every way. It is just like half of my heart is torn out right now. . . .

There are so many people praying for us and I can feel it. Today is the first day (night) that I am starting to feel a little weak. But you've been gone for about 8 weeks so maybe adrenaline can only carry me so far. . . .

I love you very much and I am so ready for you to be home with me and Brady and Hunter Grace. We miss you! Come home soon.

I love you,
Drew
Drew Jernigan

After Major Jernigan's tour as executive officer of 1st Combat Engineer Battalion, 1MARDIV, he was chosen as a Marine Corps corporate fellow. He lives in Atlanta with Drew and their children. His brother is also a Marine. They ran into each other a few times while deployed in Iraq.—FS

28

Matthew was twenty-three when he wrote this letter.—FS

April 21, 2003

Hey there Mom and Dad. How is everything? Great I hope. Well this letter is going to be a little off base but I don't want you to think anything is wrong because things are great. But during my time over here and all that I have seen and experienced makes you take a step back and just look at your life and think about the past, present and future. I have come to realize many things while I have been here. One is that life here on earth is extremely short. Also that life is very precious. And no matter how shitty things may get, it's *always* just a great day to be alive.

You have a lot of time to yourself when you are out here. And I can't help but to think about all the great and wonderful times I have had during the 23 years I have been alive. First there is the past. And where do I begin? When I think of all of the things that I have been blessed to be able to do and have and the BEST thing that I have is my family. . . .

I think all the way back to pre-school. I remember when dad would come to pick me up at Pinecrest and I'd be playing and look up and see him. Then I would run as fast as I could to him and give him a big hug and he'd pick me up in his arms and hug me back. I also remember the orange Toyota and how I'd stand up in it while Dad drove. That was Cool! Also when I was in grade school at Pinecrest [I remember] him always picking me up and reaching in the back seat and pulling out packs of baseball cards and giving them to me. And when I started playing baseball at William S. Hart, I remember Mom always saying how cold it was at the 7:30 PM games but no matter how cold it got I could always look into the stands and see her sitting in there cheering her heart out for me and dying to shout out "GO BIFFER!" And Dad would park the car by the out-field fence and say "Break the windshield I'll give ya 100 bucks!"

Those were a great 10 years. Then came Jr. High and High School, which also meant adolescence. There were a lot of ups and downs during this time. But no matter what decision I made whether it was right or wrong, you guys were right there by my side to see me through it and to help me learn from it . . . and we all know and remember all the trips to the courthouse for all the tickets I got. . . . It was like 12 speeding tickets in a year. EEK!!

. . . And through everything that I have done in my life, be it good or bad, you guys have always supported me. I know I can never repay you for what you have given me in my short 23 years on God's green earth. I have no regrets and wouldn't have changed ONE thing that has happened. I'm just thankful to have the best family that a kid could ask for.

I know I don't say it enough but I love you more than anything in this world and I would do anything for you. I'm glad I joined the Marine Corps, also that I could make you so proud of me, because that's all I want is for you guys, to be able to say "That is our son" with pride.

I LOVE YOU SOOOO MUCH.
Love always, MATTHEW.
Cpl. Matthew Mertz, USMC

Cpl. Matthew Mertz is back at Camp Pendleton, California.—FS

29

These letters are from Sergeant First Class (E-7) Jack Wilder, U.S. Army and his wife, Susan Wilder. Jack turned forty-three while at war.—FS

February 20, 2004

Frank

Here is the first of several letters between me and my husband, Jack Wilder, United States Army, Active duty. Sergeant First Class (E-7) 3d Infantry Division that I am going to send you.

Susan Wilder

Jack Wilder, United States Army, Active duty, Sergeant First Class (E-7)
To: Susan Wilder
March 14, 2003

Hey baby,

This will probably be the last letter that you get from me for a few weeks. I expect that we will be busy. . . . My platoon has been training hard. We will mark and bust the burm for the division's thrust into Iraq. The guys are tired, but are ready to start, so we can finish.

Last night, my guys and I were sitting around talking, and they asked me if I was scared. I told them yes, because I am. But I also told them that we are prepared to fight and we will win. This is a responsibility that weighs heavily on my heart—the lives of those men. I have vowed to myself and to them that we will all return safely and in one piece. I pray daily that I can keep that promise.

How are you? I expect you are working horribly long hours. Please remember to take care of yourself. I know that you are expected to care for all those families,* but I need you to take care of yourself too.

How are my girls? Please tell them how very much I love them and that I miss them.

Susie, I love you. The past 6 moths in Kuwait have been long, but hopefully, I will return to you soon.

Take care my darling. . . . and remember that I adore you.

I LOVE YOU
Jack
Jack Wilder, United States Army,
Active duty, Sergeant First Class

Susan Wilder
To: Jack Wilder, United States Army, Active duty, Sergeant First Class (E-7)
Sunday, March 30, 2003

Hello my darling,

Happy Anniversary! Wow, can you believe that we have been together for 19 years! Happy Birthday! [Jack turned forty-two] But you are not getting older, just better!

---

*Susan Wilder is the Mobilization, Deployment, Support Stability manager, Fort Stewart 3rd Infantry Division: she cares for families during deployments.—FS

Thank you for loving me, I am missing you terribly on our special day. Do you know how many days 19 years is? 6935 Days, 988 Weeks, 228 Months, but not enough!

I miss you today, I miss your smell, your touch, how you hold me, looking into your green eyes, the sound of your voice, I just miss you.

Stay safe, Take care, and know that I love you.
Always
Susan
Susan Wilder

Jack Wilder, United States Army, Active duty, Sergeant First Class (E-7)
To: Susan Wilder
Sunday, March 30, 2003

Hey Baby

Well, I am sitting here thinking of you—as usual. When we are not on a mission or in a fight, I take off my Kevlar [helmet] and look at your picture. Have I told you lately that you are beautiful? I love you so much and I miss you terribly. Happy Anniversary baby, I promise I will make this up to you. Sometimes I wonder why you still love me, after all I have missed, birthdays, anniversaries, sickness, happy times. I don't deserve you—but I am keeping you!

I miss your touch, the smell of your hair and your beautiful blue eyes. I miss waking you up with a cup of coffee and watching you get dressed. I guess that you could say that I really miss you.

How are the girls? Please tell them how much their dad loves them.

You are doing such a great job at home, raising the girls, working full time and taking care of everything while I am here. How is the new stove? I want you to know that I really appreciate everything that you do for our family.

. . . I heard a song the other day "Husbands and Wives," by Brooks and Dunn, the words have nothing to do with us, but in my mind I pictured you and I two-stepping to it all night long.

I realize that over here you never know if there will be a tomorrow. When I come home, I want to hold you in my arms and see your beautiful smile everyday. Darling, you are the reason that I am able to make it through this war. I miss you terribly, I love you and I will be home soon.

I love you,

Jack

Jack Wilder, United States Army, Active duty, Sergeant First Class

---

Susan Wilder

To: Jack Wilder, United States Army, Active duty, Sergeant First Class (E-7)

April 1, 2003

My Darling Jack,

I love you so very much and I am missing you especially bad today. We are seeing on the news that the 3d Infantry Division is leading the charge to Baghdad. Fear grips my heart, I worry so over you, I need you to come home to me, I love you so much—PLEASE, PLEASE Stay safe.

I went to my weekly briefing yesterday, and the G staff tells us that the push to Baghdad will be the worst. I love you darling. Things in the Division are tense; the families are waiting for the big push as we all hold our breaths.

I worry that you will be different when you come home. Is that silly? I worry that war will change you. I love you my darling. I know that you can tell I am scared from this letter, its not that I don't believe in you, I know what a great soldier you are and the best Platoon Sergeant in the Army, it's just those bastards that you are fighting against. Know that I love you and I believe in you AND THAT I AM SO VERY PROUD OF YOU.

Things at home are OK, the girls and I have bonded so much together. Often in the night, I wake to find Amy in our bed; war is hard for them also. Rachel's sleepover went well last week; she really needed a diversion from the war.

Dad is still calling daily—I can hear the fear in his voice also, but he puts on a brave front for me. This must bring back memories from Vietnam for him. The Korean couple who own the store up the street ask about you every single day and they send their love.

Jack, do you know how much I love you? I will remain ever faithful and loving until you return to me. Stay safe and look at the stars at night. I am sending my love to you on them.

Always yours
Susan
Susan Wilder

Susan Wilder
To: Jack Wilder, United States Army, Active duty, Sergeant First Class (E-7)
April 9, 2003

My darling Jack,

As I write this letter, I am just getting home from being at work for 2 straight days. When the 2d Brigade TOC got hit on the 7th, it was all over the news. The waiting to hear about casualties has been so very hard. I know that you are OK; I feel it in my heart.

Jack, Paul Smith got killed last week. I went to Birgits the next morning, she is coping the best she can. This is so damn hard. When I looked into Birgits face, I saw a reflection of me. You and Paul have the same jobs, please stay safe. My darling I love you.

I wonder if you are getting my letters. I have not heard your voice in so long. Dad calls almost every day. He always asks if you have called. . . .

The girls are OK, I am trying to keep some normalcy in their lives, but Amy is struggling with you being at war. I often find her up in the middle of the night watching TV, crying and looking for a glimpse of you. Usually she comes to bed with me and we both cry ourselves to sleep. Rachel is good; she has been having a lot of friends over so that helps her cope with things.

Your sister and brother (Faye and Charles) have both called several times. Charles is really worried. I tell him not to worry, that Jack is the greatest soldier who ever lived! He laughed at me as usual!

The flowers in the front yard are starting to bloom, and of course your grass is growing.

Jack, please stay safe, I cannot imagine how my life would be without you in it. I need you to come home to me.

I am so proud of you and I love you so very much.

Always Yours
Susan
Susan Wilder

Frank:

Here are the last two that I will send, and probably the most personal.

Susan Wilder

Susan Wilder
To: Jack Wilder, United States Army, Active duty, Sergeant First Class (E-7)
May 1, 2003

Hello my Darling,

Well its official, ground combat is over!!!!!!!!!! I cannot tell you how elated I am that you are safe and will be coming home soon.

Jack, this is a really hard letter for me to write and will be for you to read, bear with me and understand my reasons for keeping this from you.

When you left last September, right after I had the breast biopsy, I lied to you. The tumor was malignant. I knew that if I told you the truth that you would have stayed with me and not have deployed to Kuwait then to Iraq. I also know that you would have been torn the entire time, between me and your men. So I made the choice for us.

I started radiation therapy in Nov and today was my last treatment! I still have most of my hair, and all but about 10 pounds. As far as the doc can tell, I am cancer free. I am going to hold off on a decision about having reconstructive surgery until you return home, but I am leaning toward doing it.

Jack, I know that you will be angry at me, and I understand why, but please understand that I did what I thought was best at the time.

I promise I am fine now.

I LOVE YOU
Always Yours
Susan
Susan Wilder

Jack Wilder, United States Army, Active duty, Sergeant First Class (E-7)
To: Susan Wilder
May 17, 2003

Hey Honey,

I received your letter today, and you are right, I was angry, but only for about 1 minute. Are you sure that you are OK? I cannot believe how strong you are. Most women would have crumbled under the pressure that you have had. Your job is enough to strain anyone, the girls, and how sick you have been.

Do you know that you are my hero? You are the true hero of this war. Things for you have been so hard, but as usual, you rose to the challenge. Susie, I love you, and I admire you for your strength and courage.

I am not angry. I love you and I do understand the decision you made.

You are the greatest soldier who ever lived. I love you with all my heart and soul and I cannot wait to hold you in my arms again.

Jack
Jack Wilder, United States Army, Active duty, Sergeant First Class (E-7)

Jack Wilder, United States Army, Sergeant First Class is in Fort Stewart preparing to return to Iraq. Susan is in remission and still taking care of the other families on the base.—FS

OCCUPATION
IRAQ

30

LCpl. Joseph Giardino, whose letters also appear in the boot camp section of this book, is in 37 India Company, USMC, and is now serving his second deployment to Iraq. He will be there until at least October/November of 2004.—FS

August 10, 2003

Mom and Dad,

How's life on your continent? Sorry I haven't written much but it's not exactly fun and happy times here. Things are still really crazy. We're doing work with the Army and encountering a lot of resistance.

I liked the pictures of my softball team you sent over. . . . All the letters and pictures help but they don't, if you know what I mean. I saw one of my good buddies today for the first time since we got here, it was so nice to talk to him but at the same time it was sad. We got to exchanging names of people we know that were WIA [wounded in action]. We counted 10 people we know and that's only between 2 companies of 200 Marines each. . . .

It's 150 degrees here today and we did a mid-day raid. You get to being so hot with all the gear on and the heat that you're ready to black out but I'm becoming used to it. It's almost funny, the heat dropped to 90 degrees one night and I needed a sleeping bag!

So you like Becky, huh? Me too! Thanks for sending the pictures of Chicago; there are 7 guys here with me from Illinois so pictures of Chicago are nice.

Everyone really liked the picture you took off the back of the boat with the flag waving off the boat. I can't wait to come home and see everyone. How's Grandma doing? Annie's going to be a senior this year, huh? That's amazing! Well, I'm going to get going now. Please take care of yourselves and know that I'm taking care of myself too. I'll call whenever I can.

Love,
Joe
LCpl. Joseph Giardino, 37 India Company, USMC

March 26, 2004

Dear Mr. Schaeffer,

Enclosed is a copy of a letter our son sent to us last November. He has been serving in Iraq since April 2003. He is a member of the 652nd engineering company. His name is Steven J. Begle Specialist (SPC) Army.

Thank you.
Sincerely,
Linda Begle (mother)

Steve was twenty-one when he wrote this letter.—FS

November 22, 2003

Dear Everyone,

Well I can't recall when I last wrote, so it is probably long overdue.

So I figure I'd take some time today and write. To start with, we had a car bomb go off at the police station about 2 blocks away this morning. Details are still sketchy but I guess it was one of 3 that were simultaneously detonated in the area. I am pretty sure no Americans were hurt, that it did injure 20+ Iraqis. So things were pretty hectic around here this morning. It was a very loud explosion.

As you know, we are still at the govt building doing the same old thing. The company is making it through mid-tour leave pretty steady. Hopefully I will get my turn [to come home] in the next couple of months. The weather here has cooled off considerably in the past month or so. . . .

Well I just called you asking about Grandma's phone number, and since I have guard duty in 10 minutes I am going to set this aside until later.

It's now 2230 Monday night, not the timeliest return to this but I figured I'd finish up. I received your package the same day I talked to you . . . much appreciated. I kept the one from Mom to open on Christmas. Hopefully I'll have a chance to get on the phone and at least say hi to everyone while you are opening presents and such on Christmas. . . .

Today was the end of Ramadan, so it was pretty much the Middle East equivalent of Christmas—stayed pretty quiet, which was nice. I guess even terrorists celebrate holidays. Ha, ha. . . .

The media does tend to highlight the nasty stuff over here, mainly because that's what they excel at. For the most part, the peace process and rebuilding are going along quite excellently, though we still must keep our guard in a heightened state because you never know what the next day, the next minute for that matter, is going to bring.

Keep in mind that the strength and dedication of the coalition forces, along with the majority of the people here who are working for the same goals we are, are 100 if not 1,000 times stronger and more dedicated than those who are trying to undermine our goals and operations. It's inevitable that we will face setbacks and attacks that have no logical point behind them, but we must accept these risks and do everything in our power to counteract and overcome them, while diligently fulfilling our missions here. . . .

In conclusion, tell Rachel that her poem had a very strong emotional impact on me. I am doing a job here that many people do not understand and many oppose. Yet this is a job that must be accomplished and I am proud to be one of the select few tasked to reach this goal. . . .

Thanks for the countless prayers, and understand that though it is not a guarantee that I will return home, know that every day, I am trying my damndist to make sure I, and all my fellow troops, do make it home.

Well, it is late and I have early guard so I am going to bring this to a close. Hopefully, Thanksgiving all went well and Christmas is not approaching too soon for your liking.

Take Care,
Steve
Steven J. Begle, Specialist (SPC) Army

Steve is still in the Army reserves and is headed back to school.—FS

31

Frank:

Here are some of the letters and emails. Our son Steve (Army Reservist Sgt. Stephen McDowell) knew I watched the news religiously so didn't spare many details. Thank you for caring about our sons & daughters.

Sandra McDowell

Local newspaper article about our son:

> Army Reservist Sgt. Stephen McDowell reported for active duty on Wednesday, Feb 20, 2003 following two weeks of training in Southern Missouri. McDowell, who will be going to Fort McCoy, is in the 652nd Engineering Battalion in Elsworth, WI. He has been in the reserves since 1996. Stephen graduated from East Dubuque High School in 1997, and is also a 2001 graduate of Northern Illinois University. He is currently employed at Insurotech in Naperville as a computer programmer.
>
> Before leaving for active duty Stephen married his college sweetheart, Megan Grippe, on Jan 25, 2003. They

plan a celebration of their marriage in the spring of 2004, following Stephen's return. (Rescheduled for Sept. 5, 2004)

Stephen is the son of Arnie and Sandy McDowell of East Dubuque.

May 9, 2003

. . . . We're sitting at Baghdad Airbase which is 30 odd miles north of Baghdad. We've set up a base camp with bag showers, wooden tent floors, and burn barrel shitters; all the luxuries of home. Last week we (my squad) built the overhead anchorage system for a 46 bay ribbon bridge across the Tigris River. The bridge cuts 150 miles off a major supply route that leads north from Baghdad. Due to security—car bombers—they pulled us off of controlling the bridge and sent us back here to do supply runs and base security.

Now it's guard duty, haul missions, and shit burning detail until they find something else for us to do. Rumor has it we'll be going on "presence patrols" through some towns. That is we'll walk the streets until someone shoots at us or we'll hang out on a corner as a show of force.

They say the area is "secure" to "semi-secure" but we still hear machine gun and small arms fire almost nightly. They say the locals are fighting with each other over government land that been tossed up. I've seen some "Hajjies" with AK [rifles] but we can't shoot unless threatened and they wave a lot of the time.

Anyways, I imagine the new McDowell family will have returned from their honey moon by now. How was it?

[Jeremy, Steve's only brother, was married April 26, 2003. Steve was to have been the best man.—FS]

There's talk/rumors we'll be out of here by midsummer—I hope so. I'd love to be back for the mini-poker run! If we're deployed for 30–179 days I'll have 30 days to report back to work and plan on using a good portion of it. At the least I'll spend 4 or 5 days back home.

As of today, no mail but a few guys did receive a letter. I guess all the address changes probably have huge stacks of mail waiting for us somewhere. I would say that the worst part about being over here is not hearing anything from the home front. I last talked to Megan on the 25th of April. She was dealing with the job hunt burdens and an up-coming graduation. I'd go the rest of the time here without showering to be there.

The best we can do for laundry here is a bucket or the river and the two pairs of pants they issued us are starting to fall apart. So regardless of how clean you come out of the shower you're not really putting on clean clothes.

It would be good to hear from you guys so write when you can. Care packages have to be shoe-box size or smaller and anything in them would be used by me or one of the guys. Maybe a couple of computer magazines or something of that sort would help to kill some of the down time. I'm sure we'll be out of here in no time & I'll see you guys on the flip-side. I'll write when I can.

Love ya guys,
Steve
Army Reservist Sgt. Stephen McDowell

July 23, 2003

. . . . Another day almost gone by in Iraq. We conned a Baath Party police chief to come to a meeting in the building we are guarding and then arrested him and his body-guards. Chump!

That's awesome news that Saddam's sons got taken down. I see it as one step closer to home. I have a feeling that we are going to be here for the long haul though. My only hope is that they rotate out reservists before the 4th ID. Our company have become the grunts for a bad reputation battalion so we keep getting little support and lots of shitty missions. I guess you get used to it.

Happy Birthday, Mom! I hope this gets to you by then. I wish I could call and say hi but the phone situation over here is next to non-existent. It's been over three weeks now since I last talked to Megan. I know it's hard on her with my being gone so long and not hearing from me regularly. I hope she decides to go to the family reunion but I have to understand if she doesn't—we do have some weird relatives!

What I wouldn't give for a plane ticket out of here! I got some golf balls in the mail from some people at work. They said I should "work on my sand wedge" while I was over here. A round of golf about now would be great. . . .

August 8th is the 180 day mark which means that I'll have 90 days to report back to work [to my civilian job]!

. . . But! Who know when we're getting out of here. . . .

Anyways, I need nothing! I have enough suntan lotion, lip balm and toothpaste to last 4 years. Chips and salsa con-caso would be a treat though! I have day dreams about hot dogs and pizza (Happy Joe's!) Don't take anything for granted when it comes to food. T-rats (family size MREs) and MRE make the meals. We also eat the local food but you usually get facet ass afterwards.

. . . Give Megan a hug for me. My head's down and I'm working through the grind. I'll be home b4 you know it.

Love ya guys,
Steve
Army Reservist Sgt. Stephen McDowell

Sept. 11, 2003

What's going on, Mom? Bad news over here. Extended.

We are [now] looking at one year in country/theater. Insanity. So much for buying a house this year. It's crazy when you think about it but I've got 6 more months over here. . . .

OK, we're still training Iraqi army wannabes. Not too exciting. Anyways here's a story for ya: We're at our training site which is on the far eastern end of our camp outside our perimeter. Some old Iraqi army buildings are still standing over there. Anyways, a bunch of squatters moved into one of the buildings and turned it into a whore house. We're out there training these guys—actually on a lunch break—and we hear AK-47s fire about a quarter mile away at the fricky fricky (Arabic for whorehouse). We mount up in 2 humvees and go tearing up there. You can see people running every which way and cars started peeling out. The bad guy got away but we got the big pimp daddy with a butt load of money. Long story short—just another day in Iraq. Just another war story for the grandkids.

I'm going to ask Megan to send over a Christmas tree I guess. I could cry just thinking about it but—someone has to do it. The UN won't, so young Americans will.

I hope our phone situation improves but I highly doubt it considering how much we're taken it in the ass from our parent battalion. We've got the short end of every stick—I guess it's to be expected—they watch their own, we [reservists] just suck on it. Oh well.

I'm thankful for a loving family & a great wife. Thank you guys for all the support so far. I'm sure there'll be some rough roads ahead but we'll make it. Talk to Brian Kuhle and get the poem Invictous— William Henley. Read it and send a copy. Inspiration I guess. I'll try and call soon.

Love you guys,
Steve
Army Reservist Sgt. Stephen McDowell

October 2, 2003

What's going on, family? Long time no letter—sorry. It's been pretty crazy here with training the new Iraqi Civil Defense/Army lately. It's funny that these guys (or most) were on the other side of our sights up until April. I gave a class on squad tactics the other day to my (yes, *my*) platoon & I scared the shit out of them. I don't think they like the whole army thing—they asked all kinds of questions on how to break contact/retreat!

Sorry for the sloppy writing—we're under tight discipline right now because of the fear of mortar attack. A base up the road just got hit with 82s—the nasty ones—about 30 minutes ago.

We did a river crossing raid not too long ago—can't remember if I told you guys. We have these 15 man assault rubber boats. We paddled some infantry across the river to the objective site and then pulled security on the far shore. A red fox came running up on us— didn't see us but I think it smelled my stink ass.

Anyways, it was a bitch getting the boats down this cliff and then we couldn't get ashore on the far side because of the elephant grass growing in the water. This infantry guy jumped off a 4 foot drop-off on the near shore and got stuck up to his junk in the mud. It took 4 guys to pull him out, add all his groaning into the mix and it was quite the entertaining predawn show. They hit the target house and got the guys—mission success. . . .

Jeremy, as far as cool shit— I got 8 M@ 50 cal machine guns today. I'm picking up 8 more tomorrow, plus some Russian grenade launchers. There's a burned out building I found on some of our patrols with a small arsenal in the basement. We destroyed all the mortar tubes but can only carry so much. They all have pretty bad fire damage but I had my guys soak one in the solvent tank today and it's operational.

I'm placing an order for the springs that were weakened by fire so ya ya! I have to give one to my LT but the rest I'm going to mount on my truck. Or at least 2, I'll have to horse trade for ammo. AKs trade even up for ac units. It's going to be easier to get with the M@ 50 cal than the AK though. I'll try. Happy Birthday if I do.

So the boat is in? Where is my picture? I hopefully see it before it goes into the water next spring. I'll be pissed if they transfer us to the 1st AD when they get here in January. Anyways, the clocks turn back tonight for us so + one hour of sleep—hell ya!

It gets cold as hell here at night. Only in the 60s but still— Ali, the interpreter I work with, says that the area we are in floods when it rains. The rainy season starts late this month so we'll see what happens. . . .

Alright—almost out of room. I'll try calling soon. I need nothing and want nothing. For Christmas I'll take—? I have no idea. No more hard candy though! My Halloween bag is already overflowing.

Love ya guys. My head is to the sky and my ass is down.

Steve
Army Reservist Sgt. Stephen McDowell

October 17, 2003

Hey Mom. . . . Yes, I'm picking up on the language . . . fairly well. I can follow simple conversations if I know what they are based on. I follow the military ones quite well. I can count to 999 in Arabic. . . .

To eat soup we set it out in the sun for about a half hour. Or we just eat it cold.

The Iraqi's eat our MREs but a lot don't eat at all and take the food home to their families. We buy local food a lot and eat lots of the fruit. There is a thing called a ramond (which is the fruit's name but also Arabic for grenade). It's a round citrus, I think with read seed like things—damn good. . . .

One of our ICDC platoons was split onto 4 Baqubah banks. I was on the roof of one of the banks when a pro-Saddam demonstration walked by—I thought I emailed you that already. Crazy shit. Watch the movie "Rules of Engagement" and that was what it was like— minus the shooting. A police officer fired 3 shots into the air and they just kept on coming. One of our trucks pulled around the corner and a bunch took off running— funny as shit. They got their balls back though and proceeded to march by the bank with incident.

I've got check points, foot patrols, and bank security planned for the ICDC company tomorrow so fun, fun—another day in Iraq.

> Love ya,
> Steve
> Army Reservist Sgt. Stephen McDowell

> *October 23, 2003*
> *652 EN CO, 588 BN, 2nd BCT, 4th ID*

You asked about abuse. One BN [battalion] has their head up someone's ass. They don't have a clue three quarters of the time. Here's a quick story of us "winning the hearts and minds" of the Iraqi's.

We're on bank guard. [The] 588 EN BN [a battalion] supplies 2 track vehicles as the armor support to each bank. The kids over here sell plastic BB guns. Some of the 588 guys are shooting the kids with the [BB] guns and waving them around like they are real (they look real). Anyways, a kid threw a rock back after being shot by a BB. He runs away, these guys roughed up some people and caught the kid, duck-taped his ass. The BN is all around messed up. We get jack and shit for support from them.

Enough. Take care.

> Love,
> Steve
> Army Reservist Sgt. Stephen McDowell

Subject: re babysitting report
February 28, 2004

Hey there. The internet was down for a few days here but we're up and running now. I'm excited to see Megan. I wonder if she is going to remember me?

The days are getting longer over here. Same shit different day. Roadside bombs blowing up. A car ran a check point in town today and the driver got two to the head!

Knock on wood but I don't think anyone in Baghdad was killed in the last three days! Still looking at the middle of April to be stateside. . . .

I'll keep you posted. Gotta run.

Love ya, guys.
Steve
Army Reservist Sgt. Stephen McDowell

Subject: re: Spring Break
March 11, 2004

Hey Mom, another rough week over here. Not good. I'm so glad it's almost over. Our replacements are here and we're doing the change-over thing tomorrow. My battery is dying so I've got to type fast and cut this short. I'm good and will be on my way home in a couple of days— hopefully in one piece. I'll write you back when I hit Kuwait. No worries.

Love,
Steve
Army Reservist Sgt. Stephen McDowell

Army Reservist Sgt. Stephen McDowell was released March 31, 2004, from active duty and has returned to work as a computer programmer.—FS

32

Frank,

Here is another email I got from my son, Scott Wicklund, when he was stationed on the Syrian border. . . .

Roy Wicklund

January 17, 2004

Hey Dad,

Got back yesterday from the mission. Very, very interesting. Figured I would tell you and of course, don't tell Mom.

We were running the Syrian/Iraqi border checkpoint for 7 days in the town of Husaybah. Bad, bad town. During our stint there we had one day when 24 mortars fell and another when 37 fell into the compound.

The first day I was getting ready to eat dinner and was starving when I look up and damn mortars are landing 75-100 meters away. Loud. 82 mm variety. That wasn't too bad. A lot of buildings to run and hide in.

This is the part you should like. It was 2 nights ago when the compound took the 37 mortar rounds and myself and one of the other Bradley's were at an observation post on the border. Our drill is that if anything happens we get ready to move out (we were not set as a reaction force but sometimes we like to make things happen). Well, we got ready and the commander told us to move out.

Moving into town, they fired two rockets at my Bradley. One went just over my head and the other one hit a wall next to me. Bad mistake. The Bradley has a full automatic 25 mm chain gun that fires high explosive rounds. My gunner was scanning in another direction so he didn't see it, so I took the gun and started traversing it and walked the rounds into the area so he could see, then he took over, launched 60 HE rounds into the area and killed two of the bastards. These two died very gruesome deaths. Had to put one of the bodies in trash bags.

Morale shot up a lot in our troop after they found out that we had confirmed enemy deaths. They still had one rocket they hadn't fired. Very bad rockets that will punch thru anything we got, so it was good that we blew them up. Thought you might like that story.

These are not the first guys we've killed over here, just the most satisfying because of the rockets they first fired at us, the mortars, etc. Tell Mom everything remains boring like usual and nothing ever happens over here.

Don't need anything at all right now. Living conditions are fine and everything is good. Mid March to early April is when we are coming home, but that seems so far away that I don't even think about it right now. Still running a lot of missions, so I don't even focus on home. . . .

My men have no problem going out on missions with me. Love it. They'd follow me anywhere and my job is to try and make sure we all get back in one piece.

> Well, take care Dad and I'll talk to you later.
> 1st Lt. Scott Wicklund, 3rd ACR, U.S. Army

1st Lt. Scott Wicklund and all his men returned home.—FS

The 1st Marine Division had just returned to Iraq. This is a letter from the commanding general of the division.—FS

Major General U.S. Marines
Marines up!

Letter to all Hands:

We are going back in to the brawl. We will be relieving the magnificent Soldiers fighting under the 82nd Airborne Division, whose hard won successes in the Sunni Triangle have opened opportunities for us to exploit. For the last year, the 82nd Airborne has been operating against the heart of the enemy's resistance. It's appropriate that we relieve them.

When it's time to move a piano, Marines don't pick up the piano bench—we move the piano. So, this is the right place for Marines in this fight, where we can carry on the legacy of Chesty Puller in the Banana Wars in the same sort of complex environment that he knew in his early years. Shoulder to shoulder with our comrades in the Army, Coalition Forces and maturing Iraqi Security Forces, we are going to destroy the enemy with precise firepower while diminishing the conditions that create adversarial relationships between us and the Iraqi people.

This is going to be hard, dangerous work. It is going to require patient, persistent presence. Using our individual initiative, courage, moral judgment and battle skills, we will build on the 82nd Airborne's victories.

Our country is counting on us even as our enemies watch and calculate, hoping that America does not have warriors strong enough to withstand discomfort and danger. You, my fine young men, are going to prove the enemy wrong—dead wrong. You will demonstrate the same uncompromising spirit that has always caused the enemy to fear America's Marines.

The enemy will try to manipulate you into hating all Iraqis. Do not allow the enemy that victory. With strong discipline, solid faith, unwavering alertness, and undiminished chivalry to the innocent, we will carry out this mission. Remember, I have added, "First, do no harm" to our passwords of "No Better Friend, No Worse Enemy."

Keep your honor clean as we gain information about the enemy from the Iraqi people. Then, armed with that information and working in conjunction with fledging Iraqi Security Forces, we will move precisely against the enemy elements and crush them without harming the innocent.

This is our test—our Guadalcanal, our Chosin Reservoir, our Hue City. Fight with a happy heart and keep faith in your comrades and your unit. We must be under no illusions about the nature of the enemy and the dangers that lie ahead. Stay alert, take it all in stride, remain sturdy, and share your courage with each other and the world. You are going to write history, my fine young Sailors and Marines, so write it well.

Semper Fidelis
J. M. Mattis
Major General, U.S. Marines

33

February 27, 2004

Dear Mr. Schaeffer,

I am not sure what kind of letters you are looking for. . . . My son, SGT Cory R. Mracek, was sent to Iraq, from the 82nd Airborne in Ft. Bragg, NC. He left January 16, 2004. None of us had been writing to him via e-mail as we thought he had to have a military email [address] so were waiting for him to send it. This is the first message I received from him as he was killed on January 27, 2004 from a roadside bomb. He was there eight days.

I had sent him a letter everyday since four days before he left FT. Bragg. He never received any of them, so I will always feel bad that I hadn't been e-mailing him. I didn't know I could. I did get to talk to him on MSN about 1 hour, which would have been the night before here, and the day that he was killed there. I think I received one other message from him but that was all before he died. If you can use any of this, please feel free. Or if not, it helps me to write about it a little.

Thanks so much.
Pat Mracek

An email sent two days before Cory was killed.—FS

From: Cory Mracek
Sent: Sunday, January 25, 2004 2:35 AM

What, no one can write anymore? Geez, seems as though everyone's forgotten me. Well, the GPS seems to be doing fine, Iraq is ok, very muddy, and its not nearly as bad as I'd thought it would be. There's a lot more at our little base than I thought there'd be. So life is good and I'm getting all this tax free money!* I almost like this better than being back at Bragg. We're actually doing something.

I miss you and hope you all are well. I'll try to call sometime, but the hours really don't come together well. It's almost worse than Korea, because there it was half a day. Now your off time is my sleep time. Oh well, one of these days I'll get to [call] I hope.

I could use a couple things though, CD player, or something to listen to music. Scratch that, I have no CD's that I brought. Hand Sanitizer, Notebooks and Envelopes, Gum! Definitely gum. Winter-fresh and Polar Ice and Big Red I like. Laundry Detergent and Body wash. For the detergent, get those rapid tabs. They work great. Can't really think of anything else.

How's work? How are the girls and Dad? How is that dog? How is everything? It would be nice to hear from people, kinda to know what's going on at home and all. I check my email almost every day, so don't worry about filling up my inbox, just don't send forwards, ok? Let Grandma and whoever else know that too.

Love you, Cory
Sgt. Cory R. Mracek, 82nd Airborne, U.S. Army

*Combat pay is tax-free.—FS

Frank: [Here below is] the second and last letter I received from my son Sgt. Cory Mracek the day before he died.

Pat Mracek

Monday, January 26, 2004

Hi:

That's cool that the girls whooped some butt. [Cory is responding to some information learned on the MSN chat with his cousin—FS] Hope they can make it to state. . . . No I didn't know the guys from 82nd that got killed, well I don't know of anyone I know getting killed, and no one from our company. . . .

I forgot one thing I need soon: razor blades. Mach III Turbos if you please. I haven't gotten any mail or packages yet. Still pretty good weather here. A little cold in the mornings, and the occasional rain, but I'm not complaining, because I know how hot it's going to get here. That's about all the news I have for right now. So I'll write again soon.

Love you, Cory
Sgt. Cory R. Mracek, 82nd Airborne, U.S. Army

February 29, 2004

Frank:

Here is my niece Jackie's last conversation with Cory. A friend of his has some emails from when he was in Korea that I am going to get for you. Also some of the guys from Iraq have emailed me some of their feelings and some of Cory's so will send some of them to you.

Pat Mracek

From: Mary Kay
To: Pat Mracek

Hi. . . . okay so here is my [last] MSN conversation with Cory:

It was 11:00pm my time on Monday and 0700 a.m. on Tuesday Cory's time. I'm online everyday and this was the first time Cory had been online since he left for Iraq so I was ecstatic to talk to him and see how everything was going.

After asking him how he was I [proceded] with what seemed like a thousand questions about Iraq, the people, how they live, and the geography of the area. . . . everything. I could tell Cory was equally excited to chat with me as he answered all of my questions in great detail and then some.

Some questions that really stand out are: I asked what the people were like and he said they live in mud shacks and its desert all around. I asked him about the food and he said, "Well there is definitely no McDonalds." We talked about some of our memories growing up and how his little sister Heather and our other cousin Angela were growing up so fast, we both complained that it made us feel old.

I asked Cory if he was scared and he said, "No, not really, I just don't know who I can trust."

He said that on one side of the road there would be children jumping up and down and cheering and thanking them while on the other side of the road there were very suspicious faces.

We talked about all the places the Army has taken him and how he truly has seen the world. He said he couldn't wait to someday tell his children all about the places he had been. He then joked and said by that time his kids would get bored and go play, Play Station 10! He then said he needed to get ready for his mission of the day. We told each other how much we loved and missed one another and he said he would write an email later. He also said he would be sending pictures as soon as he could.

Cory had a special gift and that was one of joy, he could brighten anyone's day by making them laugh and he would do whatever it took to see a smile. I can remember laughing endlessly for no reason at all, only because the sound of his laugh was contagious.

Mary Kay

From: Parker, Bruce LTC CJTF7-82ND AB BN CDR
To: Pat Mracek
Sent: Thursday, February 12, 2004
Subject: Iraq Jan 27

Dear Mr. and Mrs. Mracek,

I am the battalion commander for the 2nd Battalion, 505th Parachute Infantry Regiment. Your son was attached to my battalion in December as the Bravo Company Fire Support NCO for 1st Platoon. I wanted to send you a note to let you know that you are in our thoughts and prayers.

Although I have already sent out a letter of condolence, I felt it didn't do your loss justice and wanted to correspond to you by e-mail and let you know what your son meant to all of us. Words can not adequately express our loss and my heart goes out to both of you.

I had talked to Cory in the first week of January just prior to our deployment when he was introduced to me by CPT Yanda when he came down to the battalion. I wanted you to know that your son was excited to be a paratrooper and eager to serve his country.

Although new to the battalion and the company he supported, your son had the nickname of "SGT Morale Check." He was always the first to lend a hand when someone needed help. He was very good at what he was trained to do and much respected by those that he came in contact with on a daily basis.

This last week has been terribly sad for all of us. Although I have not lost a child, I feel that I lost three sons last week and the pain will always be there. Your son was a paratrooper, friend, and big brother in the company. I want you to know that Cory was not alone when he died, and that he did not suffer. He was a warrior who died doing what he believed in, and he was a terrific paratrooper.

We fare welled your son from the Forward Operating Base Kalsu on 30 January with a beautiful Memorial Service. It was attended by over 300 paratroopers and soldiers. Our Assistant Division Commander (COL Broom) flew in to pay his respects as well as the 1st Brigade Commander (COL Donahue), 3rd Brigade Commander (COL Smith), DIVARTY Brigade Commander (COL Thein), 220th Brigade Commander (Brigadier General Geoghan), and the 16th MP Brigade Commander (COL Quantock), as well as their Command Sergeants Major.

Your son was loved and respected and now missed by all of us. I sincerely express to you my sadness and condolences in your loss. Your son's sacrifice will never be forgotten. I am so sorry.

Sincerely,
Bruce Parker
Lieutenant Colonel
Commander, 2nd Battalion, 505th Parachute Infantry Regiment
82nd Airborne Division

From: Pat Mracek
Thursday, February 12, 2004
To: Parker, Bruce LTC CJTF7-82ND AB BN CDR
Subject: Re: Iraq

Dear Lieutenant Colonel Parker,

Thank you for the wonderful letter. We know that Cory loved his job and was proud of his accomplishments as we were also. He wanted to be in Iraq. We are so glad that he didn't suffer. That is the one thing that would have made it so much harder to deal with. His dream was to be a paratrooper and I just wish he would have had a little more time to enjoy it.

You were all like family and have been through this hard time. I know it can't be easy on any of you. I have had phone calls and so many messages from all of you. It helps to ease the pain. He was so worried about fitting in a new place, but seemed like in a few days he had lots of friends.

We have no regrets, as we knew that is what he wanted to do and we believe that the U.S. needs to be there so that this war does not come onto our soil. We appreciate everything that our soldiers do for us.

Cory and his two fallen comrades are heroes, but so are the rest of you. Please don't forget that. We are praying for you all to come home safely and we hope that some of the bad things that are going on there can be stopped so there won't be so much danger.

Please stay safe.
Pat Mracek

From: Parker, Bruce LTC CJTF7-82ND AB BN CDR
To: Pat Mracek
Sent: Thursday, February 12, 2004
Subject: Iraq

Pat,

Thank you for the nice note. I will pass it to our Paratroopers.

Sincerely,
Bruce Parker

From: Pat Mracek
Sent: Thursday, February 12, 2004
To: Parker, Bruce LTC CJTF7-82ND AB BN CDR

Is there anything that you need? We would like to send some pkgs for you to share. I am making cookies today but let me know of anything else.

Pat Mracek

From: Bruce Parker
To: Pat
Sent: Friday, February 13, 2004

Pat,

It is apparent where Cory's strength of character came from. The battalion is touched by your offer. Homemade cookies would be awesome! Thank you for the offer.

Sincerely,
Bruce

Frank:

This is another letter from one of the soldiers in Cory's unit.

Pat

From: Matthew Hardman
To: Pat
Sent: Thursday, March 04, 2004
Subject: Thank You

Mrs. Mracek,

Thank you so much for your kind and supportive note. It meant the world to me, and it provides me the strength I need to see this mission through. Your support of the unit is so inspiring. One more example of how blessed we are to serve with such wonderful people as Cory and be connected to their families. I am continually amazed and humbled by how strong the families we left behind are.

The number one reason I am in the Army is my love of the people that I am associated with and their families. Sandy lets me go away and live this life because the people that we get know and hopefully one day raise our children around are so incredible, supportive, and centered on values.

I read the article on Cory and his obituary. It reminded me of the burden that we all now carry: to live our lives as best we can to . . . continue to honor our friends and comrades.

My emotions are mixed: terrible sadness and the tremendous pride and joy of being a part of your son and having the honor of serving with him. I looked at the picture of your family and I want to hug you so bad. I want in some way to take away the pain that I know I am incapable lifting or mitigating. I pray that God can ease your pain as I cannot.

I shared the newspaper with the men of the company, and like your wonderful cookies it is getting passed from man to man the way paratroopers do. It meant a lot to the men to see that. Thank you so much for sharing it. I selfishly kept one copy, I plan to hold onto and share with my children one day. I want them to understand why I'll always have special place of sadness and most importantly joy for Cory, Lester, and Luke.[*]

We are all changed forever; we will always carry that sadness, the pride of comradeship, and the joy of our memories of our friends and comrades.

We look forward to seeing you and your family at Green Ramp Ft. Bragg, N.C. If you cannot see us there, I will come to see you. Having the opportunity to talk with the families is something we all look forward to and need.

Thank you again for all the support from you and your family. You are all truly amazing and a source of great strength.

All-The Way!
Matt Hardman
CPT Matthew Hardman
B CO 2-505 82D Airborne Division

June 2, 2004

Dear Frank,

Cory was 26 years old. He had just graduated jump school in November 2003. It was his dream to be Airborne. He never got to make his sixth jump. They are required to make six to graduate. On July 1st, 2004 all his unit will be making his sixth jump for him.

Pat

*The three soldiers killed by the roadside bomb that day.—FS

34

Reservists play a big part in the occupation of Iraq. We met Chaplain Kevin Wainwright before in the deployment section of this book in letters from October 16, 2003, as he got ready to leave for the Middle East. We meet Chaplain Wainwright again now six months later via dispatches he was sending to his family and church congregation back home.—FS

CH (CPT) Kevin Wainwright
Chaplain 1-113th FA BN
March 15, 2004

Scripture and Thought for the Day . . .
"In those days there was no king in Israel; every man did what was right in his own eyes."—Judges 17:6

Greetings from Iraq. With a sorrowful heart I write on this day, the Ides of March. We have lost the first soldier in our brigade. He was killed west of Baghdad two days ago. All I could think about this afternoon was how the notification process was going to happen. I have been that chaplain who had to notify a family that their loved one had died. There is absolutely nothing you can say or do to comfort that family.

I had believed in my heart that we would get through this deployment without a loss. I knew that this was not reality, but I was hopeful that we would be different. I keep thinking about his children and wife if he had any. As our battalion XO, MAJ Maynor said, "we are in a war!" I know this had a silly obviousness about it, but a part of all of us did not believe that people were not going to come home from this. . . .

I have often said that soldiers are the most noble and depraved people all rolled into one. We witnessed a sad event as we crossed Iraq that also was tinged with hope. I have mentioned the poverty in which so many of the Iraqis, especially the children, live. Almost every soldier I talk to has mentioned how much this genuinely bothered them.

We have a brick factory outside of our [base] where children as young as five and six help make and stack bricks. Our soldiers want to do something to help them. We do not know what it is, yet. It is part of my plan to come up with a way to help. I think we can minister to soldiers by helping them minister to Iraqis.

We talk much about how America has or is changing for the worse. Sometimes I have thought that this was true. We also think that the generations before us, especially the WWII generation, were somehow morally superior. The time we live in is no better and no worse than any other time. Every age has had more than its fair share of selfishness, hatred, and bigotry. If I am serving with the citizen soldiers of my age who are an accurate representation of our society, then I am not worried about the immediate future. . . .

My closing thoughts return to the family of my brother-in-arms who was killed. "There is no longer slave nor free, Jew or Greek, male or female, for we are all one in Christ Jesus." May his crossing into the Promised Land be one of peace and joy; may his sacrifice not be in vain; and may the Lord comfort the broken hearts and dry the tears of sorrow of those who loved him so dearly.

Grace, Mercy, and Peace,
CH (CPT) Kevin Wainwright
Chaplain 1-113th FA BN

"Be strong and of good courage. Do not be afraid nor be dismayed; for the Lord your God is with you wherever you go."—Joshua 1:9

CH (CPT) Kevin Wainwright
Chaplain 1-113th FA BN
March 15, 2004

"Watch over your heart with all diligence, for from it flow the springs of life."—Proverbs 4:23
"Our generation will have to repent not only for the words and acts of the Children of Darkness, but also for the fears and apathy of the Children of Light."—Rev. Dr. Martin Luther King, Jr.

Greetings from Iraq,

Homesickness has finally settled in. I have not missed home so much in my life. I keep thinking of [my wife] Heather and [son] Josh. I attended worship last night. . . . It dawned on me during the middle of [the service] that I have not prayed enough for my unborn child. It hit me that I was going to miss all of the exciting things that come with a pregnancy. As a father, I felt for the first time that not only was I going to miss much with Joshua but with Julia/Nathaniel [the names we've chosen for our unborn child] as well. The baby in Heather's womb would not get to hear my voice in the morning or hear me tell her/his mother how much I loved her.

I will not get to see my child discover his/her hands, or say her/his first word, or get to watch him/her sleep at night. I do not regret being here in Iraq, nor do I doubt that this is where God wants me to be, but it does come with a price. . . .

[We soldiers'] biggest fear is that our families will forget about us or that our spouses will not be true. The only real stability we have is knowing the home front is safe, secure, and stable. . . . We do not want to let go or compartmentalize our life, but in a way we must lessen our ties to family while we are in Iraq in order to cope with the separation. We do this in order to stay focused on the mission and on survival, but we also experience a tremendous amount of guilt. . . .

Our wives should know that we get much time to think about things over here. We should be men of more considerable depth when we return. . . .

Grace, Mercy, and Peace,
CH (CPT) Kevin Wainwright
Chaplain 1-113th FA BN

"Be strong and of good courage. Do not be afraid nor be dismayed; for the Lord your God is with you wherever you go."—Joshua 1:9

CH (CPT) Kevin Wainwright
Chaplain 1-113th FA BN
March 18, 2004

Thought for the Day . . . "In repentance and rest you will be saved. In quietness and trust is your strength."—Isaiah 30:15
"To do injustice is more disgraceful than to suffer it."—Plato

Greetings from Iraq,

. . . . With no television, Hooters [restaurants], pubs, good gyms, etc., our soldiers have had a great deal of time to think . . . This experience tends to focus the mind on the blessings and curses that we carry in our hearts. Many of our soldiers also start thinking about God. I have had many come up to me and ask when church is. They confess that they want to make it more of a priority. . . .

During a typical day our soldiers commit numerous small acts of courage. Our division, the Big Red One, had seven deaths this week: six from combat and one from an accident. Several of our [bases] in the area have been attacked. This is real.

The small acts that I mention are simple things. Getting in a vehicle and going on patrol, visiting a local official, climbing a tower for guard mount, all these acts require the individual to consciously put aside their fears and act instead of or despite them. . . .

I am amazed by the integrity of my fellow [reservist] citizen-soldiers. For example, where a banking official stood now stands a first sergeant. Failing to overcome [my] fears and thus failing our brothers is what I worry about. . . . Whether it is true or not, [as chaplain] I do feel like I represent the promises God has made to these men. If I do not act like God's representative, I let Him and them down. This causes me to lean forward in the foxhole probably too much.

I have been rightfully scolded by my Brigade Chaplain of being a little too eager to leave the comfort of the [base] and venture forth. I yearn to be credible. By going out on a mission, however, I put those who I am with in greater danger since I do not carry a weapon. I now tend to listen to CH Goodwin a little more attentively than I used to.

We are arranging to see C and B battery. The command group worries that they will think that we have forgotten about them. . . . We are trying to get a Blackhawk helicopter for the command group to go see them. I am not a great fan of flight, but I will be going along because it is the right thing to do. . . .

Three missionaries were gunned down in Mosul two days ago. They were all Baptist and included a 28 year old married couple from North Carolina. I had a first sergeant from another unit ask what they were thinking. I responded that they were not thinking, they were responding to that "unreasonable" call that puts Christians in harm's way and pastors in wars. I pray for their families, but I also pray that ten more will come over to replace them. This country needs all the material help that it can get, but it needs spiritual help even more. Centuries of Islam and decades of socialism have not made lives better. I wonder how these people would respond to a message of hope instead of blind obedience and submission. . . .

On a humorous note, Donovan ordered some communion wine through the military system the other day. Yes, the Army has a stock number for seven different types of communion wine! The Army has a number for everything. . . .

On the way to church last week my [wife told me that] my son Joshua asked [her] if [they] were going to "see daddy." . . . Stories like this break and mend my heart all at the same time. I worry about the long term effects this deployment will have on my son. . . .

One of the toughest things I do as a chaplain is to tell soldiers that they have to return for emergency leave or that they cannot go. Most of these situations arise from a child getting injured. I pray with all my heart that Heather, Josh, and the baby will be fine. I have been away so long that I had to look up my zip code. I am forgetting the address where I live. . . .

The final word I have to share is about the 1-17th FA BN. They are the unit that we are replacing. They are a fine active duty unit out of Ft. Sill, OK. They have rendered good and faithful service. Please pray for them. Also, pray for the 120th Infantry "Tusk Hogs." They are the battalion that lost the soldier to an IED [improvised explosive device]. We had our memorial ceremony today.

MG Batiste, the division commander, was present for it. I felt sick inside during the whole ceremony. . . . It struck home that it could happen to anyone of us. I am not one who sheds many tears when I grieve, but I came close today.

LTC Stevens, their battalion commander . . . spoke of the legacy that we should leave this soldier, a safe and secure Iraq that has a future. My prayer is that his death will be a fruitful sacrifice that produces some peace in this area of the world. I patted the chaplain of the 120th, CH Walter Graves, as he wept after taps.

He is a Viet Nam vet who served with First Cav. I think it brought many memories back. . . .

. . . . We are looking for children's books for boys and girls age 2-6. We are going to tape soldiers reading these books to their children on video and then mail [it] to the [soldier's] child.

Grace, Mercy, and Peace,
CH (CPT) Kevin Wainwright
Chaplain 1-113th FA BN

"Be strong and of good courage. Do not be afraid nor be dismayed; for the Lord your God is with you wherever you go."—Joshua 1:9

CH (CPT) Kevin Wainwright
Chaplain 1-113th FA BN
March 20, 2004

Good Afternoon from Iraq,

I do not know how to begin this next "dispatch." In it I will try to summarize the plight of the folks right outside our gate. . . . A few days ago we paid a visit to the "Brick Factory," a small industrial village a few kilometers from our [base]. We had seen the smokestacks from the kilns in the distance. When the atmosphere is just right, the black smog coats the horizon making our area look like something out of a Dickens novel. The commander asked that I come along with some of the key leaders. What I saw broke my heart and reminded me why we are here.

I know that there has been a great deal of both international and national debate about this war. Spain, Poland, and Korea are all wavering about whether we should be here at all. Our presidential race promises to have this as a key issue. Everyone is focused on weapons of mass destruction (WMDs), but they have forgotten about the Iraqi people.

I encourage every American to ask themselves what responsibility we will bear if, as a nation, we ignore the plight of those in our world. Our armies no longer conquer, but liberate and rebuild. I wonder what judgment our Lord will pronounce on us if we turn inward as a country and forget about our blessings. . . .

Thirty years ago Saddam Hussein moved Arab squatters from the South into the North. He did this to "resettle" the areas that were once inhabited by the Kurds, a people of different ethnicity than the Arabs. He moved them in because he had killed . . . the Kurds who lived here. Saddam proceeded to build over 54 kilns that would produce bricks for sale. He and his friends would pocket the profit. The bricks are made by placing thousands of them inside these kilns, packing them with fuel oil, and then firing them up. . . .

The population that surrounds the kilns cannot be accurately measured, but estimates range from 5,000 to 10,000 men, women, and children. . . . They are essentially untouchable slaves. . . . The children make $3/day with the adults making $5/day.

We first drove to the school and community center that the unit before us, the [U.S. Army] 1-17th FA BN out of Ft. Sill, built for $40,000. It was a pleasant complex with brightly colored walls and happy scenes of children working, playing, learning, and spending time with their parents. The walled compound had very little furniture, no school supplies, and the only inhabitant was a guard that has been hired with American money. The prior unit had done all they could with their limited manpower and time. They expressed the hope that this project would grow to really help the people.

We then drove to the center of the complex where we stopped at a kiln. About half of the 54 kilns were in current use, spewing filth into the sky and coating everything with a thin grime of soot. When we got out of our vehicles, a group of children came to greet us. The only thing they had in common with their painted counterparts was the smiles on their faces. We were encouraged to take off our sunglasses, for the children were originally afraid of the soldiers who came because they could not see their eyes.

We received permission to take pictures and began to click away, but this was not a tourist stop. I immediately saw three girls, aged about twelve years old, covered from head to toe, to include their faces, not for religious reasons but to protect their lungs from the brick dust. They were stacking bricks on a cart pulled by a very tired looking donkey. A couple of boys were watching them with rubber hoses in their hands. They usually used the hoses to beat and prod the donkeys, but our 1-17th host told us that the donkeys were not the only things that they beat, especially if the [girls] did not work.

A little boy appeared with a soccer ball and began to play. We found out that Saddam had forbidden them to build soccer fields or to have soccer balls. They were there to work. In a nation, like most of the world, where soccer is a secondary religion, think about what effect this had on the children growing up in this inferno? I was amazed that they could still smile. . . .

I told my assistants that this was the way the majority of the people in this world lived. CPT Orlando Ortega, the commander of G Battery out of Illinois, was the man tasked to organize the efforts to help improve the lives of the people of the Brick Factory. He is a capable and wise commander whose unit has been attached to us. Composed of soldiers from the Southern Illinois region, they will spearhead our efforts here. One of the biggest challenges they will face is making sure that the children will receive and keep the aid.

The 1-17th had given away some shoes this past fall only to learn that some men of the village had collected them after the soldiers had left and then sold them in the local markets. We think we have solved this issue. Our plan is to hire five teachers, build a soccer field, and pay for outside workers to help the men make the brick. We want to make it economically feasible to have the children in school. . . .

I have asked [my friends and church community back home] for many things. . . . I apologize, for I have probably asked for too much.

. . . My desire is that you think about the possibility of finding ways to help us with this project. We want you first to continue to pray for us, this project, and the millions of innocent Iraqis who have suffered for so long. Our soldiers have universally agreed that this village needs our help. Many have come to me grieving over what they have seen. I had a hardened first sergeant share how seeing these kids suffer has made him restless at night.

By helping us help this community we can help our soldiers cope with seeing their own children in the eyes of the Iraqis. I also hope that they will see the locals as a little more human in the process. . . .

Wish List Playground Equipment: . . . the hardware for playground equipment. Polaroid Instant Cameras + Film: We would like to take these cameras to the factory and take the children's pictures and give them the copy. . . . This will probably be the first picture of themselves that they ever had. Sandals/Shoes: in various sizes for boys and girls. We plan to mark them so that they will not be sold in the local markets. Candy: no chocolate (will melt in the heat). Hard Candy is preferable. Soccer Balls and Pumps: Inexpensive and rugged soccer balls are best. Please send them deflated. Our 1-17th host tossed a few of these out of his Humvee as we left. They are hugely popular. Pencils, notebooks, and other school supplies: we need items for the school. Dolls for little children: no Barbie's please. The toys need to be modest. Sunglasses: the kids love our sunglasses. Cheap sunglasses would be great. General, durable small toys: We need to make sure we can give away as many of these as we can. . . .

Some of our soldiers had been grousing, like we are all prone to do at times, about their living conditions. After seeing [the village and brick factory], they were not so upset anymore. . . .

Grace, Mercy, and Peace,
CH (CPT) Kevin Wainwright
Chaplain 1-113th FA BN

"Be strong and of good courage. Do not be afraid nor be dismayed; for the Lord your God is with you wherever you go."—Joshua 1:9

CH (CPT) Kevin Wainwright
Chaplain 1-113th FA BN
March 24, 2004

Greetings from Iraq,

. . . . It is hard, but I still believe that God has placed all of us here for a reason. . . . I still feel as if I am walking among giants. I am very proud to be a guardsman. Some of the writing on the porta-pottie walls keeps pointing out how inadequate the guard is. I beg to differ. At the risk of offending my active duty brethren and sisters, I will share the new motto for the National Guard, "The National Guard, doing the Army's job!"

Take care. . . . God is good.

Grace, Mercy, and Peace,
CH (CPT) Kevin Wainwright
Chaplain 1-113th FA BN

"Be strong and of good courage. Do not be afraid nor be dismayed; for the Lord your God is with you wherever you go."—Joshua 1:9

May 21, 2004

Dear Mr. Schaeffer,

My name is Jenny Troyer and I met you yesterday at the MCA (Marine Corp Association) bookstore at Camp Pendleton. I have gathered some letters and an email for consideration. The first letter is from my husband, after I had mentioned that he doesn't really tell me a lot when we talk. It is mostly me doing all the talking when we are on the phone. The second letter is describing what happened when there was a mortar attack on base. I was very worried about this because I am a Key Volunteer for Chad's battalion and just got word there was an "incident" on the base he is at.

Here is a little background on my husband: He is 2nd Lt. Chad E. Troyer with 3d LAAD Bn (Low Altitude Air Defense) Bravo Company 1st platoon attached to 3rd MAW. He left for Iraq on the 21st of February of 2004 and will come home in September. He enlisted in the Marine Corps at the age of 17 and served 4 years in infantry. He then went to Ball State University in Indiana where we are from. He did his undergrad in Physical Education and entered OCS in May of 2002. We will be married a year in July [2004].

I hope this is useful to you.
Sincerely,
Jenny Troyer

March 30, 2004

Jen,

Well, I just talked to you, so now I'll inform you. On the 21st three rockets landed inside our perimeter. The rest of the room and myself (three Captains, three Lt.'s) were watching a movie. We felt the 1st impact and I knew that it was incoming. I threw on my cammies, flak, and helmet and we went to our HQ (headquarters). I took a group of my Marines and secured one of the gates (ECPS). After that, the three rockets, nothing else came at us. It was weird because earlier in the day I told my Marine who mans the .50 Caliber machine gun to be diligent because I had a funny feeling about that day.

Yesterday I was at my ECP coordinating the construction that was happening. A truck came up to our drop arm (first entry point before they get searched) at a high rate of speed, so four of my Marines opened fire on the vehicle. Luckily they didn't kill the driver, but that was more scary than the rockets because I was standing there talking when I heard the M16's open up. I dove for cover, then pulled my pistol and went to assess the situation. The driver was near sighted and couldn't see that he had to stop. Everyone was okay.

Work is good and so am I. Definitely exciting here. I am happy to be a part of all the happenings here. . . . We are all going to watch a movie it is our nightly ritual.

I miss you tons and I also catch myself wondering what you are doing. We've taken in a dog (Bravo Company). Its name is Chance. Like a second chance at life. It makes me think of Myla [his dog] and what a good life she has. I miss you tons and love you.

Chad

2nd Lt. Chad E. Troyer with 3d LAAD
(Low Altitude Air Defense) Bravo Company 1st Platoon, USMC

May 14, 2004

Dear Jen,

We are now into our third month of a seven-month deployment here in Iraq. With each day my love for you grows stronger. I think back to when I was a 20-year-old kid fighting in Somalia and I wonder what kept me motivated while I was there. As a young enlisted man the biggest relationship I had was the camaraderie that I shared with my fellow Marines. Back then the only thing that I looked forward to was going home and being able to drink a beer and hang out with my friends. It seemed so simple back then, I still feel that camaraderie, probably even more so since I am a Platoon Commander, but knowing you are back there waiting for me gives me a sense of hope that on some days overwhelms me.

I watch these young Marines on a daily basis and they are performing amazing tasks. Some of them have never been trained in the job that we have been asked to do but still they have learned quickly and no one questions why they are here. The only gripes that I get are why is the mail not here, and what is being served for chow. I know some are homesick, but they won't admit it because they don't want to seem weak in front of their peers.

I sometimes get mad at myself because I love being here I love being able to lead Marines in combat, but through my pleasure I know you sit at home and wonder how I am doing, am I alive and am I thinking of you as I know you are thinking of me. Every night I pray that you travel through your days safely, that nothing happens to you because I can't imagine my life without you. There are days when I forget what it felt like to hold you. . . . Sometimes you can become very numb here. . . .

We haven't been attacked in some time now. I can see the complacency setting in among my Marines. I make it a point. . . . talking to them telling them about the intelligence I have just read, reminding them that danger is only a second away. . . . I try not to ask personal questions . . . for I don't want their minds to wander from what their mission and responsibilities are. It takes only one bad vehicle search to set off an explosion that could wipe out one entire squad. That is a squad of Marines a squad of people whose deaths I would have to live with the rest of my life. The thought of anyone getting hurt or killed keeps me up at night.

I want you to know that I am sorry that I don't get to write or talk to you as much as the other husbands do. It is not because I don't care or I don't want to. I have been given the toughest assignment within our Company and I really do call and write whenever the time comes available. Know that because of the love we share I have become a much better leader and a much better man. I feel so lucky that you and I met, that you took a chance on guy with a funny looking go-tee smoking a cigar in that bar that night.

Our first wedding anniversary is coming up. . . . Know I will love you the rest of your life. Thinking of you every day and loving you more as each day comes.

Love Chad
2nd Lt. Chad E. Troyer with 3d LAAD (Low Altitude Air Defense)
Bravo Company 1st Platoon, USMC

2nd Lt. Chad E. Troyer is still in Iraq.—FS

CH (CPT) Kevin Wainwright
Chaplain 1-113th FA BN
April 4, 2004

Greetings from Iraq,

It is a day after an absolutely wonderful and uplifting Palm Sunday Service. . . . We met at the parade field where we had our memorial ceremony for the soldier who died. The baptistery was a wooden box constructed by our chaplain assistants. It was lined with plastic and surrounded by camouflage netting. The pastors had all met to decide who we were going to baptize and how we were going to do it. We agreed that it was going to be by immersion. I felt strongly about this. While I do not, nor does the reformed tradition hold, that immersion is required or that someone has to be an adult, we wanted to put the soldier's needs first. I did not want a new Christian to return back to the States and join a church that did not agree with anything but immersion.

Since, as a Presbyterian, we can baptize as well as anoint, I wanted to cover our bases. We found out later that all who were baptized were going through it for the first time, but we also decided that it was up to the soldier, once we had explained the meaning of baptism, to decide whether he or she should be baptized. Basically, as chaplains (we are two Methodists, a Southern Baptist, and me, Presbyterian) we concluded that it was not about us but between the soldier and God. . . .

We had over 140 soldiers from across the brigade attend the service. . . . CH Goodwin gave an excellent sermon on the meaning and purpose of baptism. After the message, we called those who wanted to be baptized to come forward. We had a group of folks from a wide range of backgrounds. We had male and female, black and white, officer and enlisted, short and tall, old and young. . . .

The baptisms started while one of our female soldiers with a beautiful voice sang "Down to the River to Pray," from the soundtrack of "O Brother Where Art Thou." CH Brumsfield, our Baptist, started off. He immersed two guys and then motioned to me to take over. Now, I had never immersed anyone before. I helped baptize two soldiers, but I forgot to hold their noses, a rookie mistake. I remembered to close their nostrils on the third and fourth baptism I performed.

CH Brumsfield, who is 5'6", had to baptize one of his soldiers who is 6'8". We were able to fit him in the box. . . . Every soldier had a different path that brought them to this particular service. . . . Many had lived lives that were not very acceptable by traditional standards. This was mentioned to me, and I responded that those who have sinned the most provide the best fields for sowing the Gospel. Far too many of us, both in and out of church, operate under the assumption that we are good people who will get a pass from God or whoever when the time comes. . . .

The day was probably the most significant that we may have as chaplains in the brigade. The next morning, it was back to business as usual, but I was able to hold on to all that had happened. Even though it was back to meetings, visits, and knowing that there is never enough day to accomplish all that you can or should do, we who had been present at the service walked around with smiles on our faces.

I have been reading some poetry by the 14th century Persian Sufi master Hafiz. In Iran, his books of poetry sell more copies than the Koran. It has been interesting seeing how the Sufi extension of Islam is much less fanatical and more tolerant than its source. . . .

It has been a tough two weeks in theater. We have had outbursts in Fallujah and Najaf. When these things happen, the first thing I think of is Heather and all the wives back at home. I cringe when I think of how these events are reported. I wonder if the families at home should try to avoid the main part of the news altogether?

I think about the eleven people who were baptized and feel in my heart that, for me, this somehow makes up for all the days I am missing with Josh, for all the time away from my beloved wife. Was it not God who brought those individuals here, primed their heart, and placed other believers amongst them to allow the Spirit to communicate hope to them?

The more it seems we try to control our lives and hold on to those around us, the more we fear. The more we worry, the more selfish we become. Like Isaiah, I ask if not me, then who will serve our nation? I am not sure I want to live in a society that is so risk averse it will let evil triumph as long as evil allows everyone to get along. The opposite of love has always been apathy. . . .

Sunday morning eleven children went down to the river to pray. Sunday morning eleven brothers and sisters joined the body of Christ. . . .

Grace, Mercy, and Peace,
CH (CPT) Kevin Wainwright
Chaplain 1-113th FA BN

"Be strong and of good courage. Do not be afraid nor be dismayed; for the Lord your God is with you wherever you go."—Joshua 1:9

35

Message from the Commanding General, 1st Marine Division
April 6, 2004

The days fly by out here, and for all the improved living conditions compared to last year's deployment into Iraq, the tempo of our operations across our far-flung area is consistently high. That said, if there is one message that I need to convey, it is the unrelenting high spirits of our Sailors, Soldiers and Marines. They are undeterred by the harshness of the fighting and the casualties amongst their comrades. They clearly convey a greater appreciation of their life and of the love that they share with their families, that does so much to sustain them as we move forward in this test of wills between us and the enemy.

The connection with home — with their reasons for being here now engaged in this fight — are seen in the pictures of you, their wives, children, siblings, parents and friends that they carry in their helmets, pockets, notebooks and Bibles. Their faith remains strong and serves as the bulwark that it always is, and their humor is clearly intact as their smiles greet me on my rounds. While they dearly miss home, the already strong bonds with each other out here have grown even stronger, and together we will come through all this.

Our operations have seen many successes, from 7th Marines' dispersed units across the western desert and along the Euphrates River, to the provincial capital of Ramadi, and even into the contentious eastern zone where the elements of 1st Marines move against the enemy strengths in Fallujah and adjacent areas.

The casualties have been heartbreaking, yet nothing is weakening our Marines' resolve. Daily we grow stronger and the enemy grows weaker. In the complex environment in which we operate, the Marines' generosity of spirit, their guardianship of their buddies, and their steadfastness in the face of adversity are the things that will ultimately build our families, our communities and our Nation into even greater examples of all that is good.

The character of these fine young warriors is something to behold as I get to see each day. Yet I recognize that you don't get to see this reassuring presence and the best I can do is to try to articulate their strengths with these few awkward words. I hope that you hear from your loved ones through letters or maybe e-mail or perhaps an occasional phone call so you can know what I see every day.

The enemy has surged recently, and the alarm in the newspapers and on TV that accompanies such activities must be very worrisome to you and to all our families. Rest assured that there is no pressure on us to act hastily or move faster in our operations than we believe is prudent — no one is pushing us to do things that require us to sacrifice good judgment. We are methodical in our approach, first getting the best possible information, then setting up the best possible support for each operation, and only then prosecuting our mission, but with keen attention to any possible enemy surprise. Coupled with the prayers and support of you at home—you who represent to us what really matters in this world—we could not be in better company as we fight.

Please take care of each other and know that our high spirits and deepest prayers are with every one of you. . . .

Sincerely,
MGen Mattis

36

CH (CPT) Kevin Wainwright
Chaplain 1-113th FA BN
April 7, 2004

Greetings from Iraq,

. . . . There has been a great deal of talk about what has happened in Fallujah and Najaf. We worry about our families and the news they are receiving at home. I do not think there is a conspiracy on behalf of the media. There are bad things going on over here. This is a dangerous place, and we are in a war. . . . What is not presented in both peace and war are people going about their normal significant yet boring lives. . . .

All of us here in Iraq feel connected to you back at home; your morale affects our morale. If one family is having a hard time, their soldier will not be as ready to perform his duty, and this will affect his buddy and by extension his buddy's family.

This deployment is like the voyage of a ship with more than enough lifeboats that starts to sink. If we remain calm in the face of calamity and remember to work together, everyone will survive. If we panic and start to think only of ourselves, our needs, and our pain, the ones closest to the deck will get in the lifeboats and get out of danger leaving the rest of us to go down with the ship. . . .

What I enjoy the most is the humble nobility of the men and women who are serving over here. What has separated them from everyone else is that they have made a commitment to strangers, each other, to place themselves in harm's way and then to defend each other to the death.

I am here because every other soldier here said yes. By proxy, their families have agreed to this as well. I am thankful and in awe of the sacrifice that they are making. They have placed their family's health and well being behind a commitment, a promise made to serve. How many modern citizens in our republic would do any of this for strangers?

When the day comes where people in our nation will no longer make a sacrifice to serve others, this day will be the day that we start to decline as a nation. This is probably apostasy to say as a West Pointer, but serving the nation as defined by a flag or a governing body no longer has any romance for me. I love the flag, and I hate when it is desecrated, but it is still Caesar's flag. I serve because of all the disparate groups coming together and saying that the world's classifications no longer carry any weight or meaning. I love serving because it reminds me of what the church can and should be.

I have made a new friend who serves with the civil affairs unit. I am working with them to help interface with the local communities. Chaplains are considered to be the Subject Matter Experts on religion! It has also helped that I have traveled in the region before.

My new friend is an American who was born in Iran. He moved from Tehran when he was ten and grew up in Silicon Valley. He is a very nice guy. I am not sure if he is a practicing Muslim. He joined the Army out of high school to make a statement that he was thankful for all that America had given him. He also wanted to show that he, too, was an American who was willing to sacrifice for his country. He shared a very painful story about how an ex-girlfriend of his would have her friends give her a hard time about how she was dating an Arab (which is wrong because Iranians are considered Persians. In fact, they do not speak Arabic in Iran but Farsi.). He has been a valuable cultural resource here. He is just another example of how you cannot judge someone in our country by where they come from.

All Arabs (and, another FYI, most Arabs in the United States are Christians. They are Christians who have moved to the U.S. because they have been persecuted by the Muslims in their own country. My soccer coach when I was in high school was a Lebanese [Arab] Christian) are not terrorists. I know that statement is facile, but sometimes we need to be reminded of that. It is like saying that all Irishmen (which I am part) are terrorists (IRA) or Catholic (I am Protestant). . . .

We have three women in our battalion. It must be like living in the boy's locker room. All three are moms. Two of them are single mothers. We have one who has three kids and is a prison guard. She should have no trouble handling us. I had a nice conversation with our new female medic. She is a single mother who has left her three year old son at home with her mother. Say what you want about women in the military, but I will not say that they are making any less of a sacrifice than the men. She is needed to help take care of the Iraqi women we might encounter, and a mortar shell does not discriminate according to gender.

The ladies are pretty tough and live under the same conditions that we do. I am glad they are here. I am embarrassed though at how some of the guys treat them. The vast majority of our soldiers, especially those in our battalion, are gentlemen. I just get disappointed at what is written on the latrine walls. We have begun tasking people with cleaning them up. I am afraid that it will be a never ending job.

For those wives who might be concerned, the ladies sleep in a different tent, and there is no hanky-panky. Adultery is still punishable by UCMJ [Universal Code of Military Justice].

I spent quite a bit of time yesterday speaking with our soldiers. Their emotions are all over the map. The length of this deployment is beginning to hit them. . . .

We had an interesting thing happen last week. One of the ICDC (Iraqi Civil Defense Corps) soldiers brought his two year old son into work to meet some of the American soldiers. His son was dressed in a suit, complete with tie. The soldier went around thanking the soldiers for what they are doing and had his son wave a little American flag. His son also wanted to be held and kissed a few of our soldiers on the check. This little act of civility helped melt some hearts that had very little tolerance for the people.

I have made an observation of the two cultures of America and Iraq. Many Muslims in the Middle East believe ours is a culture of depravity and that Islam offers a better way. I used to think that there were some merits to their critique even if I disagreed with their solution. Now that I am here, while I still have many criticisms of my native culture, ours is by far more moral than the culture of the Middle East.

Multiculturalism begins with the implicit assumption that all world cultures have equal value. This . . . is a false assumption. This culture has many merits, but it also contains a massive amount of denial and repression. The way women are treated, the way property is not respected, they way others of different faiths and beliefs are treated leads to the conclusion that this culture is on the borderline of being nihilist.

While I may not agree with an atheist, I do not want to kill him. The best way to describe the difference is through the following truism. The West accepts the following statement that has emerged from its Judeo-Christian tradition, "Every human is my brother." In the Islamic world, the only statement that is true is, "Every Muslim is my brother."

Life over here should serve as a warning to those who seek to reduce America to tribal sub-groupings that have competing interests. We either believe that there are some truths that are self-evident, or we are clans competing for limited resources. . . .

Grace, Mercy, and Peace,
CH (CPT) Kevin Wainwright
Chaplain 1-113th FA BN

"Be strong and of good courage. Do not be afraid nor be dismayed; for the Lord your God is with you wherever you go."—Joshua 1:9

LCpl. Joe DePew, USMC, was nineteen years old when he wrote this letter.—FS

April 11, 2004

Hi Mom,

How are you? Damn, I miss you a lot. I can't stop thinking of you guys especially after they told us we are definitely over here for 14 months. Well, I'm going back to Fallujah on Wednesday. I hate it there. So much shit goes on there. They said it's like Vietnam all over again, it's true. I was there when that fire fight broke out, that was some messed up shit. 20 were injured and 12 were killed. This one kid lost half his leg, it was sick. His tendon or whatever was hanging from it. I didn't see it happen, but I saw him when he was getting carried to the 7 ton. But those fire fights scare the shit out of you. You never know if you're gonna get hit, I'm not telling you anything else, cause your gonna worry even more. But, before I came to Iraq, I was like "I'm going to war." I didn't think it actually would be this bad, you know, I'm not trying to sound like a bad ass, but I'm actually seeing some shit you see in the movies.

I'm telling you, Blackhawk Down is the way it is over here in Fallujah, Tikrit, and Baghdad. Around here they just shoot rockets at us from the next city. Everybody always says, "Oh I could easily kill someone or seeing someone all fucked up is tight." *Well it ain't!*

I hate seeing fellow Marines dead or missing parts of their body or a 1.62 round in their body. I can see why people that went to war don't like talking about that shit because it really bothers you a lot. I'm just telling you because I like talking to someone about it. Some people won't believe half the shit I'm saying but they aren't here.

Normally I wouldn't be going to Fallujah and stuff but I'm on the QRF. But anyway I really appreciate you sending me the packages.

This is a few things would like: Tang, DVDs (Missing in Action, Chuck Norris), if you can find them. Cigarettes, magazines, facial wipes, Gillette shaving cream, blades, stuff like that. Candy would be cool. . . .

How'd you like the pictures? Here in a few days I'm gonna send another camera and a recorded tape for you and the girls and Dad. I've been thinking about Dad a lot, I love him so much. It makes me feel so good knowing how much he appreciates what I'm doing and how proud he is of me. Don't get me wrong in any way, I think of you the same, but I don't talk to him nearly as much as I do anyone else and it makes me feel real bad. Just to let you know, you are the *BEST MOM* someone could ever have, just wanted to let you know that. I miss you a lot and love you very much, bye.

PFC DePew
(Fighting For My Family's Freedom)
Joe

LCpl. DePew, USMC, has been deployed in Iraq since February 2004 and is still there.—FS

CH (CPT) Kevin Wainwright
Chaplain 1-113th FA BN
April, 19 2004

Greetings from Iraq,

. . . We have been watching the news, and it appears back at home that nothing is going right. Columnists like Andy Rooney write disparaging articles about us, and it can be quite demoralizing at times. . . .

Life has been a challenge the last two weeks . . . nerves are starting to show the strain. We do have some soldiers that are hurting. We are not, however, in a state of panic, nor are we without hope. A good gauge of a unit's morale is how the worship services go. . . .

We had 200 worshippers for our 6AM Sunrise Service. Yesterday, we were so full in our morning worship that we could not fit any more folks in our room/chapel. The chain of command from the General on down attend worship. Remember, this is not mandatory. . . .

While we cannot wait to come home, we are not the bitter, disgruntled soldiers that some either want or hope us to be. We are serving just like our fathers and grandfathers did before us. We are holding ourselves accountable for the promises we have made, and we do this because we are men (and women), not boys and girls.

God Bless,Grace, Mercy, and Peace,

CH (CPT) Kevin WainwrightChaplain 1-113th FA BN

"Be strong and of good courage. Do not be afraid nor be dismayed; for the Lord your God is with you wherever you go."—Joshua 1:9

May 22, 2004

Mr. Schaeffer:

I am [sending you my letters]. Unfortunately some of the letters leave out the dangerous stuff, like being shot at, because they go to my mom and my wife.

Sincerely,
Richard W. Spiegel
Major, U.S. Army Public Affairs Officer
13th Corps Support Command & Logistic Support Area
Anaconda Balad, Iraq
Deployed March 7, 2004, to Ongoing. Contact by return e-mail to Iraq, no phone. . .

April 11, 2004—Balad, Iraq

Dear Family and Friends,

How ironic that I am writing you on Easter from the land where many of our biblical stories are known to have taken place. . . . Unfortunately rather than being exited about the coming of Easter we are caught up in the turmoil surrounding the Arbe'en, a Muslim religious holiday that involves a pilgrimage from the surrounding lands to the town of Karbala.

In ancient times a Muslim Imam was besieged and called for help to the people of the surrounding lands (including what is now Iran), they said they would come but refused when the going got rough. The pilgrimage is the symbolic making up of the journey to come to the Imam's aid. Some flail themselves out of guilt.

You may have read or heard in the press that this festival is the reason for the heightened violence and tension or that there is a Shi'a uprising but this is not the case. Those that oppose us are nothing more than terrorists and criminals that seek to deny the vast majority of Iraqis the freedom and stability they deserve.

There has been an upsurge in violence but again, despite what you see in the media, I can assure you we are in firm control. Because things have been a little "hotter" life has changed a little here at LSA Anaconda. We do not step outdoors without our helmets and body armor which makes for some interesting times. Imagine placing 25-30 lbs of gear on just to go to the shower or bathroom trailers. Perhaps you would like to be the preacher looking out on over 200 soldiers, dressed for success and armed to the teeth, not your typical Easter Sunrise congregation (by the way the Chaplain wears everything but the weapon—talk about sweating on the pulpit!).

Lately I have been quite busy late into the evening with the unfortunate duty of preparing press releases on our fallen and wounded soldiers; I have done over 15 in the last 7 days as we have soldiers all over Iraq and not just here in Balad. My fellow PAOs [public affaires officers] in the maneuver divisions have it much worse. I haven't been out the gates in over a week but we expect some normalcy to resume in a few days.

My office is a little short staffed until the end of the month so I am doing more editing and writing than I had planned. This week we released a story I did with my senior sergeant on a fallen soldier memorial service. . . .

Rich
Richard W. Spiegel
Major, U.S. Army Public Affairs Officer
13th Corps Support Command & Logistic Support Area
Anaconda, Balad, Iraq

Major Richard W. Spiegel, U.S. Army, is still in Iraq.—FS

May 22, 2004

Frank,

You don't remember me I'm sure, but I'm the cheap bastard that checks out your books from the library and buys a used version on Amazon.com.

My son's name is Lt. JG William Joseph Fiack, U.S. Navy, SEAL Team II, deployed somewhere around Mosul. He's been there since the first part of April.

Paul Fiack

Easter Sunday, April 11, 2004

Dad,

This morning the Easter bunny brought me a basket of golden eggs, the 40mm type.

The chow hall is the best I've seen, no brownie care packages. Nice facilities for a hot zone. We're busy.

Will
Lt. JG William Joseph Fiack, U.S. Navy, SEAL Team II

––––––––––

April 11, 2004

Dad,

The news on how those detainees were treated sure had a "knee jerk" reaction. A lot of new rules on how we can treat POWs, obviously— not that there is anything to worry about with us, we consider ourselves professionals.

Will
Lt. JG William Joseph Fiack, U.S. Navy, SEAL Team II

Lt. JG William Joseph Fiack is still in Baghdad and still with Navy Seal Team II. We will meet him again a little later in this book.—FS

––––––––––

CH (CPT) Kevin Wainwright
Chaplain 1-113th FA BN
April 24, 2004

Greetings from Iraq,

. . . . What follows in this "dispatch" is a response to an article by

Andy Rooney. . . . It is rather amazing to me that this little piece slipped by the editorial staff at CBS. . . .

OUR SOLDIERS IN IRAQ AREN'T HEROES
April, 12 2004
by ANDY ROONEY

Most of the reporting from Iraq is about death and destruction. We don't learn much about what our soldiers in Iraq are thinking or doing. There's no Ernie Pyle to tell us, and, if there were, the military would make it difficult or impossible for him to let us know.

It would be interesting to have a reporter ask a group of our soldiers in Iraq to answer five questions and see the results:

1. Do you think your country did the right thing sending you into Iraq?

2. Are you doing what America set out to do to make Iraq a democracy, or have we failed so badly that we should pack up and get out before more of you are killed?

3. Do the orders you get handed down from one headquarters to another, all far removed from the fighting, seem sensible, or do you think our highest command is out of touch with the reality of your situation?

4. If you could have a medal or a trip home, which would you take?

5. Are you encouraged by all the talk back home about how brave you are and how everyone supports you?

Treating soldiers fighting their war as brave heroes is an old civilian trick designed to keep the soldiers at it. But you can be sure our soldiers in Iraq are not all brave heroes gladly risking their lives for us sitting comfortably back here at home. Our soldiers in Iraq are people, young men and women, and they behave like people—sometimes good and sometimes bad, sometimes brave, sometimes fearful. It's disingenuous of the rest of us to encourage them to fight this war by idolizing them.

We pin medals on their chests to keep them going. We speak of them as if they volunteered to risk their lives to save ours, but there isn't much voluntary about what most of them have done. A relatively small number are professional soldiers. During the last few years, when millions of jobs disappeared, many young people, desperate for some income, enlisted in the Army. About 40 percent of our soldiers in Iraq enlisted in the National Guard or the Army Reserve to pick up some extra money and never thought they'd be called on to fight. They want to come home.

One indication that not all soldiers in Iraq are happy warriors is the report recently released by the Army showing that 23 of them committed suicide there last year. This is a dismaying figure. If 22 young men and one woman killed themselves because they couldn't take it, think how many more are desperately unhappy but unwilling to die.

We must support our soldiers in Iraq because it's our fault they're risking their lives there. However, we should not bestow the mantle of heroism on all of them for simply being where we sent them. Most are victims, not heroes. . . .

This is my response:

Dear Mr. Rooney . . . I can only assume. . . . that you do not think me or any other soldier serving in Iraq, especially guardsmen, as real, professional, military men and women. This is unfortunate for us. . . . You have come to think of our nation's military as nothing more than a . . . corps that our politicians have purchased through economic manipulation and educational incentives.

You call us victims, thereby robbing us of any accountability and responsibility for our actions. You make it sound as if we were conscripted to fight this battle.

Every person who is serving in our military has made a commitment of their own free will. We were not drafted. I believe your intention is noble when you say we are victims, for victims must be rescued from the big and bad enemy called the state. However, you make us powerless when you label us as victims. A victim can only be freed and has no say in his or her future, and a victim has had a little of his humanity taken away. While we may be suffering on our way to our own personal Golgotha, I can assure you that while we may go with fear in our heart, we do go willingly.

It has been the practice of late to parade on the news scene after scene of disgruntled military personnel and their families. This is fine, because they do exist. What we are missing is the other side of the story. You fail to present the single mother who has left her son in the care of her mother so that she can be over here. She misses her boy, and she is missing her chance to start college this year, but she would not think about abandoning her post as a medic because she is a professional. . . .

I will respond to your five questions. Keep in mind that they are a response, not "the" response. I claim to speak only for myself.

1. What I think about my civilian chain of command's decision to send me to Iraq does not make any difference. The military remains one of the few places where one cannot opt out of one's commitment when the terms of fulfillment become difficult. I do not remember in my oath that I said that I will protect and defend the constitution when I feel like it. . . .

2. I believe that we cannot make anyone be anything. I do not think we can successfully force a government on anyone. I do believe that we can aid a nation in setting up the conditions for democracy to take root. . . . I believe that democracy is the fruit of the tree of freedom. Iraqis have never known what it was like to be

free. I would also argue that this tree is watered by the blessings of God. While I know in some circles that the invocation of manifest destiny is blasphemy, I still believe that our nation has a responsibility to help other peoples experience freedom. . . .

3. When has the highest command ever been in touch with the reality of my situation? Every single military book, journal, or article has mentioned the "disconnect" between the soldier on the ground and the general in command. . . . This question is just plain silly. . . .

4. I spent my four years at West Point reading about how too many of our graduates hunted for medals. We heard story after story of how lieutenants were fragged because they wanted glory above the safety of their soldiers. . . . Frankly, I would worry about any soldier who said that he would prefer a medal to a trip home to his family. In fact, I would be tempted to take his weapon away from him. . . . Being a hero does not mean that you have to be stupid. If we conducted a survey, I doubt that a single Medal of Honor recipient woke up the morning of event and said that it was his goal to win a medal that day. What we do want to do as soldiers is to perform with courage and resolve, not because we want medals, but because we do not want to let our buddies down.

5. . . . Am I encouraged when a fifth grade class writes telling our soldiers that they are thankful for our service and how proud of us they are? Am I encouraged when our employers assure [us reservists] that we will have our jobs waiting for us when we return home? Why, yes, I am.

. . . As far as the motivations for service, you seem fairly eager to make a generalization that all of us in the National Guard only joined up because of the money and never thought we would go to war. [What of the] young person who signed up for the service out of a desire to serve her nation and give something back to the country that had given her so much? [There is the] appeal that the military might actually make us less selfish, more mature, and better people. [What of the] desire for camaraderie and equality?

Your article. . . . sparked a lively debate amongst my fellow soldiers, and we unanimously concluded that we were glad to live in a country where you are free to express your opinion, no matter how misguided it might be. It is my hope that your news organization will have the courage to come out to visit us and hear our story. You will find that you are right about one thing—we can be good and bad. We are normal people, not heroes.

We are proud to serve our country, we miss our families, and we cannot wait to return home. We have our tough days and our proud days, but most of all we are thankful that we have each other. We are thankful that, when we look into each other's faces, be they black or white, male or female, Christian, Jew, or Muslim, that we have each other. We do not want to serve with heroes, we want to serve with real people . . . who are proud of who we are and where we come from. . . .

Grace, Mercy, and Peace,
CH (CPT) Kevin Wainwright
Chaplain 1-113th FA BN

"Be strong and of good courage. Do not be afraid nor be dismayed; for the Lord your God is with you wherever you go."—Joshua 1:9

Letters written to LCpl. David K. Sandifer's wife, Katie, while he was serving in Iraq. We met David in his boot camp letters earlier in this book.—FS

April 21, 2004

My squad got shot at for the first time last night, but nobody was hurt. We were putting up concertina wire and an RPG [rocket-propelled grenade] flew over our heads and slammed into something behind us. It was quite a rush, but I was mad that we couldn't see who shot it.

We got shot at again today, but the impacts weren't very close and we didn't see who shot those either. If we did, they'd be dead.

The place we're staying at has been nicknamed "Camp Incoming" because of all the mortar rounds that hit. Don't worry, there haven't been that many since we got here. Let's just say I've listened to more war stories than I've told.

My platoon has earned a couple of purple hearts, but nothing really bad. . . . there are 2 KIA [killed in action] and yes, I knew them both. One of them was at SOI with me and came to our room all the time back at Horno. . . . The other played a lot of Skipbo with us back in Kuwait.

I'm not really scared, Babe, except that I hate to think of how it would be for you to deal with if I got hurt. I don't know how I could handle it if anything happened to you, so I can imagine what it must be like. . . .

LCpl. David K. Sandifer, USMC

April, 24 2004

Living here is like living at a landfill, only with more flies and more nasty dogs. And with a permanent sound track of Arabic wailing from one of the eight mosques I can see from our compound. Those things never shut up.

We all want to break in and play "American Baddass" by Kid Rock loud enough for all . . . to hear. I'm tempted to feel sorry for these people, but I can never quite see them without remembering the wives of the two Marines we've lost (yes, they were both married, one with a baby due in July) and the families of the four American contractors that were burned, hacked to pieces and hung from a bridge by a cheering mob of 300+ people. I've been to that bridge, and it's all too real for me to truly feel pity.

Only God's grace could extend to people like this, so when I refrain from treating these people like I want to, I know it's His mercy and not mine. I don't have pity for these people, but God does. After all, I'm as responsible for the gruesome death of Christ as much as they are for those Marines and contractors, and His mercy covers me. You can pray that I won't ever forget that. . . .

LCpl. David K. Sandifer, USMC

May 15, 2004

Another guy that I knew was killed. . . . He slept a few racks down from me in both boot camp and SOI. He was in a Humvee that got hit by an IED. Every time somebody I know gets killed, I think about the last time I saw them. I used to see [him] at the armory back at Horno when the Battalion was drawing weapons for an OP. He was a tall, lanky guy that was hard to miss. . . . His memorial service was today. . . . I found out from another friend of mine from SOI.

I'd rather not lose another friend over here. It sounds heroic to "die for your country" and all that, but there is no glamour in a KIA. It breaks my heart that a 19-year-old kid had his life taken in a filthy place like this. We all know the risk we take by choosing to fight, but it still hurts to send home shortened lives in wooden boxes because a chickenshit Jihadist planted a bomb on the side of the road and basically got away with murder. . . .

I think there are two real reasons I'll keep fighting: to honor the men whose lives were taken away, and to preserve the lives of those who are still alive and continuing the mission, regardless of what it is. . . .

LCpl. David K. Sandifer, USMC

LCpl. David K. Sandifer is now twenty-two years old and in Fallujah, Iraq, with the 1st Marine Division. He is supposed to be coming home on October 1, 2004, though that might change. He has been in Iraq since mid March 2004. Katie and David were married in a small civil ceremony January 2, 2004, but are waiting to have a church wedding with all their friends when David gets home, "whenever that is," as Katie said.—FS

CH (CPT) Kevin Wainwright
Chaplain 1-113th FA BN
April 28, 2004

Read the reports coming out of Fallujah this morning. It appears that negotiations are over. I know it does not sound very chaplain-like, but it is about time that we get the assault underway. Both Marines and Soldiers have been taking casualties from insurgents that are hiding in shrines and mosques. While we do not want to touch holy sites, the enemy leaves us no choice. The truth of the matter is that most of the fighters lack the support of the local populace. The people in Najaf and Fallujah are themselves hostages at the mercy of the thugs with the weapons. One paper reported that an underground militia group within Najaf had already killed eight members of Sadr's militia. The residents cannot stand them, for they are lawless and ruthless, not a good combination.

Many in Fallujah are coming from Saudi Arabia, Chechnya, Pakistan, and other Islamic countries. In one case they had ascended a minaret and were sniping at Marines. They forced the Marines to level the minaret, something they were loath to do. Part of the problem over here is the Arab news agency, Al-Jazeera. They call themselves a newsgroup, but they function more like the propaganda wing [of] Al-Qaeda and the other fanatics. Most of the Arab world gets their "news" from their station. They are so unprofessional that they reported that Marines were indiscriminately shooting children. Of all the armies throughout history that have conquered this region of the world, our military has bent over backwards to ensure the safety and dignity of the inhabitants. We are moving old shot-up hulks of military equipment from beside the road because we do not want the Iraqis to feel any shame. We are drilling wells for the small communities so the women do not have to walk miles to get water from an irrigation canal filled with pollutants, waste, and carcinogens. We are busily painting over any sign or mark that shows we are here. Al-Jazeera broadcasts nothing but lies. I would like to see what a spare tomahawk missile would do to their broadcasting dish.

Grace, Mercy, and Peace,
CH (CPT) Kevin Wainwright
Chaplain 1-113th FA BN

"Be strong and of good courage. Do not be afraid nor be dismayed; for the Lord your God is with you wherever you go."—Joshua 1:9

CH (CPT) Kevin Wainwright
Chaplain 1-113th FA BN
May 4, 2004

I keep thinking of the guys who are pulling rear detachment duties. These are the soldiers who are at our home armories supporting the families and other soldiers in North Carolina.

Theirs is a thankless job. I fear that all they receive each and every day are problems to solve and complaints to field. I wonder if they are getting any compliments. We could not do what we do in Iraq without them. . . .

Lately, the treatment of Iraqi prisoners has been a hot topic in the news. I want everyone to know that our treatment of prisoners in our base has been humane, professional, and respectful, which is what our nation expects out of its military. One of my duties as the chaplain is to inspect our detention center and to make spot checks concerning prisoner treatment. I take this responsibility seriously. I remember studying the My Lai massacre at West Point and hearing that no chaplain was present in the particular battalion that committed the atrocities. This memory proved to be so powerful that it is probably one of the reasons that I am a chaplain today. Our soldiers know that I will back them up with all of my heart, mind, and soul, but, if they abuse the Iraqis, they will hear about it from me. All of the chaplains in the brigade make sure that we are keeping as much of our humanity as we can. I think what happens is that, as the deployment drags on, we can tend to confuse the enemy with the innocent Iraqi people. In our messages, our visits, our counseling, and our prayers, the chaplains make sure we do not let them forget that all the people here, regardless of ethnicity or belief, are God's children. We do not want our soldiers to hesitate when they are in harm's way, but we also do not want them to lose their integrity by acting on pure emotion.

The biggest moral struggle that most of our soldiers have is that they are frustrated by the tactics of a very cowardly and sinister enemy. The challenge for soldiers is to still meet and defeat the enemy while not resigning ourselves to use the morally depraved techniques of those who attack us. The anti-coalition forces do not have a problem detonating a roadside bomb that kills innocent civilians in the process. They have accepted this collateral damage as a satisfactory consequence of their resistance to making Iraq free. The final reason why soldiers must fight and behave with dignity is that we will have to redeploy home. Casualties do not stop once the bullets cease to fly. We will have to look our children, our spouses, and our communities in the face and say that we acquitted ourselves in a way that would make them proud.

If we do not adhere to high standards for behavior, it will be increasingly difficult to reintegrate back into society. The chaplains are here to ensure that the soldiers, when faced with combat stress, have a constructive way in which to deal with it. We are here to make sure prisoners, noncombatants, and our fellow soldiers are treated like human beings. One of the most telling comments came from one of our chaplains who is a Viet Nam veteran. He did not see his chaplain very often, if at all, and he said he wished that he had received the support that our brigade was receiving today. . . . Several rumors have been circulating about when we will redeploy. I think that I have heard that we will be back by before Christmas, some have even said we are coming back in August so we can redeploy to Afghanistan. All of these are untrue. We still do not know when we will be back. I tell soldiers that the best thing they can do is prepare to be here at least a year, and if we are home before this it will be a pleasant surprise. I also remind them that we need to focus on our mission and our fellow soldiers who are temporary family. We need to do this so we can all go home. My last thought concerns the stories we hear about our children. Heather has told me how Joshua now prompts her to pray for daddy before bedtime.

Many of my buddies have shared similar stories. We all agree that this is one of the most blessed gifts we could receive. We often think about how we need to pray for our children, but it was not until this deployment until I realized how much I need the prayers of my son. The "boy" prays that his daddy and all of the soldiers in Iraq will be safe and will return home. May God answer his prayers.

We love you all.

Grace, Mercy, and Peace,
Chaiplain 1-113th FA BN (CPT) Kevin Wainwright

We met Lt. JG William Joseph Fiack, U.S. Navy, SEAL Team II, several pages ago. Here is another letter to his father.—FS

May 4, 2004

Dad, your advice is in synch with all of the other combat veterans, many from Vietnam. . . . "When you land in country, it is tactical. Period. Never get complacent." One of my buddies . . . said the same on Sat. night: "Don't trust anybody, watch your choke points in vehicle convoys, and always be locked and cocked." I don't have to tell you all the different feelings you have going into a war zone. Defining moments come with new chapters. It is the unknown/unpredictable that fuels our breed. I am so proud to be a part of the fighter class that you were once a part of. . . . I see and hear a lot of men and women in the service who are complaining about the war and questioning the President's decisions [and his] integrity. I always think of what you once said: "It's not for you to ask for what or why, but only to do or die."

I signed those six articles of the code of conduct the day I joined the Navy; the first code stating "I am an American fighting in the forces that serve and protect my country and our way of life. I am prepared to give my life in their defense." I think the people of our community are the most secure with this belief because we know that everything about [our] country is worth living for. It is serving a call to duty. Yes, we have our internal problems but they pale in comparison to other countries not so fortunate. I read in the *Armed Forces Officer* the other night: "All of our senses leave an imprint or traces of themselves on our minds; in other words, every experience we have touches the circumference of our daily lives and shapes us as a person."

I couldn't be more prepared. . . . Every guy who hasn't been to war has no idea what it's going to be like, and all of their questions and answers prove it with their ambiguity. The only thing left to do is go.

It's go-time, Dad.

Will

Lt. JG William Joseph Fiack, U.S. Navy, SEAL Team II

Lt. JG William Joseph Fiack was still in Baghdad as of June 13, 2004.—FS

We first met Richard W. Spiegel, Major, U.S. Army Public Affairs Officer several pages ago.—FS

Balad, Iraq
21 May 2004

Dear Family and Friends,

. . . . The Abu Gareib scandal is on our minds here as I'm sure it is on many of yours. The investigation is ongoing and the first court proceedings were in Baghdad this week, it's important that, regardless of the outcome, the Iraqi people understand how a fair, just and democratic criminal justice system works. One misconception that I must clear up: one of the first things we teach a soldier in basic training, and reinforce every year, is the Geneva Convention and the laws of war. Soldiers also learn very early that illegal and immoral orders are NOT to be obeyed; perhaps we have also all forgotten that ignorance of the law is not a recognized defense.

Please remember that the vast majority of soldiers are working everyday, in difficult and dangerous conditions, often under fire, to bring hope to this troubled country. Their spirit will not be diminished by the acts of a few. I read a great article the other day in one of my daily media sweeps. The author was making the point that his media colleagues only reported death, scandal and misconduct, he told the untold story of a Marine Captain, recently awarded the Navy Cross. His unit was ambushed on in Iraq with enemy fighters entrenched on the side of the road, according to the citation; the Captain drove his humvee straight into enemy fire and dismounted, jumping into the trench with, "his rifle, a pistol and 228 years of Marine Corps pride." These are the Soldiers, Sailors, Airmn and Marines that belong in the headlines.

The civil affairs effort in the Balad area continued here last week as we took our doctors and a dentist into one of the local villages for a short medical and dental clinic.

Rich
Richard W. Spiegel
Major, U.S. Army Public Affairs Officer
13th Corps Support Command & Logistic
Support Area Anaconda Balad, Iraq

Major Richard W. Spiegel, U.S. Army, is still in Iraq.—FS

37

Major John Thomas, USAF, was thirty-eight when he wrote these letters. He is married to Stephanie. They have five children, ages ten to two. He has been in Iraq since March 29, 2004.—FS

May 23, 2004

Mr. Schaeffer,

My sister-in-law sent me a note that said you were looking for emails home. I'm assigned to the Coalition Provisional Authority in Strategic Communication—(tasked in common parlance with "winning the hearts and minds . . . ") So, I don't have the perspective of the front lines. We do get mortars here periodically and I have gone outside the "Green Zone" compound—once to Abu Ghraib. I've attached some emails that span a few different topics. There's also one pasted below about a letter that I sent to NPR that they then read in part on the air.

John
Major John J. Thomas, USAF
Office of Strategic Communications

Here is my response to an NPR report in May of 2004: "There Is

Overwhelming Support For The Iraq War Among U.S. Military Personnel, But For More Complicated Reasons Than One Might Think." NPR's Jeff Brady reports. . . .

Dear NPR:

Of course there are countless reasons why service members serve, and how we respond to the wars we are sent to and about which we are not consulted. I've had conversations about the morality of this and other wars with many of my fellow service members before and during my current service here in Baghdad. But Jeff Brady's report on why military people support the war was unfortunately condescending because it presumes the negative: his unstated premise is how can soldiers support such an unethical war—how can we be so gullible. His report suggested service members are "carefully" trained how to think; that we are nothing but brainwashed products of the military machine, unable to think for ourselves.

Give our soldiers credit. Don't try to psychoanalyze away our reasons for serving. Military people are diverse and represent a wide range of political views about this war and every other issue. If we choose to serve our country in peacetime and in war, don't make patronizing excuses for our behavior. As much as you'd commend environmentalists or artists or teachers for their dedication to their chosen courses in life respect service members for their dedication and patriotism. We make the choice to serve. Respect that for what it is. We do not need excuses for our service.

Major John J. Thomas, USAF
Office of Strategic Communications

This next letter from John was in response to a friend's questions about the morality of military service.—FS

From: Thomas John J Maj AFPC/PA
Sent: Monday, November 10, 2003 9:54 AM
To: Kenneth Thomas

Kenneth, you raise interesting points. Here's my thoughts, off the top of my head.

None of us can be sure if we understand, on the grand scale, what actions are right—like our country going to war. We can trust and pray that our leaders are acting ethically. But even they have to make decisions without omniscience, with their human intellect and, we hope, by also asking God's guidance.

So we are left, all of us, not just those in the military, to act as best we can to do good given the circumstances we are put in. Just like anything else, in the military it is more a series of decisions. Most people don't act by reassessing which road they are traveling, but by assessing which turn to take next. We don't question our last step as much as decide which next step to take. You find yourself in a situation and are faced with acting within the situation. You can't hit the reset button to start over. So you wake up each day and do your job.

It goes something like this, I think: Is it right to defend freedom? Then we raise our hands and swear to do so by joining the military. And at that point we also pledge to follow "the President of the United States and those appointed above us." Is it right to go to war? No one is asking us. We follow the decisions of the elected officials, who represent the will and wisdom of the American people. What they ask us to do is fight that war— morally, without malice, without giving in to evil. We are asked to follow the "law of armed conflict" by not shooting at medical operations and by not targeting civilians, and such. We conduct the war and try to spare lives by ending it quickly.

So we get orders to go to Iraq, and we go. The right thing is to honor our oaths. The right thing to do is to make the part of the conflict we touch as good as we can. To, with prayer, bring good to an evil situation; to cradle and feed the orphans; to destroy those who are given to evil; to tend the wounds of an enemy soldier; to smile at a group of scared civilians; to be a Good Samaritan. What we do even unto the "least of these . . . "

When you're someplace across the world, you don't feel you're a world away. It becomes your daily life and you act just as you might if you were back home and saw someone with a flat tire and stopped to help. Or if someone were trying to kill your neighbor and you had the means to stop them. You don't think every minute about the grand scale of things. You do what you can to be good where you are.

That's not so much courage, that's focusing on doing what you are there to do. You've given your oath. If you weren't doing it someone else would be and you'd rather be there trying to do good than have someone else there who might not. The courage comes when having to leave your family at the airport. The rest is just trying your best to get through the days until you are with them again.

Major John J. Thomas, USAF
Office of Strategic Communications

An email from John to a high school friend.—FS

Thu, 29 Apr 2004 20:13:32 +0400

David,

. . . . We have a credibility problem, for certain. We've so far lost the information war. (And of course that's what I'm here doing!) My boss here is a Brit. . . . What a resume! Perhaps the most interesting thing he told me is about Northern Ireland. He graciously says that the

Brits took 30 years to figure these things out and the U.S. is not there yet (God forbid 30 years in Iraq). But what they finally did among other things in N Ireland was to have their troops patrol without body armor, without tanks . . . nothing. . . .

The whole situation calmed down. Look at Basra compared to Falluja and Ramadi and Najaf . . . the Brits control Basra. It is far more peaceful. Look at Israel. I think you are right. Violence breeds enemies, when it's misapplied. We need to fight some of them, but we're indiscriminant. I think we learned the wrong lesson from Vietnam: that we should let the military always use overwhelming force, that if we unshackle the military and let them fight the wars we can beat anyone. Instead, we should remember larger issues of national policy. . . . There is not enough strategic thinking going on.

What all this says is that I think that things will work out. We're learning fast. But it's more painful and [causes] more loss of life than we should be inflicting or suffering. We also seem to want to pick the leaders and install puppets. Not wise. In America we tolerate robust debate. Here we want to handpick people to be our lackeys. . . .

Will Iraq be "stable" ? Depends. How much "instability" can we tolerate? Will we let them find their own way? If we do, they will be our allies. If we don't they will resent us forever.

The good news is that for political reasons we're turning things over 30 June. Thank Goodness. That's only going to lead to a "mostly sovereign" Iraq, but it's a great start. Do I think we're going to be evacuating like we did from Saigon? Doubtful. There really aren't that many people who want us dead, or even out of here. We just have to stop being patronizing.

These people thought the U.S. meant jobs, money, a chicken in every pot and safety. Well the terrorists are making it so that we can't even spend the 18.6 billion to get the jobs started. They are smarter than we are. So the people resent us for both not bringing jobs and for no security. Otherwise things would be great. But that's a significant "otherwise."

Kill all the terrorists? Unlikely. Kill one, two more hate you. That's what we've done wrong in responding to this. But there's still a lot going right here. The news only covers the bad stuff, well, not only, but that's what TV covers. This will work, if we can figure out Fallujah. If we get it right there, we have figured it out. If not, it will be a while. And there are smart Iraqis counseling us. And we listen, mostly. It should work.

But we need to let the Iraqis govern themselves and not try to set up a little America. They are not Americans. Some would favor a dictator who makes the trains run on time rather than some concept called "freedom" that doesn't let them be safe enough to leave their houses. . . .

Like I said to Col Tunnicliffe (my Brit boss) they've had a lot more practice with this Empire thing than we. He agreed.

By the way, I don't agree with your professor smugly saying I told you so. This war was not a mistake, although we've made mistakes fighting it. His is a nice satisfied stance for people to take. . . . The question is what now. What to do about the future?

People who point to the past, as if it makes a difference, are not helpful, you're right, either in an academic sense, or practically. Point is, we're here. What are we going to do about it to make it work for the Iraqis? . . .

And it continues. . . .

John
Major John J. Thomas, USAF
Office of Strategic Communications

This e-mail was sent to John's youngest sister Kristy, who was worried that CBS should not be showing pictures of abused Iraqi prisoners.—FS

Subject: RE: CBS To Show U.S. Mistreating Iraqi Prisoners

Date: Thu, 29 Apr 2004 08:23:57 +0400
Thread-Topic: CBS To Show U.S. Mistreating Iraqi Prisoners
From: "Thomas, John J. (O-4)
To: Kristy Thomas

Kristy,

This is not "aiding and abetting the enemy." It's a crime and it needs to be punished and stopped immediately. We should never cover-up what we do wrong. We should broadcast and punish people.

Let your friends who want to support the military know that we don't close ranks and protect criminals. We punish them. And we should not cover up when they [commit crimes], we should trumpet to the world that we will not tolerate criminals among us.

I'm not directing this at you. I'm just worried that there are people who would advocate 60 Minutes NOT broadcast this [program showing pictures of Iraqi prisoners being abused by American soldiers].

Hope your day is going well,
John
Major John J. Thomas, USAF
Office of Strategic Communications

John is still in Iraq and now working for the Coalition Provisional Authority on loan from the USAF. He should be coming home in July 2004.—FS

May 24, 2004

Dear Mr. Schaeffer,

My son, LCpl. Scott Dunnicliff is presently serving in the western Al

Anbar region of Iraq with the 2nd Marine Div. Small Craft Co. that has attached to the 1st MEF.

You recently wrote an article about his roommate from LeJeune who was injured by a landmine in April. My son, Scott, and Josh Davey were roommates for almost a year. Scott will not say much about the accident but I do know that he was there. His e-mails and notes are very short and usually deal with making sure everything is OK at home.

I was called a week ago by a friend who had read a short message written by my son to a Mom, Becky Mizener. Her son, Jesse Mizener (Army), was killed in Baghdad on Jan. 7, 2004 when a mortar hit his barracks. She had sent my son a care package with a survey of things he might need. He wrote this message:

"Please pray for my Mom and Dad since I know they know it is dangerous here and they worry. Pray that they won't worry or be afraid for me."

Scott's messages are usually short since he won't share what he is doing. We received a thank you card from him a few weeks ago.

"Thank you for helping me weather the storms of life. . . . Love, Scott"

Another letter:

". . . . I am still at Al Asad but will be heading back to the field soon. . . . I can't wait to come home and sleep in my own bed. . . . It will have been 2 years since I went camping with you. . . . It's hard to believe that Sarah is almost finished with her Sophomore year in High School. I remember when I started my Junior year. . . . It's pretty amazing that I came from there to where I am now. . . . "

My son is a man of few words and won't say anything about combat because he doesn't want us to worry. He carries the SAW [machine gun] for his team and I'm afraid that he has had to use it. I pray that God will protect him physically and spiritually as well as emotionally. He does not want to come back a SECOND GENERATION VIETNAM VET!

I know this is not much but his few words mean the world to me.

Sincerely,
Penny Dunnicliff

Cpl. Joshua A. Mandel USMC 1st LAR Bn H&S Co is an intelligence specialist. He was deployed to Iraq February 19, 2004. Josh was twenty-six when he wrote this. He graduated from law school December 2003 and is also a city councilman in Lyndhurst, Ohio.—FS

May 7, 2004

Dear Mom & Dad,

Word has reached us about some soldiers who are in trouble for allegedly abusing war prisoners. I don't know the details of the situation, but from what we've heard, it's pretty ugly and all over the news. I wanted to tell you a story about a night in the desert a few weeks ago that you won't see in the news, but is more representative of what's going on over here.

Due to operational security constraints, I can't go into great detail in this story, but I think you'll get the picture.

In the course of my unit's operations, it's very common that suspected bad guys are captured and detained for interrogation. I'm sure the media is making interrogations out to be bad or wrong, but they are not. Interrogations are a necessary tool to extract intelligence that helps us destroy the enemy and protect Americans from terrorism.

Sometimes we have a roofed facility in which detainees are held and interrogated, but if we are on the move, often times they are placed in whatever temporary detainee area we can create.

One night last month, we were stopped in the desert outside of Fallujah. We had three detainees under our control that were captured in the act of [attacking] Marines. Because we were in the open without any facilities around, the detainees were temporarily being held on a patch of desert closed off by concertina wire. [But for] the wire and guards watching them, they were out under the stars just like all of our Marines.

Around 3:00 a.m., the wind started blowing hard and a sandstorm hit our position. As Marines covered themselves with their sleeping bags, the sky opened up and the flying sand was joined by a downpour of rain. Most of the Marines hopped into vehicles to get some cover.

In the back of a truck, which was the closest vehicle to the detainees, four Marines were trying to stay dry and get some sleep. The lieutenant who was in charge of providing security for the detainees approached this truck and opened up the back hatch. He ordered the Marines out of the truck and told them that they couldn't stay in there. The Marines asked why and he explained to them that he had to put the detainees in the back of the truck to protect them from the rain and sand.

Word of this spread very quickly and everyone was livid. We couldn't believe that our Marines were being kicked into the sandstorm/rainstorm so these three detainees, who were caught trying to kill Marines, could stay dry. The next day I was still angry and everyone was still talking about what had happened that night. Later in the day, after having time to cool down and think about the situation, I switched from being angry to being proud.

Who else, other than Americans, would kick their own men into a storm so their enemy could sleep in peace? Who else, other than Americans, feel so strongly about laws and rights that they would go to such extremes to protect captured terrorists during a war on terrorism?

When these guys are under our control, they eat better than they do when not in captivity, receive medical attention that they would never otherwise receive, and are treated . . . . professionally.

I assume whatever happened with the alleged prisoner abuse is leading headlines back home, but I wanted to share this story with you. . . . What I've described in this letter is indicative of how my unit operates, and I would venture to guess that it's representative of the other ninety-nine percent of detainee handling throughout Iraq.

My spirits remain high, my body's holding up, and all's well. . . . I hope the same is the case with everyone back home. I love you and miss you lots.

Your son,
Josh

Cpl. Joshua A. Mandel USMC 1st LAR Bn H&S Co is scheduled to return to the U.S. in mid October 2004.—FS

HOMECOMING

38

More from the Lussi family, whose first letters appear in the deployment and Afghan combat sections of this book and who sent their father and three sons to serve.—FS

May 8, 2004

Hi Frank,

Here's the "update" letter you requested from me. Sorry again for the delay. It's just been a crazy week, busy and hectic. It's much quieter now; all but Matt and Bethany have left.

What a wild and crazy two weeks it has been since April 24th, 2004. Jeremy (our middle son, age 22, Army/10th Mountain Division) arrived back in the states on April 19th from a ten-month deployment to Afghanistan. He was granted early leave so he could see his Dad (Navy Chaplain, presently with 3rd Battalion, 6th Marines) and younger brother, Aaron (age 19, USMC, 3rd Battalion, 6th Marines—yep, they are in the same battalion!) before they deploy for six months to Afghanistan.

What a glorious reunion we had at the airport on April 24th! Most everyone was crying we were so happy to see Jeremy. He was stunned because he did not know we were all going to be there to pick him up: Signs, balloons, whooping and hollering, the whole nine yards! It was wonderful. I was so thankful to God he was home, alive and unharmed.

We spent the next day celebrating Grandmamma and Grand-daddy Lussi's 50th Wedding Anniversary. We were all there—Matthew, the oldest at 24, Jeremy, Aaron, Bethany, age 11, Mom (that's me), and Dad, Emory.

We decided later, after talking to Jeremy, to forego our traveling plans to see other relatives, and head home to Hubert, North Carolina and stay put and just enjoy each other. We usually run ourselves ragged trying to see relatives, but decided that sometimes one has to do what one has to do. Jeremy needed some time to transition from being in Afghanistan. It was the right decision. We spent the remainder of Jeremy's leave just hanging out, no specific schedule from day to day.

Because Emory and Aaron were leaving for Afghanistan soon, there were lots of last minute things that needed to be done: things around the house and in the yard, packing, calling friends and relatives to say goodbye, sorting through stuff, getting Jeremy's truck repaired before he headed back to Fort Drum. The boys were gracious in helping us out with some of the outside work of which we were greatly appreciative. We ordered pizza, watched movies, went to the movies, ate mom's home-cooked favorites, sat around and talked and listened to Jeremy recount his war stories and adventures, watched the videos he had recorded with the video-camera we had sent him for Christmas while in Afghanistan, baked pecan pies, went to church, went out to eat, stayed up late, played, laughed, loved each other, developed many rolls of film and looked at Jeremy's pictures from Afghanistan, and enjoyed hysterical, nonsensical, and rowdy fellowship around the dinner table. It was a momentous time.

As I stood outside and watered some plants late this afternoon, I realized that once again I have entered the ranks of several of my neighbors—single parent at home to raise the kids and hold down the fort. Only difference for me is that I've sent not one loved one, but two. My husband Emory and son Aaron departed for Afghanistan this morning; they'll be gone at least six months. Jeremy left this afternoon to return to Fort Drum; he reenlisted and will be stationed in Alaska come fall. Matt will head back to Atlanta in a day or two to help out the grandparents for a while before going full-time Army (he was in the Wyoming Army National Guard from 1997 to 2003).

My tear ducts are rather full at the moment. I'm not a big crier; I tend to hold things in. But tears are good and I need to shed them. For me they cleanse and give me the strength to carry on. There's always an empty spot in my heart when Emory is gone. My best friend is not here to share the day to day experiences. The bed is not as warm. His presence is missed.

People ask me from time to time, "How do you do it?" I tell them, "God." He gets me through. He is my strength and my song. I know that He is always there; He will never leave me nor forsake me. And that gives me the hope to carry on each day.

Bethany [now age eleven] and I will carry on. We'll stay busy and have fun. We'll proceed with daily life as usual. We have each other to lean on because we know at some point along the way we'll need that shoulder to cry on; we'll need a big, long hug; we'll need a good funny movie and popcorn to pass the time; we'll need the laughter and conversation of friends and family to keep us from worrying and dwelling on the fact that our guys are gone for now. We'll miss our men folk, but Lord-willing they'll return to us soon.

Blessings,
Beverly Lussi

May 2, 2005

Frank, it was a pleasure meeting you at Camp Lejeune this week. . . .

To remind you, Josh was one of the Marines that were in a Humvee that hit a landmine on April 20, 2004. You saw the bandage on his right hand at the Bachelor's Quarters at Lejeune Friday morning 4-30-04. His middle finger on his right hand is gone from about the middle knuckle up. The fact that he is still alive is a miracle.

The Marine that was sitting next to him is still in critical condition with head trauma, and compound fractures. . . . Josh and Sergeant Poe (in critical condition in Germany) were sitting over the passenger side wheel well. . . . I appreciate your prayers, and we pray for your son as well, and all our servicemen and women defending us.

The people I met in Lejeune were amazing. The duty, honor and care all the Marines exhibited is an inspiration to us. The sincerity of the Marines themselves and their families has taught me more about patriotism than anything I have encountered in my life. My son Josh will heal.

Unfortunately, Josh will head back to Iraq to his unit as that is what he desires when he is physically able. Josh came home to a hero's welcome with banners, flags, hugs and kisses from friends and family here in Atwater, California. Although he is very glad to be home, he is finding it difficult to cope with not being there in Iraq with his fellow Marines. That is common valor among our service men and women, our heroes. . . . Thanks for the support and care.

God Bless.
Rob Davey
Marine Dad
High School Bio Teacher
Atwater, California

P.S. Here is one of the last e-mails Josh sent me before he was injured.

Friday, 19 Mar 2004

Hey Dad:

I'm writing you this to tell you that I made it safely to Iraq. We convoyed through southern Iraq and are now at our base. I drove my boat on a lake all day today. It kind of reminded me of Lake McClure only the water is a turquoise color. In the south of Iraq on the convoy over all you saw was little kids by the road wearing rags and begging for food along a desolate desert. There were about 300 kids that we passed up. They were the Shiite Muslims. They were the poor ones. The further north we traveled the better clothes the kids had. They were all cheering for us and smiling and walking to school. This area is pretty hostile though and we couldn't get caught up in the distractions. We are living in big tents that hold our whole company for now. In the beginning we were sleeping on the ground outside. It wasn't so bad though. The stars out here are like the ones at Yosemite. You can see all the constellations. Time goes by quickly over here too because we are so busy. . . . I haven't had a whole day off in over a month, hopefully though we might get one on Sunday. I'll probably write you again on that day. Tell everyone that I said hello and that I'm doing fine.

Josh

May 5, 2004

From: Frank Schaeffer
To: Rob Davey
Dear Rob,

Meeting you and Josh made a big impression on me. Below please find something I wrote to express my feelings about your brave son. It will be printed as an op-ed in USA TODAY tomorrow, Thursday,

May 6, 2004 under the headline: "For War Families, It's Not Political."

With respect,
Frank

USA TODAY May 6, 2004
FOR WAR FAMILIES, IT'S NOT POLITICAL
by Frank Schaeffer

This morning, I hugged Josh Davey, a young Marine whose finger was blown off in Iraq. Josh was one of the Marines in a Humvee that hit a land mine on April 20. His father introduced me to him at Camp Lejeune, N.C. It was his son's first day out of the hospital.

My son, also a Marine, was deployed to the Middle East for 11 months. Unlike the young wounded Marine, my son came home unharmed. Having a son at war has made me part of a close family that lives and suffers through each moment of our children's deployments. This fact made it possible for me to hug Josh and thank him, though we'd never met before. I was not embarrassed that there were tears on my cheeks. We were strangers, yet he was also a "son" of mine.

There is a debate raging about how to appropriately deal with the "issue" of the deaths of our men and women in uniform. For instance, some people objected to Ted Koppel reading the names of our war dead on *Nightline* or USA TODAY publishing the pictures of those killed in April.

As a Marine's father, I have a different perspective. To me, the issue is personal. What I object to is not pictures of our dead soldiers and Marines but the fact that so many people seem eager to politicize the issue of our war dead for short-term political gain. President Bush seems to want to minimize the suffering of our military family to help his election chances in the fall. He chooses his photo opportunities carefully. And his Democratic opponents seem eager to exploit every dead and wounded soldier to defeat him. Neither side seems genuinely interested in the human cost and sacrifice.

Maybe this is because some of the people who run for national office these days, or who manage their campaigns, do not have a child deployed in harm's way. I find that the whole debate about how to treat the subject of our war dead is mostly being carried on by people with no skin in the game. This is hypocritical. Each side wants to use the war on terrorism and the fighting in Iraq and Afghanistan for political ends. They should earn the right in lost sleep over a child sent to war before they speak to the issue. And they should stop trying to find military parents or personnel to quote to support their political agendas.

Right now, I don't care about politics as much as I care about the dazed look on that young Marine's face. Josh's eyes were still bloodshot from the explosion. To me, they were the most beautiful eyes in the world. They brimmed with tears when he spoke of his friend who was riding shoulder-to-shoulder with him when they hit the mine. Josh went home damaged but alive. His buddy lies in a coma at death's door in a German hospital.

Josh may be sent back to Iraq in about 30 days. He wants to return. He's worried about his buddies. "I only lost a finger," he said. By the time he is back in action, the political leaders will be on to the next event they are spinning into a political web of "issues" with which to catch their ideological opponents.

The young Marine will be facing danger again. His parents will be sleepwalking through another day, feeling as though they have just been kicked in the stomach, feeling as though time has stopped, as though their lives are over. I know.

It is time for my fellow citizens to remember that whole families feel as though they have gone to war with their sons and daughters. We who have children in danger feel powerless to help them. Our lives have been changed forever. And right now, we care about something a lot more immediate than election results or how the death and suffering of our flesh and blood affect this or that opinion poll or candidate's chances.

To us, our children are not political cannon fodder to win elections with. They are all we have.

May 6, 2004

Dear Frank, I just read your article. I am not ashamed to tell you that I sit here with tears streaming down my face. I saw how you hugged Josh. I saw your emotion as you sincerely thanked him for his service and sacrifice. I will never, never forget that. My only regret is that I did not hug you as well. I don't know if you knew it or not, but the lump in my throat as you spoke to him almost paralyzed me. . . .

I sit here at the computer writing this note as family members sit out back next to the pool enjoying the wholeness of our family because Josh is home. For me, "wholeness" lies with Josh returning safely from Iraq again and again. That is not a sure thing. For now, however, I will rejoice. Josh is home for 30 days. We will love as never before because soon, all too soon, he will be back in hell, and our "normal" lives will be disrupted again with the terror of the 24 hour nightmare of having our beloved son at war in Iraq. My Very Best Wishes to you and your family, and especially your son in the Marines.

With utmost sincerity,
Rob

Dear Mr. Schaeffer,

My name is lance corporal Joshua Davey. We met at Camp Lejeune in late April. In fact you made a reference about me in USA Today. I was the Marine who had came back from Iraq after running over a landmine. I understand that you need letters for your book. . . . I don't know if it is what you are looking for, but I can give you a letter that I wrote my dad while I was in the hospital in Iraq.

Josh wrote this letter to his father when he was nineteen.—FS

March 2004

Dear Dad,

I have some bad news. Before I continue I want you to know that I am in a hospital but I am doing fine. They had to amputate part of my middle finger on my right hand, but other than that I'll be o.k.

Earlier yesterday me and the guys in my platoon were coming back from a mission. There were seven of us in the back of the humvee and we were getting pretty close to our base. We all kind of let out a sigh of relief when the base was in view, and we started talking about life back home and our future plans. All of a sudden I heard a loud explosion. Our humvee had hit a landmine.

I must have blacked out during the explosion, but when I had awakened I was a good 15 ft from the humvee and I was lying on my back. I was in shock. . . . I tried to get up and I realized that I couldn't move.

At the time I couldn't feel my legs or move my right arm. I heard someone say "Grab your weapons we have possible enemy vehicles approaching!"

I felt helpless. I knew that there were other people who must have been injured and I couldn't grab my weapon to protect them. Luckily for us the guys from second section heard the blast and came to our aid. They quickly resolved the situation with the incoming vehicles and then helped us out with whatever they could.

At this point I looked over my shoulder and saw my sergeant lying down about 3 ft away. I can't give out his name right now, but he was one of the best sergeants that I know. He was bleeding everywhere, but I noticed there was a particularly bad wound on his head. His legs were obviously broken by the way that he had landed. I heard one of my buddies in the distance yell that he couldn't move because he had hurt his back.

There was someone tending to all of the guys who were injured. Hook had run over to me and was talking to me the whole time. I was glad to see that he was o.k. Our doc was doing the best he could to stop the bleeding on the sergeant until we had been medivaced out of there.

There were only three of us in the chopper so I knew everyone else must have been alright. Once we got to the hospital they started working on the sergeant. Then they operated on me. They took me to a different room and amputated my finger. I haven't seen the sergeant since. I did see Bryan though. He was the one I heard saying after the explosion that he hurt his back. They put us in beds right next to each other. I'm glad that they did that so that we don't feel like we have to go through this alone. It looks like both of us will be fine.

I can't stop thinking about my sergeant though. He was talking to me about what he was going to get his mother for Mother's Day. He said he wanted to do something special for her this year, and when he got back he was going to buy her a necklace that she had always wanted. We were having a normal conversation one moment, and he's a casualty the next.

Dad, I don't know if he's going to make it or not. It's the not knowing that kills me. I don't know where he's at or what exactly is wrong with him. He was sitting shoulder to shoulder with me, and here I am lying in bed writing you this letter while he's fighting to stay alive. It really makes you think. The doc told me that I'll be going home in a couple of weeks. I don't want you to take this the wrong way, because you know how much I love everyone and I want to see everyone, but I don't feel right coming back early while everyone is still going to be over here fighting.

I wouldn't feel right eating at a restaurant or sleeping in a bed while all of my friends are taking fire and sleeping in the sand. But the doc said that I don't get to decide. So I will be back soon, probably before this letter gets to you. And I will be glad to see the family. Tell everyone that I said hello and that I'm doing fine. Tell Nana that I had the angel charm that she gave me in my pocket during the accident, and that I still have it with me. I love you and will see you soon.

Your son,

Josh

Josh was sent back to Iraq after a few days at home.—FS

Jane was thirty-one when she wrote to me. She is the same Jane (Vizzi) Blair who made appearances in both *Keeping Faith* and F*aith of Our Sons*. I wrote about attending her wedding to Lt Peter Blair, USMC.—FS

April 20, 2004

Dear Frank,

Just over a year ago, around mid-March 2003, when we were still in Kuwait waiting for Operation Iraqi Freedom to kick off, I remember running into a buddy of mine from the Basic School. He was one of the first people I ran into that I knew while over there. I was overjoyed to see him because he had been a friend during our training together.

His name was Lt. Oscar Jimenez. We had gone through both Marine Officer Candidacy School and the Basic School together. Since we were both prior enlisted NCOs [noncommissioned officers], we had become friends eagerly trading experiences and looking forward to getting back into the fleet, this time as officers.

During the Basic School, a dreary but important six months training period for all new officers, I remember one of our first classes there. Two hundred and fifty new officers all sat in a classroom expectantly waiting for our instructor. A silence fell over the room when he entered. The self-assured Captain stepped in front of us, and without emotion said, "Before your first tour is up 25% will get out of the Marine Corps. At least three of you will get DUIs [driving under the influence of alcohol] . . . and two of you in this classroom will be killed in action."

Could that be true? Here we were young, healthy Lieutenants with our lives ahead of us, practically indestructible warriors. So I thought.

When we graduated from the Basic School, many of us would part ways. Thirty lucky warriors got stationed in the infamous 29 Palms—a place scorned by any Marine who's visited this distant duty station. Many of my closest friends and I were "the lucky ones." Many were assigned to Infantry or ground combat units. But before we could settle in, suddenly we all got deployed to Iraq in support of what would become Operation Iraqi Freedom.

After Operation Iraqi Freedom ended, we thought our class had been fortunate: a few Purple Hearts and war stories, but nothing more. Things had not ended though. We were all told we would deploy again within months. . . .

With combat operations long ago declared "over," Operation Iraqi Freedom II was supposed to be a cake walk—basically doing patrolling and convoy operations in support of peacekeeping efforts. We had all known about the threats of Al Sadr and his militia, the Imam Mehdi Army, but had not considered that he would go on the offensive and attack Marines.

I had not expected what was to shape up in the early weeks in

April, 2004 in Fallujah, Ramadii, and throughout Iraq. By the 22 April, nearly 100 Marines had been killed in one month alone, making it the highest death toll for us ever in Iraq. Since many of my friends were deployed, I frequently scanned the web sites reading of the stories and casualties. Most of the casualties were from 1st Marine Division, and many from 29 Palms. As I read the web pages on Easter Sunday, I saw a familiar name—that of my friend and fellow officer 1st Lt. Oscar Jimenez.

Sickness overcame me. He had been killed in Al Anbar Province during the offensive of Al Sadr forces, and was shot, once directly to the head, dying of multiple gunshot wounds. He had been the Battalion Motor Transportation Officer of 3rd Battalion, 4th Marines.

Two other Marines were killed alongside him. What shocked me is that Oscar had always been so prudent and smart. What I realized then was that anyone could be killed out there, no matter how vigilant they were.

Oscar was the last person I would have ever worried about. He was a calm, collected person. He had been the type of candidate during training that helped everyone else through OCS and TBS. He was the type to lead the way. That's exactly what he was doing when he died in Iraq.

Finding his CACO (Casualty Assistance Call Officer), 1st Lt. Brian Solomon, was a great relief. Not only was he courteous and professional, but he took the time to talk to me. Lt. Solomon, part of 1st Tank Battalion also in 29 Palms, received a call in the middle of the night from his Battalion Commanding Officer and told him he would be assigned to tell Oscar's widow, Alejandra, that her husband had been killed.

Lt Solomon put on his blues, called the Chaplain and GySgt Justice, and got ready to drive over to tell the family. Lt. Solomon told me all this while I spoke to him only two days after Oscar's death. "I'm sorry your friend has been killed," he said, "this has been one of the hardest things I have ever had to do." He described to me how they drove in to base officer housing where all the officer spouses live.

He said, "We drove into the housing just as people were waking up and going to work . . . most of the wives' husbands are deployed. As we drove down the street, everyone began staring; they saw our blues and that could only mean one thing. They all wondered if we were going to stop at their home, if it was their husband who had been killed. I felt like death. It was the most awful feeling driving through there with my blues on."

Alejandra and Oscar had been married for fifteen years and have three children, a girl and two boys. Both are of Mexican heritage, they also have a huge extended family in San Diego.

"I never expected it to be as hard as when I was standing at her door knocking, and when she opened the door I saw her face and she knew," Lt. Solomon said.

I had just gotten back from an exercise in Yuma, Arizona and immediately began emailing fellow TBS classmates from all over the Corps. Lt. Solomon phoned me with the funeral information and said, "Oscar's body is in Dover . . . he'll be in San Diego tomorrow."

At least ten of us, fellow TBS classmates of Oscar, with one or two days notice were able to make it to his funeral. All two hundred and fifty of us would have been there if we could have.

At the burial service several hundred people paid their respects including about fifty Marines. Many of the Marines were from Oscar's old reserve station, 4th Tank Battalion. Oscar received the Purple Heart, and a Major who read the citation handed the medal to Oscar's grieving widow.

As his body was lowered into the ground, a Mariachi band played a solemn and hauntingly beautiful Mexican funeral song. The Marines all rendered a slow salute as his widow and family wept. Many of the Marines including myself were struggling to hold back tears. I had to stare into the distance so as not to see the pain that his family was experiencing.

When his body was buried, we walked away. I turned away and could no longer hold back my tears.

The downtown Marriott in San Diego hosted the reception after the funeral. Friends, family members, fraternity brothers and Marines all gathered in Oscar's remembrance. . . .

As the ten of us, all Marine Officers, all in our blues, walked back toward our cars, an unforeseen thing happened. Passersby offered thanks, some offering us dinner and drinks. We could scarcely walk twenty feet before we were stopped again by someone wishing us well. One gentleman insisted and we had a drink with him. He was a former Marine and he also had just buried his godson killed in Iraq. He offered us a toast, "Your friend Oscar was a patriot, and you are also all patriots, and you must never forget that."

Love, Jane

1st. Lt. Jane (Vizzi) Blair, USMC

Jane is at Twenty-nine Palms Air-Ground Combat Training Center. She has served one tour of duty in Iraq along with her Marine lieutenant husband, Peter Blair, who is now deployed to Okinawa.—FS

May 3, 2004

Frank:

I got your book [Faith of Our Sons] and have to admit, it took me a couple of weeks to pick it up to read it. I got to page 50 and had to put it down, so raw are my feelings still when it comes to remembering my sons and their homecomings.

Something that is not generally known outside our family is that my stepson Matt [Sgt. Matt Dickinson, 82nd Airborne, in Iraq from March 13, 2003, to January 27, 2004], my oldest, while in Baghdad, got a notification that my youngest, Billy, [Billy Mitten (my first husband's name) Pvt. 27th Engineering Battalion], had been shot in Afghanistan. [Billy was in Afghanistan January 27, 2003 to June, 27, 2003.]

. . . It ended up being a huge misunderstanding. . . . Billy was absolutely fine, but we were all reeling from being told one of our own had been shot. Billy was not even told of this until about a week later, and then understood my tearful response to his calling, filled with "I love you". It was all I could say. Outside the family, everyone has had the same response of "Well, he wasn't shot so why were you so upset?" Gee, I don't know why. . . .

How do you explain to someone who is not living your life, or one that is similar, just what it is like, having a son in a war zone? You don't sleep, you don't eat. When you do sleep, it is fitful, when you do eat, it is piddling and tastes like cardboard.

I also have a 10 year old son, Elias. [He] is so proud of his brothers; he took them in for show and tell when they came home on leave, just before their successive deployments. He took it so hard, their leaving. He was getting into fights every day and finally got suspended for it. We were so numb from worrying about the soldiers in our family; we had forgotten that others around us hurt too. When Elias got suspended, that was the wake up call for me to notice he needed our help. I finally got him to admit to me how worried he was and how angry he was at the boys calling [home from their deployments] when he couldn't talk to them [because he was always at school]. He finally cried. It wasn't just a little boy letting out some hurt feelings. I had never seen him sob like he did. His soul was being bared in the form of crying. I could feel every bit of his heartache with every tear that came from his eyes.

We live in a farming community and the school was clueless as to how to help him. We had to drive him to the military hospital an hour away to get him help. . . . Like our soldiers, we all were working so hard to not show fear that it was tearing us all apart. I thank God every day for Dr. Countryman at Wright Patterson Air Force Base for all her help. She was our light and our saving grace.

The military goes out of their way to "be there" for the spouses and children of the soldiers and they do nothing for the parents and siblings. When we were notified that [our sons were] coming home, a number of the parents wanted a reunion briefing to know how to help them. We were told by the command of the 82nd Airborne that we didn't need one. Somehow, we didn't matter, though we are the ones that gave them our children to serve.

I am still raw over the whole matter. Matt was gone for almost a year. When he came back he was angry and bitter and shell shocked. I think that what upset him the most was the poverty he saw, the situation the Iraqis were in. He has been deeply hurt. He blows up so easily now. I talked to him just yesterday and he is in the process of ETS'ing [end of time in service processing]. He shared with me that he is not authorized by command to go to counseling because he is "short" [short time left in service]. . . . Using his words, "Just three months ago, I trusted these guys to keep me alive and now they couldn't care less about me."

This is why I had to stop at page 50 of your book. We left for Fayetteville, NC on 23 Jan, the day before he was due to arrive home. He got stuck in Germany for 4 days, with many units coming home before him, ones that had arrived after the ground war had ended. We were called at least twice a day that he was on his way, only to be called later to be told, "No, their plane broke." When he landed at Ft. Bragg, he was so drained, we all felt it. When he was released from formation, I was the last one to hug him. I cried on his shoulder, telling him over and over, "Thank you, son, for coming home." When he started to pull out of the hug, I begged him to hang on, I wasn't ready to let go.

This war was one of the most difficult events in my life and it consumed me for a year. How does one shut that off, once your child comes home? What makes this even harder is that there was a mom in my online support group who had a son in my son's unit—same company, they knew each other. Two weeks before they were to return, she and I were chatting online, as I was kind of the "Mom" of the group—having gone thru this all with my military husband and my second son, returning from a deployment like this—I was helping her find a hotel room for her trip to "Bragg" to be there for her son's return. Just 24 hours later, she opened her front door to see two Army officers there, telling her "On behalf of a grateful nation . . . " her son, Marc Seiden had been killed.

[The soldier was killed on Jan. 2, 2004, in Baghdad, Iraq, when his convoy was ambushed by the enemy, who used an improvised explosive device (IED), small arms fire, and a rocket-propelled grenade (RPG). Killed were: Spc. Solomon C. Bangayan, twenty-four, of Jay, Vt. Spc. Marc S. Seiden, twenty-six, of Brigantine, N.J. The soldiers were assigned to 2nd Battalion, 325th Airborne Infantry Regiment, 82nd Airborne Division, Fort Bragg, N.C.—FS]

How does one shut this off when your child is killed? I also carry the guilt that it was her son, and the relief that it wasn't mine. All I could do was send flowers and a note. Gail is Jewish so she sat Shiva for 8 days, so she was reliving the loss again and again with people visiting.

. . . I am a military parent in a non-military community, as you are. There is no one near me I can discuss this with. We are the forgotten ones in all of this. We feel their pain thru all the broken bones and skinned knees. We feel their love when they rejoice in the goodness of God. But, somehow, the military doesn't think we feel anything once they turn 18. As a result of the war, I have lost the son I had. . . . So deep is the pain he feels, it is an elephant in the room that all of us tiptoe around. . . .

Thanks for letting me bend your ear, so to speak. I hope all is well with you and John, especially John. My son, Billy, missed his unit's latest deployment as a result of a leg injury that now requires more operations. . . .

Thanks for all you do, bringing the "forgotten ones" to the forefront of people's minds.

Nancy M. Dickinson

Lieutenant Colonel Michael Strobl, USMC, is currently head, Officer Distribution Section, Manpower & Reserve Affairs Headquarters. It is somewhat unusual that someone of his rank volunteer for the duties described below.—FS

From: Lieutenant Colonel Mike Strobl, USMC
To: Frank Schaeffer
April 23, 2004

Frank: Chance Phelps was wearing his Saint Christopher medal when he was killed on Good Friday [2004]. Eight days later, I handed the medallion to his mother. I didn't know Chance before he died. Today, I miss him.

Over a year ago, I volunteered to escort the remains of Marines killed in Iraq should the need arise. The military provides a uniformed escort for all casualties to ensure they are delivered safely to the next of kin and are treated with dignity and respect along the way.

Thankfully, I hadn't been called on to be an escort since Operation Iraqi Freedom began. The first few weeks of April [2004], however, had been a tough month for the Marines.

On the Monday after Easter I was reviewing Department of Defense press releases when I saw that a Private First Class Chance Phelps USMC was killed in action outside of Baghdad. The press release listed his hometown—the same town I'm from. I notified our Battalion adjutant and told him that, should the duty to escort PFC Phelps fall to our Battalion, I would take him.

I didn't hear back the rest of Monday and all day Tuesday until 1800. The Battalion duty NCO called my cell phone and said I needed to be ready to leave for Dover Air Force Base at 1900 in order to escort the remains of PFC Phelps.

Before leaving for Dover I called the major who had the task of informing Phelps's parents of his death. The major said the funeral was going to be in Dubois, Wyoming. (It turned out that PFC Phelps only lived in my hometown for his senior year of high school.) I had never been to Wyoming and had never heard of Dubois.

With two other escorts from Quantico, I got to Dover AFB at 2330 on Tuesday night. First thing on Wednesday we reported to the mortuary at the base. In the escort lounge there were about half a dozen Army soldiers and about an equal number of Marines waiting to meet up with "their" remains for departure. PFC Phelps was not ready, however, and I was told to come back on Thursday. Now, at Dover with nothing to do and a solemn mission ahead, I began to get depressed.

I was wondering about Chance Phelps. I didn't know anything about him; not even what he looked like. I wondered about his family and what it would be like to meet them. I did pushups in my room until I couldn't do any more.

On Thursday morning I reported back to the mortuary. This time there was a new group of Army escorts and a couple of the Marines who had been there Wednesday. There was also an Air Force captain there to escort his brother home to San Diego.

We received a brief covering our duties, the proper handling of the remains, the procedures for draping a flag over a casket, and of course, the paperwork attendant to our task. We were shown pictures of the shipping container and told that each one contained, in addition to the casket, a flag. I was given an extra flag since Phelps's parents were divorced. This way they would each get one. I didn't like the idea of stuffing the flag into my luggage but I couldn't see carrying a large flag, folded for presentation to the next of kin, through an airport while in my Alpha uniform. It barely fit into my suitcase.

It turned out that I was the last escort to leave on Thursday. This meant that I repeatedly got to participate in the small ceremonies that mark all departures from the Dover AFB mortuary.

Most of the remains are taken from Dover AFB by hearse to the airport in Philadelphia for air transport to their final destination.

When the remains of a service member are loaded onto a hearse and ready to leave the Dover mortuary, there is an announcement made over the building's intercom system. With the announcement, all service members working at the mortuary, regardless of service branch, stop work and form up along the driveway to render a slow ceremonial salute as the hearse departs. Escorts also participated in each formation until it was their time to leave.

On this day there were some civilian workers doing construction on the mortuary grounds. As each hearse passed, they would stop working and place their hard hats over their hearts. This was my first sign that my mission with PFC Phelps was larger than the Marine Corps and that his family and friends were not grieving alone.

Eventually I was the last escort remaining in the lounge. The Marine Master Gunnery Sergeant in charge of the Marine liaison there came to see me. He had Chance Phelps's personal effects. He removed each item: a large watch, a wooden cross with a lanyard, two loose dog tags, two dog tags on a chain, and a Saint Christopher medal on a silver chain. Although we had been briefed that we might be carrying some personal effects of the deceased, this set me aback. Holding his personal effects, I was starting to get to know Chance Phelps.

Finally we were ready. I grabbed my bags and went outside. I was somewhat startled when I saw the shipping container, loaded three-quarters of the way in to the back of a black Chevy Suburban that had been modified to carry such cargo. This was the first time I saw my "cargo" and I was surprised at how large the shipping container was. The Master Gunnery Sergeant and I verified that the name on the container was Phelps's then they pushed him the rest of the way in and we left. Now it was PFC Chance Phelps's turn to receive the military—and construction workers'—honors. He was finally moving towards home.

As I chatted with the driver on the hour-long trip to Philadelphia, it became clear that he considered it an honor to be able to contribute in getting Chance home. He offered his sympathy to the family. I was glad to finally be moving yet apprehensive about what things would be like at the airport. I didn't want this package to be treated like ordinary cargo yet I knew that the simple logistics of moving around a box this large would have to overrule my preferences.

When we got to the Northwest Airlines cargo terminal at the Philadelphia airport, the cargo handler and hearse driver pulled the shipping container onto a loading bay while I stood to the side and executed a slow salute. Once Chance was safely in the cargo area, and I was satisfied that he would be treated with due care and respect, the hearse driver drove me over to the passenger terminal and dropped me off.

As I walked up to the ticketing counter in my uniform, a Northwest employee started to ask me if I knew how to use the automated boarding pass dispenser. Before she could finish another ticketing agent interrupted her. He told me to go straight to the counter then explained to the woman that I was a military escort. She seemed embarrassed. The woman behind the counter already had tears in her eyes as I was pulling out my government travel voucher. She struggled to find words but managed to express her sympathy for the family and thank me for my service. She upgraded my ticket to first class.

After clearing security, I was met by another Northwest Airlines employee at the gate. She told me a representative from cargo would be up to take me down to the tarmac to observe the movement and loading of PFC Phelps. I hadn't really told any of them what my mission was but they all knew.

When the man from the cargo crew met me, he, too, struggled for words. On the tarmac, he told me stories of his childhood as a military brat and repeatedly told me that he was sorry for my loss. I was starting to understand that, even here in Philadelphia, far away from Chance's hometown, people were mourning with his family.

On the tarmac, the cargo crew was silent except for occasional instructions to each other. I stood to the side and saluted as the conveyor moved Chance to the aircraft. I was relieved when he was finally settled into place. The rest of the bags were loaded and I watched them shut the cargo bay door before heading back up to board the aircraft.

One of the pilots had taken my carry-on bag himself and had it stored next to the cockpit door so he could watch it while I was on the tarmac. As I boarded the plane, I could tell immediately that the flight attendants had already been informed of my mission. They seemed a little choked up as they led me to my seat.

About 45 minutes into our flight I still hadn't spoken to anyone except to tell the first class flight attendant that I would prefer water. I was surprised when the flight attendant from the back of the plane suddenly appeared and leaned down to grab my hands. She said, "I want you to have this" as she pushed a small gold crucifix, with a relief of Jesus, into my hand. It was her lapel pin and it looked somewhat worn. I suspected it had been hers for quite some time. That was the only thing she said to me the entire flight.

When we landed in Minneapolis, I was the first one off the plane. The pilot himself escorted me straight down the side stairs of the exit tunnel to the tarmac. The cargo crew there already knew what was on this plane. They were unloading some of the luggage when an Army sergeant, a fellow escort who had left Dover earlier that day, appeared next to me. His "cargo" was going to be loaded onto my plane for its continuing leg.

We stood side-by-side in the dark and executed a slow salute as Chance was removed from the plane. The cargo crew at Minneapolis kept Phelps's shipping case separate from all the other luggage as they waited to take us to the cargo area. I waited with the soldier and we saluted together as his fallen comrade was loaded onto the plane.

My trip with Chance was going to be somewhat unusual in that we were going to have an overnight stopover. We had a late start out of Dover and there was just too much traveling ahead of us to continue on that day. (We still had a flight from Minneapolis to Billings,

Montana, then a five-hour drive to the funeral home. That was to be followed by a 90-minute drive to Chance's hometown.)

I was concerned about leaving him overnight in the Minneapolis cargo area. My ten-minute ride from the tarmac to the cargo holding area eased my apprehension. Just as in Philadelphia, the cargo guys in Minneapolis were extremely respectful and seemed honored to do their part. While talking with them, I learned that the cargo supervisor for Northwest Airlines at the Minneapolis airport is a Lieutenant Colonel in the Marine Corps Reserves. They called him for me and let me talk to him.

Once I was satisfied that all would be okay for the night, I asked one of the cargo crew if he would take me back to the terminal so that I could catch my hotel's shuttle. Instead, he drove me straight to the hotel himself. At the hotel, the Lieutenant Colonel called me and said he would personally pick me up in the morning and bring me back to the cargo area.

Before leaving the airport, I had told the cargo crew that I wanted to come back to the cargo area in the morning rather than go straight to the passenger terminal. I felt bad for leaving Chance overnight and wanted to see the shipping container where I had left it for the night. It was fine.

The Lieutenant Colonel made a few phone calls then drove me around to the passenger terminal. I was met again by a man from the cargo crew and escorted down to the tarmac. The pilot of the plane joined me as I waited for them to bring Chance from the cargo area. The pilot and I talked of his service in the Air Force and how he missed it.

I saluted as Chance was moved up the conveyor and onto the plane. It was to be a while before the luggage was to be loaded so the pilot took me up to the board the plane where I could watch the tarmac from a window.

With no other passengers yet on board, I talked with the flight attendants and one of the cargo guys. He had been in the Navy and one of the attendants had been in the Air Force. Everywhere I went, people were continuing to tell me their relationship to the military. After all the baggage was aboard, I went back down to the tarmac, inspected the cargo bay, and watched them secure the door.

When we arrived at Billings, I was again the first off the plane. This time Chance's shipping container was the first item out of the cargo hold. The funeral director had driven five hours up from Riverton, Wyoming to meet us. He shook my hand as if I had personally lost a brother.

We moved Chance to a secluded cargo area. Now it was time for me to remove the shipping container and drape the flag over the casket. I had predicted that this would choke me up but I found I was more concerned with proper flag etiquette than the solemnity of the moment. Once the flag was in place, I stood by and saluted as Chance was loaded onto the van from the funeral home. I was thankful that we were in a small airport and the event seemed to go mostly unnoticed.

I picked up my rental car and followed Chance for five hours until we reached Riverton. During the long trip I imagined how my meeting with Chance's parents would go. I was very nervous about that.

When we finally arrived at the funeral home, I had my first face-to-face meeting with the Casualty Assistance Call Officer. It had been his duty to inform the family of Chance's death. He was on the Inspector/Instructor staff of an infantry company in Salt Lake City, Utah and I knew he had had a difficult week.

Inside I gave the funeral director some of the paperwork from Dover and discussed the plan for the next day. The service was to be at 1400 in the high school gymnasium up in Dubois, population about 900, some 90 miles away. Eventually, we had covered everything. The CACO had some items that the family wanted to be inserted into the casket and I felt I needed to inspect Chance's uniform to ensure everything was proper. Although it was going to be a closed casket funeral, I still wanted to ensure his uniform was squared away.

Earlier in the day I wasn't sure how I'd handle this moment. Suddenly, the casket was open and I got my first look at Chance Phelps. His uniform was immaculate—a tribute to the professionalism of the Marines at Dover. I noticed that he wore six ribbons over his marksmanship badge; the senior one was his Purple Heart. I had been in the Corps for over 17 years, including a combat tour, and was wearing eight ribbons. This Private First Class, with less than a year in the Corps, had already earned six.

The next morning, I wore my dress blues and followed the hearse for the trip up to Dubois. This was the most difficult leg of our trip for me. I was bracing for the moment when I would meet his parents and hoping I would find the right words as I presented them with Chance's personal effects.

We got to the high school gym about four hours before the service was to begin. The gym floor was covered with folding chairs neatly lined in rows. There were a few townspeople making final preparations when I stood next to the hearse and saluted as Chance was moved out of the hearse. The sight of a flag-draped coffin was overwhelming to some of the ladies.

We moved Chance into the gym to the place of honor. A Marine sergeant, the command representative from Chance's battalion, met me at the gym. His eyes were watery as he relieved me of watching Chance so that I could go eat lunch and find my hotel.

At the restaurant, the table had a flier announcing Chance's service: Dubois High School gym; two o' clock. It also said that the family would be accepting donations so that they could buy flak vests to send to troops in Iraq.

I drove back to the gym at a quarter after one. I could've walked—you could walk to just about anywhere in Dubois in ten minutes. I had planned to find a quiet room where I could take his things out of their pouch and untangle the chain of the Saint

Christopher medal from the dog tag chains and arrange everything before his parents came in. I had twice before removed the items from the pouch to ensure they were all there—even though there was no chance anything could've fallen out. Each time, the two chains had been quite tangled. I didn't want to be fumbling around trying to untangle them in front of his parents. Our meeting, however, didn't go as expected.

I practically bumped into Chance's step-mom accidentally and our introductions began in the noisy hallway outside the gym. In short order I had met Chance's step-mom and father followed by his step-dad and, at last, his mom. I didn't know how to express to these people my sympathy for their loss and my gratitude for their sacrifice. Now, however, they were repeatedly thanking me for bringing their son home and for my service. I was humbled beyond words.

I told them that I had some of Chance's things and asked if we could try to find a quiet place. The five of us ended up in what appeared to be a computer lab—not what I had envisioned for this occasion.

After we had arranged five chairs around a small table, I told them about our trip. I told them how, at every step, Chance was treated with respect, dignity, and honor. I told them about the staff at Dover and all the folks at Northwest Airlines. I tried to convey how the entire Nation, from Dover to Philadelphia, to Minneapolis, to Billings, and Riverton expressed grief and sympathy over their loss.

Finally, it was time to open the pouch. The first item I happened to pull out was Chance's large watch. It was still set to Baghdad time. Next were the lanyard and the wooden cross. Then the dog tags and the Saint Christopher medal. This time the chains were not tangled. Once all of his items were laid out on the table, I told his mom that I had one other item to give them. I retrieved the flight attendant's crucifix from my pocket and told its story. I set that on the table and excused myself. When I next saw Chance's mom, she was wearing the crucifix on her lapel.

By 1400 most of the seats on the gym floor were filled and people were finding seats in the fixed bleachers high above the gym floor. There were a surprising number of people in military uniform. Many Marines had come up from Salt Lake City. Men from various VFW posts and the Marine Corps League occupied multiple rows of folding chairs. We all stood as Chance's family took their seats in the front.

It turned out that Chance's sister, a Petty Officer in the Navy, worked for a Rear Admiral—the Chief of Naval Intelligence—at the Pentagon. The Admiral had brought many of the sailors on his staff with him to Dubois pay respects to Chance and support his sister. After a few songs and some words from a Navy Chaplain, the Admiral took the microphone and told us how Chance had died.

Chance was an artillery cannoneer and his unit was acting as provisional military police outside of Baghdad. Chance had volunteered to man a .50 caliber machine gun in the turret of the leading vehicle in a convoy. The convoy came under intense fire but Chance stayed true to his post and returned fire with the big gun, covering the rest of the convoy, until he was fatally wounded.

Then the commander of the local VFW post read some of the letters Chance had written home. In letters to his mom he talked of the mosquitoes and the heat. In letters to his stepfather he told of the dangers of convoy operations and of receiving fire.

The service was a fitting tribute to this hero. When it was over, we stood as the casket was wheeled out with the family following. The casket was placed onto a horse-drawn carriage for the mile-long trip from the gym, down the main street, then up the steep hill to the cemetery. I stood alone and saluted as the carriage departed the high school. I found my car and joined Chance's convoy.

The town seemingly went from the gym to the street. All along the route, the people had lined the street and were waving small American flags. The flags that were otherwise posted were all at half-staff. For the last quarter mile up the hill, local boy scouts, spaced about 20 feet apart, all in uniform, held large flags. At the foot of the hill, I could look up and back and see the enormity of our procession. I wondered how many people would be at this funeral if it were in, say, Detroit or Los Angeles—probably not as many as were here in little Dubois, Wyoming.

The carriage stopped about 15 yards from the grave and the military pallbearers and the family waited until the men of the VFW and Marine Corps league were formed up and school buses had arrived carrying many of the people from the procession route. Once the entire crowd was in place, the pallbearers came to attention and began to remove the casket from the caisson. As I had done all week, I came to attention and executed a slow ceremonial salute as Chance was being transferred from one mode of transport to another.

From Dover to Philadelphia; Philadelphia to Minneapolis; Minneapolis to Billings; Billings to Riverton; and Riverton to Dubois we had been together. Now, as I watched them carry him the final 15 yards, I was choking up. I felt that, as long as he was still moving, he was somehow still alive.

Then they put him down above his grave. He had stopped moving.

Although my mission had been officially complete once I turned him over to the funeral director at the Billings airport, it was his placement at his grave that really concluded it in my mind. Now, he was home to stay and I suddenly felt at once sad, relieved, and useless.

The chaplain said some words that I couldn't hear and two Marines removed the flag from the casket and slowly folded it for presentation to his mother. When the ceremony was over, Chance's father placed a ribbon from his service in Vietnam on Chance's casket. His mother approached the casket and took something from her blouse and put it on the casket. I later saw that it was the flight attendant's crucifix.

Eventually friends of Chance's moved closer to the grave. A young man put a can of Copenhagen on the casket and many others left flowers.

Finally, we all went back to the gym for a reception. There was enough food to feed the entire population for a few days. In one corner of the gym there was a table set up with lots of pictures of Chance and some of his sports awards. People were continually approaching me and the other Marines to thank us for our service. Almost all of them had some story to tell about their connection to the military. About an hour into the reception, I had the impression that every man in Wyoming had, at one time or another, been in the service.

It seemed like every time I saw Chance's mom she was hugging a different well wisher. As time passed, I began to hear people laughing. We were starting to heal.

After a few hours at the gym, I went back to the hotel to change out of my dress blues. The local VFW post had invited everyone over to "celebrate Chance's life." The Post was on the other end of town from my hotel and the drive took less than two minutes. The crowd was somewhat smaller than what had been at the gym but the Post was packed.

Marines were playing pool at the two tables near the entrance and most of the VFW members were at the bar or around the tables in the bar area. The largest room in the Post was a banquet/dinning/dancing area and it was now called "The Chance Phelps Room." Above the entry were two items: a large portrait of Chance in his dress blues and the Eagle, Globe, & Anchor. In one corner of the room there was another memorial to Chance. There were candles burning around another picture of him in his blues. On the table surrounding his photo were his Purple Heart citation and his Purple Heart medal. There was also a framed copy of an excerpt from the Congressional Record. This was an elegant tribute to Chance Phelps delivered on the floor of the United States House of Representatives by Congressman Scott McInnis of Colorado. Above it all was a television that was playing a photo montage of Chance's life from small boy to proud Marine.

I did not buy a drink that night. As had been happening all day, indeed all week, people were thanking me for my service and for bringing Chance home. Now, in addition to words and handshakes, they were thanking me with beer. I fell in with the men who had handled the horses and horse-drawn carriage. I learned that they had worked through the night to groom and prepare the horses for Chance's last ride. They were all very grateful that they were able to contribute.

After a while we all gathered in The Chance Phelps room for the formal dedication. The Post commander told us of how Chance had been so looking forward to becoming a life member of the VFW. Now, in The Chance Phelps Room of the Dubois, Wyoming, Post, he would be an eternal member. We all raised our beers and The Chance Phelps Room was christened.

Later, as I was walking toward the pool tables, a Staff Sergeant from the Reserve unit in Salt Lake grabbed me and said, "Sir, you gotta hear this." There were two other Marines with him and he told the younger one, a Lance Corporal, to tell me his story. The Staff Sergeant said the Lance Corporal was normally too shy and modest to tell it but now he'd had enough beer to overcome his usual tendencies.

As the Lance Corporal started to talk, an older man joined our circle. He wore a baseball cap that indicated he had been with the 1st Marine Division in Korea. Earlier in the evening he had told me about one of his former commanding officers; a Colonel Puller.

So, there I was, standing in a circle with three Marines recently returned from fighting with the 1st Marine Division in Iraq and one not so recently returned from fighting with the 1st Marine Division in Korea. I, who had fought with the 1st Marine Division in Kuwait, was about to gain a new insight into our Corps.

The young Lance Corporal began to tell us his story. At that moment, in this circle of current and former Marines, the differences in our ages and ranks dissipated—we were all simply Marines.

His squad had been on a patrol through a city street. They had taken small arms fire and had literally dodged an RPG round that sailed between two Marines. At one point they received fire from behind a wall and had neutralized the sniper with a SMAW round.

The back blast of the SMAW, however, kicked up a substantial rock that hammered the Lance Corporal in the thigh; only missing his groin because he had reflexively turned his body sideways at the shot.

Their squad had suffered some wounded and was receiving more sniper fire when suddenly he was hit in the head by an AK-47 round. I was stunned as he told us how he felt like a baseball bat had been slammed into his head. He had spun around and fell unconscious. When he came to, he had a severe scalp wound but his Kevlar helmet had saved his life. He continued with his unit for a few days before realizing he was suffering the effects of a severe concussion.

As I stood there in the circle with the old man and the other Marines, the Staff Sergeant finished the story. He told of how this Lance Corporal had begged and pleaded with the Battalion surgeon to let him stay with his unit. In the end, the doctor said there was just no way—he had suffered a severe and traumatic head wound and would have to be medivaced.

The Marine Corps is a special fraternity. There are moments when we are reminded of this. Interestingly, those moments don't always happen at awards ceremonies or in dress blues at Birthday Balls. I have found, rather, that they occur at unexpected times and places: next to a loaded moving van at Camp Lejeune's base housing, in a dirty CP tent in northern Saudi Arabia, and in a smoky VFW post in western Wyoming.

After the story was done, the Lance Corporal stepped over to the old man, put his arm over the man's shoulder and told him that he, the Korean War vet, was his hero. The two of them stood there with their arms over each other's shoulders and we were all silent for a moment. When they let go, I told the Lance Corporal that there were recruits down on the yellow footprints[*] tonight that would soon be learning his story.

[*] The "yellow footprints" are painted in rows on the road at Parris Island. New recruits form up and stand on them when they first arrive.—FS

I was finished drinking beer and telling stories. I found Chance's father and shook his hand one more time. Chance's mom had already left and I deeply regretted not being able to tell her goodbye.

I left Dubois in the morning before sunrise for my long drive back to Billings. It had been my honor to take Chance Phelps to his final post. Now he was on the high ground overlooking his town.

I miss him.

Regards,
Mike
Lieutenant Colonel Mike Strobl, USMC

Lt. Col. Strobl's duty at the time he was Pfc. Chance Phelps's escort was manpower analyst, Total Force Structure Bivision, USMC Combat Development Command, Quantico, Virginia.—FS

Afterword

There are two Americas: One is at war. One is at play. In one America parents are waking up with a sickening jolt as they yearn for news of beloved sons and daughters in harm's way. The other America sleeps soundly, barely aware of the fact that there are young men and women who are living rough, if they are lucky, and getting shot if they are unlucky, for the sake of the rest of us.

Those Americans who do not serve or do not have family serving are disconnected from our all-volunteer forces and their families. I know. I never served in the military and before my son was in uniform I was busy writing my novels and raising my family while giving little thought to the men and women who guard us. My attitude changed when my son enlisted, sweated his way through three months of boot camp and then, in November of 1999, stepped off the parade deck at Parris Island a proud Marine. It changed even more when he went to war in the Middle East for eleven months in 2003. I take no credit. I did not choose to change, I was forced to. And I am glad I was. In the process I stumbled into a circle of new friends in the military family and encountered the best people I have ever met.

For all the talk about a politically divided America, of the "blue and red states," of the "coasts versus the middle," of "left versus right", it seems to me that there is a bigger division with far greater long-term implications: the gap between those who serve and those who don't. I experienced this very personally. When my son was at war I sometimes felt anger toward my oldest friends—mostly well-off, well-educated people who inhabit the comfortable suburbs of Boston and the world of arts and letters in New York and Los Angeles. In this social circle I didn't know one other parent with a son or daughter in harm's way or even in the military. For my friends life was going on as usual while my son and tens of thousands of others were at war. No leaders were asking Americans outside the military to make any sacrifices. Were we at war or not? Were we all in this or not?

In talking to other military parents what I heard most was "They just don't get it," when referring to the Americans who didn't have family serving. And it did not go unnoticed by my military friends and family that these other nonserving Americans just happened to mostly be our wealthiest, best educated, and most powerful citizens, including most members of our governmental media and business elite.

It was not always this way. Not long ago literary types, intellectuals and even the sons and daughters of millionaires, presidents, and senators served, and not only because they were drafted. Many men from privileged families, volunteered, even for service in Vietnam. World War II, Korea, and to some extent Vietnam were wars fought by all classes of Americans, though by the end of the Vietnam War many Americans in the upper classes were finding ways to avoid serving.

In the era of the all-volunteer military most members of the "upper classes" do not volunteer. Once the Vietnam War ended there was no longer the fig leaf of being politically opposed to an unpopular war. And the refusal to volunteer was not only standard practice in left-wing privileged families. The wealthy and well-connected on the right also discouraged their children from volunteering. Clearly, when it came to who served and who didn't, class was now the issue.

There was a time when most of our political leaders were military parents. Honor demanded that the men and women who sent other people's children to war lead by example. Decency demanded that those who benefited most from our way of life also served shoulder-to-shoulder with those less fortunate. Eleanor Roosevelt expressed this egalitarian outlook when she wrote: "I think my husband would have been very much upset if the boys had not wanted to go into the war immediately, but he did not have to worry very much because they either were already in before the war began, or they went in immediately. . . . " Not only presidents but many members of congress had sons and daughters serving and had served themselves. A lot has changed. According to an article by Tom Ford in the *Minneapolis-St. Paul Star Tribune*, only 30 percent of the 535 members of Congress have a military background (this number is down from 1969, when more than two-thirds had served). And only six representatives and one senator are currently known to have children serving. And it has been a long time since we've had a president with a child in uniform.

These days some members of our elite are even so hostile to the idea of service that they have all but banned military recruiters from our best private high schools and college campuses, lest anyone even suggest to *their* sons and daughters that military service is an honorable option to a headlong rush into elite colleges and high paychecks. Sometimes this hostility toward the military is still dressed up as political opposition to this war or that, this administration policy or that. But I think the truth is that resistance to military service reflects a the-military-is-beneath-me snobbery, not to mention a let-them-eat-cake attitude of unvarnished selfishness. I am not the only person to have noticed these problems. On the morning I was writing this I got an e-mail that seemed to crystallize the issue.

June 13, 2004

Dear Frank,

I was in the U.S. Navy during the Vietnam War and lost some good friends in country. I now have a friend in the USMC in Iraq. . . . Back in the 70's the words "all volunteer military" sounded so beautiful, so democratic. . . . I now think we should re-institute the draft. I feel. . . . that all of us who enjoy our freedom should earn it. . . . We see bumper stickers that proclaim "freedom isn't free" but we seldom put our own bumpers on the line. . . .

Robert M. Fehling

I am not advocating a return to the draft—I am not qualified to speak to that issue—but I do know that it does not bode well for our democracy that most of the dead from our current wars in Afghanistan and Iraq are being buried in small towns and the blue-collar, or middle- and lower-middle-class neighborhoods of our cities, and so rarely in the enclaves of the very wealthy and most powerful. I think we do need some sort of national service that levels the playing field again. We are unwittingly codifying a very un-American class distinction that will harm our country.

Perhaps a time is coming when both Americas, the America that serves and the America that rarely does, will have to get to know each other again. Perhaps it is time that our elites feel some shame. In Pericles' Funeral Oration, he says: "For a man's counsel cannot have equal weight or worth, when he alone has no children to risk in the general danger." To me this summarizes a looming national catastrophe: we are led by a political, media, business, and intellectual elite that mostly sends only the sons and daughters of others to war.

Maybe it is time we all begin participating in our defense the way the Roosevelts did. In time of war it is shameful for any family, especially the most privileged, not to stand should-to-shoulder with the rest of their fellow citizens. We are all in this together. We have to find ways to share the sacrifice.

Frank Schaeffer
June 14, 2004

Acknowledgments

I want to thank my friend and editor and publisher Will Balliett for suggesting that I collect and edit these letters. His friendship and skill are invaluable. My agent Jennifer Lyons is a good friend, and as with all my projects shepherded this through.

My wife, Genie, as always, was helpful in every way. Genie graciously typed many of the letters from the handwritten originals. Thank you!

My son John, my Marine, was of course the real reason for this book. If it were not for his service I would not have the honor to be, by proxy, a "military parent."

And of course the only reason this book exists is because of the generosity of the contributors. I thank them all for sharing their lives and especially for the service of their families to our country. I thank them too for the pain and loss, especially those whose hearts did not return from battle. May God give you peace and your warriors rest.

Frank Schaeffer, June 9, 2004